COURTHOUSE ARCHITECTURE, DESIGN AND SOCIAL JUSTICE

This collection interrogates relationships between court architecture and social justice, from consultation and design to the impact of material (and immaterial) forms on court users, through the lenses of architecture, law, socio-legal studies, criminology, anthropology, and a former high court judge.

International multidisciplinary collaborations and single-author contributions traverse a range of methodological approaches to present new insights into the relationship between architecture, design, and justice. These include praxis, photography, reflections on process and decolonising practice, postcolonial, feminist, and poststructural analysis, and theory from critical legal scholarship, political science, criminology, literature, sociology, and architecture. While the opening contributions reflect on establishing design principles and architectural methodologies for ethical consultation and collaboration with communities historically marginalised and exploited by law, the central chapters explore the textures and affects of built forms and the spaces between; examining the disjuncture between design intention and use; and investigating the impact of architecture and the design of space. The collection finishes with contemplations of the very real significance of material presence or absence in courtroom spaces and what this might mean for justice.

Courthouse Architecture, Design and Social Justice provides tools for those engaged in creating, and reflecting on, ethical design and building use, and deepens the dialogue across disciplinary boundaries towards further collaborative work in the field. It also exists as a new resource for research and teaching, facilitating undergraduate critical thought about the ways in which design enhances and restricts access to justice.

Kirsty Duncanson is Senior Lecturer in the Department of Social Inquiry at La Trobe University, Australia.

Emma Henderson is Director of Graduate Research in the Law School at La Trobe University, Australia.

Space, Materiality and the Normative

Series Editors: Andreas Philippopoulos-Mihalopoulos and Christian Borch

Space, Materiality and the Normative presents new ways of thinking about the connections between space and materiality from a normative perspective. At the interface of law, social theory, politics, architecture, geography and urban studies, the series is concerned with addressing the use, regulation and experience of space and materiality, broadly understood, and in particular with exploring their links and the challenges they raise for law, politics and normativity. https://www.routledge.com/Space-Materiality-and-the-Normative/book-series/SMNORM

a GlassHouse book

COURTHOUSE ARCHITECTURE, DESIGN AND SOCIAL JUSTICE

Edited by Kirsty Duncanson and Emma Henderson

Routledge
Taylor & Francis Group
a GlassHouse Book

First published 2022
by Routledge
2 Park Square, Milton Park, Abingdon, Oxon OX14 4RN

and by Routledge
605 Third Avenue, New York, NY 10158

a GlassHouse book

Routledge is an imprint of the Taylor & Francis Group, an informa business

British Library Cataloguing-in-Publication Data
A catalogue record for this book is available from the British Library

Library of Congress Cataloging-in-Publication Data
Names: Duncanson, Kirsty, editor. | Henderson, Emma (Emma M.), editor.
Title: Courthouse architecture, design, and social justice/edited by Kirsty Duncanson and Emma Henderson.
Description: Milton Park, Abingdon, Oxon [UK]; New York, NY: Routledge, 2021. |
Series: Space, materiality, and the normative | Includes bibliographical references and index.
Identifiers: LCCN 2021013348 (print) | LCCN 2021013349 (ebook) | ISBN 9780367181635 (hardback) | ISBN 9781032071039 (paperback) | ISBN 9780429059858 (ebook)
Subjects: LCSH: Justice, Administration of–Social aspects. | Courthouses–Social aspects. | Courthouses–Social aspects–Australia. | Courthouses–Design and construction. | Sociological jurisprudence.
Classification: LCC K2100 .C6675 2021 (print) | LCC K2100 (ebook) | DDC 725/.150994–dc23
LC record available at https://lccn.loc.gov/2021013348
LC ebook record available at https://lccn.loc.gov/2021013349

ISBN: 978-0-367-18163-5 (hbk)
ISBN: 978-1-032-07103-9 (pbk)
ISBN: 978-0-429-05985-8 (ebk)

DOI: 10.4324/9780429059858

Typeset in Bembo
by Deanta Global Publishing Services, Chennai, India

For Product Safety Concerns and Information please contact our EU representative: GPSR@taylorandfrancis.com

Taylor & Francis Verlag GmbH, Kaufingerstraße 24, 80331 München, Germany.

CONTENTS

FIGURES

CONTRIBUTORS

Thalia Anthony is Professor in the Faculty of Law at the University of Technology in Sydney, Australia. Dr Anthony researches in the areas of criminal law and procedure and First Nations people and the law, with a particular specialisation in criminalisation of First Nations people and First Nations community justice mechanisms. Her research is grounded in legal history and understandings of the colonial legacy in legal institutions. She has developed new approaches to researching and understanding the role of the criminal law in governing First Nations communities and how the state regulates First Nations-designed justice strategies. Her research is informed by fieldwork in First Nations communities and partnerships with First Nations legal organisations in Australia and overseas.

The Hon Michael Black was Chief Justice of the Federal Court of Australia from 1991 until 2010. In that capacity he had an involvement on behalf of the Court with the projects for the construction of the Commonwealth Law Courts in Melbourne (completed 1999), in Adelaide (2006), the reconstruction of the Federal Court's principal courtroom in its Hobart court (2008), and the substantial refurbishment of the Federal Court areas of Law Courts Building, Sydney (2010). He has a long-standing interest in architecture, urban planning, and conservation and in his practice as a barrister (1964–1990) appeared in some notable cases raising issues in these fields.

Anna Carline is Senior Law Lecturer at the University of Liverpool, UK, specialising in the areas of criminal law and criminal justice (specifically violence against women and sexual offences) and feminist/gender theory. Dr Carline has recently published a co-authored monograph (with Drs Clare Gunby and Jamie Murray) entitled *Rape and the Criminal Trial: Reconceptualising the Courtroom as an Affective Assemblage* (Palgrave, 2020). This book brings new materialism and affect theory into a conversation with barristers' insights into the rape trial process and the impact of reforms to argue that the courtroom needs to be reconceptualised as an 'affective assemblage'.

Annie Cossins was Professor of Law and Criminology in the Faculty of Law at the University of New South Wales, Australia, and was appointed an Honorary Professor in that Faculty after her retirement in October 2020. She spent most of her 28-year academic career researching and writing about all aspects of adult and child sexual assault in order to promote reforms to the criminal justice system with many successes along the way. Her latest book is *Closing the Justice Gap for Adult and Child Sexual Assault: Rethinking the Adversarial Trial* (Palgrave Macmillan, 2020).

Kirsty Duncanson is Senior Lecturer in the Department of Social Inquiry at La Trobe University, Australia. Her research interests lie within the field of cultural legal studies, and she teaches Crime Justice and Legal Studies. While much of her research examines how our bodies are engaged by cinema to practice popular jurisprudence, she also works with Emma Henderson in their endless exploration of what influences jury decision-making in rape trials. Her most recent publications include a chapter about the embodied jurisprudence of a video clip in the collection *Law, Lawyers and Justice: Through Australian Lenses* (Routledge, 2019).

Elizabeth Grant is Associate Professor of Architecture and Urban Design at RMIT University in Melbourne, Australia, and Adjunct Professor, Design and the Built Environment, at the University of Canberra, Australia. An architectural anthropologist, Dr Grant is an elected fellow of the Australian Institute of Aboriginal and Torres Strait Islander Studies (AIATSIS) and a Winston Churchill Fellow (2008). She was awarded the International Corrections and Prison Association's 2015 Excellence in Research Award and invited as a Visiting Scholar to the Prison Research Centre at the University of Cambridge in the same year. In 2017 she was elected by the Aboriginal community as the Independent Expert Director to the Aboriginal Prisoner and Offender Support Service (APOSS). She co-edited the *Handbook of Contemporary Indigenous Architecture* (Springer, 2018).

Clare Gunby is Research Fellow in the Institute of Applied Health Research at the University of Birmingham, UK. She manages a National Institute for Health Research (NIHR) funded study, examining the role of the specialist voluntary sector in supporting survivors of sexual violence, with a focus on the funding and commissioning of these services. Her research interests include gender-based violence, rape law and policy, emotional labour, and mental health. She has held a number of research grants in these areas and published widely on them. She is committed to participatory research methods and the co-production of knowledge.

Emma Henderson is Director of Graduate Research in the Law School at La Trobe University, Australia. Emma teaches human rights law, public law, and criminal law, and researches in the areas of feminist legal theory, rape law reform, and international criminal law. Working with Dr Kirsty Duncanson, Emma's recent projects include the Spaces of Justice symposium, which led to a special issue of the Griffith Law Review in 2018, *Spaces of Justice: Courtrooms, Innovation and Practice* and this volume, and articles on jury directions in rape trials in *Feminist Legal Studies* and the *University of New South Wales Law Review.*

Martyn Hook is Deputy Pro Vice-Chancellor Partnerships in the College of Design and Social Context at RMIT University in Melbourne, Australia. He also holds the position of Dean at RMIT's School of Architecture and Design alongside his role as Professor of Architecture. In addition to his work at RMIT, Martyn is a director of multi-award-winning iredale pedersen hook architects, a studio practice based in Melbourne and Perth dedicated to appropriate design of effective sustainable buildings with a responsible environmental and social agenda.

Carolyn McKay is Senior Lecturer at the University of Sydney Law School, Australia, teaching Criminal Law, Civil and Criminal Procedure, and Digital Criminology. She is also Co-Director, Sydney Institute of Criminology, Australia. Her research focuses on technologies in justice and remote hearings. She is author of *The Pixelated Prisoner: Prison Video Links, Court 'Appearance' and the Justice Matrix* (Routledge, 2018).

Jamie Murray is Senior Lecturer at Liverpool Hope University, UK. His research interests centre on complex systems theories and regulation/law, particularly in relation to the macroprudential regulation of the global financial system. Applying new materialism, complexity theory, and the work of Deleuze and Guattari to law, his publications include *Deleuze & Guattari: Emergent Law* (Routledge, 2013) and 'Earth Jurisprudence, wild law, emergent law: The emergent field of ecology and law' (parts 1 and 2). Most recently Murray co-authored *Rape and the Criminal Trial: Reconceptualising the Courtroom as an Affective Assemblage* (Palgrave McMillan, 2020) with Anna Carline and Clare Gunby.

It is with deep regret that we acknowledge the death of Jamie Murray in April 2020 and extend our condolences to his partner Anna Carline. It is a shocking loss and a terrible sadness.

Julian R Murphy is a PhD candidate at the University of Melbourne, Australia. His doctoral thesis examines the constitutional values informing the practice of statutory interpretation in Australia and the United States. He has previously held positions as a Postgraduate Public Interest Fellow at Columbia Law School, as Associate to Justice Nettle at the High Court of Australia, and as Criminal Appeals Manager of the North Australian Aboriginal Justice Agency. In 2017–2018, Julian undertook an LLM at Columbia University, where he was a Human Rights Fellow and received the Walter Gellhorn Prize for the highest academic average in the class.

Judith Resnik is Arthur Liman Professor of Law at Yale Law School, New Haven, CT, and Founding Director of the Liman Center for Public Interest Law. She teaches courses on federalism, procedure, courts, prisons, equality, and citizenship. Her scholarship focuses on the relationship of democratic values to government services such as courts, prisons, and post offices; the roles of collective redress, class actions, and arbitration; contemporary conflicts over privatisation; the relationships of states to citizens and non-citizens; the forms and norms of federalism; and equality and gender.

Emma Rowden is Senior Lecturer in Architectural History and Theory in the School of Architecture at Oxford Brookes University, UK. Previously a Chancellor's Postdoctoral Research Fellow at the Faculty of Design, Architecture and Building at the University of Technology Sydney, Australia, she has conducted research into justice environments across a number of externally funded research projects including a Leverhulme Trust funded project with Professor Linda Mulcahy (LSE) on the history of court design in the UK.

Peter D Rush is Associate Professor in the Law Faculty at Melbourne University, Australia. He writes, teaches, and researches in jurisprudence and the humanities, with specialisms in criminal law – domestic, international, comparative, and transitional. He has published numerous books, edited collections, and articles in these interdisciplinary fields of legal thought, as well as a film and photo essay. Specific current work includes the Lives Lived with Law project, a book on Japanese criminal justice, and a jurisography of audio-visual jurisprudence.

FOREWORD

Iconic, complex, and contested institutions

Judith Resnik[1]

Courthouses are so familiar that one might assume that they have always existed, just as the rights that adjudication has come to signify feel deeply entrenched, even as their boundaries and effects are debated. This volume maps the innovations in courthouse design that aim to respond to diverse users and communities so as to reconfigure authority and take into account the impact of new communication technologies.

Before readers delve into the rich discussion that follows, more context is needed about the spaces denoted as 'courthouses' and the activities that fall within the rubric of 'adjudication'. First, even as the rendering of judgment has a past that stretches back throughout recorded history, undertaking that form of decision-making in a discrete structure called a courthouse dates back only a few hundred years. Second, and yet more recent, are the commitments of courts to enable access to all members of the body politic. The linkage of courts' legitimacy to making adjudication accessible across the spectrum of humanity is an artefact of the worldwide human rights movements over the last century. Third, the burst of courthouse construction and iconographical innovations during the last several decades mixes aspirations for a trans-temporal and transnational legibility with a context-specific responsiveness.

Fourth, new technologies have been driving a movement away from in-person activities, as online dispute resolution (ODR) promises more accessibility

1 My thanks to Emma Henderson, Kirsty Duncanson, and the other participants in the symposium from which this book is built, as I learned a good deal from my participation. The themes in this essay build on Judith Resnik and Dennis Curtis, *Representing Justice: Invention, Controversy, and Rights in City-States and Democratic Courtrooms* (Yale University Press, 2011) and more recent work, some of which is cited here.

by lowering the costs of seeking redress.[2] The closing of hundreds of courthouses in England is but one example of the shift away from in-person adjudication. Proponents of both ODR and alternative dispute resolution argue for the utilities of formats other than a trial-focused procedure. These reconfigurations of process predate the COVID-19 pandemic to which social distancing is the recommended response. Justifications are therefore plentiful for reimagining what a host of activities – from education to healthcare to dispute resolution and punishment – entail. Discussions of the centrality of physicality and of place in adjudication need now to take into account when and how to use web platforms.

Thus, and fifth, the future vitality of courthouses, with their public adjudication and recent efforts at egalitarian redistributive practices, is far from assured. The rise of exclusionary sovereigntism; the extent of profound economic, racial, and gender inequalities; and the efforts to privatise dispute resolution authority make all the more important this volume's descriptions and analyses of values that aspire to provide a buffer against these developments. Below, I briefly explain these issues and their relationship to the chapters that follow.

★★★

Many historians identify dispute resolution as an early function of (and as a reason for) communal governance. For thousands of years, such decision making took place out of doors. When it moved inside, the venue was often a multi-purpose building, sometimes denoted a 'town hall', that provided a panoply of services of which adjudication was but one.

Over time, multi-purpose town halls and municipal centres no longer sufficed to contain these expanding functions. In response, governments erected 'purpose-built',[3] segregated facilities, which today we call courthouses, jails, prisons, government office buildings, post offices, tribunals, and agencies. During the last centuries, the courthouse gained its more familiar form as a structure dedicated to adjudication and as an icon of government. That shift was driven by a mix of governments' ambitions to expand their ambit of control, the proliferation of commerce, and the political acumen of professional lawyers, judges, and architects who succeeded in persuading legislatures to allocate funds for this form of construction.

Civic leaders of recent centuries have continued to create symbols of presence, power, and prosperity. In both common law and civil law jurisdictions, these

2 Maurits Barendrecht et al., 'ODR and the Courts: The Promise of 100% Access to Justice?' (HiiL Online Dispute Resolution, 2016); see also Judith Resnik, 'A2J/A2K: Access to Justice, Access to Knowledge, Economic Inequalities, and Open Courts and Arbitrations' (2018) 96 *North Carolina Law Review* 605.

3 See Clare Graham, *Ordering Law: The Architectural and Social History of the English Law Court to 1914* (Ashgate, 2003).

buildings served as social gathering places and 'theatres of justice'. As governments' functions expanded, their footprints did as well.

Using the federal system in the United States (US) as illustrative, the federal judiciary once decamped in what were modestly termed 'court quarters' for judges.[4] By the end of the twentieth century, the federal government had funded the largest building programme since the 1930s' New Deal for the renovation and construction of new courthouses. 'Excellence in design' became the byword,[5] as courthouse commissions went to high-profile architects who were rewarded for crafting signature buildings.

A parallel expansion of court resources can be found in many countries. During the latter part of the twentieth century, France launched a programme that resulted in several 'palais du justice modernes'; Israel commissioned a new building for its Supreme Court; and, as discussed in this volume, Australia funded new courthouse construction programs.[6]

Courthouse building (as well as prison construction) became a major industry, with specialised associations focused on designs for the justice system. Local variations were complemented by a transnational idiom propelled by a marketplace of lawyers, judges, architects, and court administrators who crossed national boundaries and shaped construction plans at the regional, national, and international levels.

★★★

These many buildings around the world are testaments to the centrality of courthouses and adjudication to government. Governments *need* their members and residents to participate in adjudicatory processes as a means of promoting peaceful resolutions, of supporting economic growth, and of generating and reinforcing states' own authority to do so. Adjudication (whether in civil, criminal, or administrative tribunals) both confirms and produces the power to impose authority. The courthouse buildings that are at the heart of this volume are iconic embodiments of sovereignty.

Efforts to shift the technologies of sovereignty to web-based platforms alter interpersonal experiences but do not necessarily shrink the footprint of governments. Design aspirations and decisions are central to whether reconfigurations and reliance on new technologies expand or contract opportunities to bring claims.[7] In contrast, mandates that potential disputants use privately based and

4 See, for example, 'Judicial Conference of the United States', *Proceedings of the Judicial Conference*, September, 1945, vols 18, 26, 28.

5 See *Vision + Voice: Design Excellence in Federal Architecture, Building A Legacy* (Washington, DC: US General Services Administration, Public Buildings Service, Office of the Chief Architect, 2002).

6 See *La Nouvelle Architecture Judiciaire: Des Palais de Justice Modernes pour une Nouvelle Image de la Justice* (La Documentation Française, 2000).

7 See Natalie N. Byron, Developing the Detail – Evaluating the Impact of Court Reform in England and Wales on Access to Justice (2019) <https://www.srln.org/system/files/attachments/Developing%20the%20Detail-%20Evaluating%20the%20Impact%20of%20Court%20Refo

closed decision-making in lieu of courts does, and such obligations have in the last decades become commonplace in the United States and enforceable under contemporary interpretations of federal law. When implemented, those obligations limit state authority to regulate and constrict the public's capacity to debate processes and outcomes.[8]

That privatisation movement has been mobilised in part in response to and as a backlash against what the authors discuss, as the reconfiguration of judicial space aims to empower formerly marginalised groups. The results can be seen in how new courthouses look and how judges have reformatted their work. Many of the architectural and procedural choices are designed to reflect the commitment that courts find ways to welcome diverse users, some of whom have long been excluded by law from full participation in the body politic and come to court with limited economic resources.

The changing 'law' of courts has contributed to pressures to reconsider building choices and to reconfigure practices within courts, as analysed in this volume. Two decisions from the United States and the United Kingdom (UK), rendered a half-century apart, provide a window into the new egalitarianism of courts, as judges understand themselves compelled to require state subsidies for some litigants and therefore to protect court access despite wealth disparities among disputants.

In the early 1970s, a class of 'welfare recipients residing in Connecticut' argued that state-imposed fees of US$60 for filing and service to obtain a divorce, coupled with no mechanism to waive that requirement, violated the federal constitution by precluding them from ending their marriages. In 1971, in *Boddie v Connecticut*, Justice Harlan agreed; he wrote for the Court that the combination of 'the basic position of the marriage relationship in this society's hierarchy of values and the … state monopolization' of lawful dissolution imposed on the state a due process obligation to provide access.[9] In support of this first decision in US history that identified the constitutional obligation to waive fees in civil litigation for people unable to afford the filing costs to obtain a divorce, Justice Harlan wrote:

> Perhaps no characteristic of an organized and cohesive society is more fundamental than its erection and enforcement of a system of rules defining the various rights and duties of its members, enabling them to govern

---

rm%20in%20England%20and%20Wales%20on%20Access%20to%20Justice%20FINAL.pdf>; Natalie N. Byron, Digital Justice: HMCTS data strategy and delivering access to justice, Report and recommendations (The Legal Education Foundation, October 2019); Hazel Genn, 'Online Courts and the Future of Justice', Birkenhead Lecture, 16 October 2017; Hazel Genn, *Judging Civil Justice* (Cambridge University Press, 2009).

8 See Judith Resnik, 'Diffusing Disputes: The Public in the Private of Arbitration, the Private in Courts, and the Erasure of Rights' (2015) 124 *Yale Law Journal* 2804; see also Judith Resnik, Stephanie Garlock and Annie Wang, 'Collective Preclusion and Inaccessible Arbitration: Data, Non-Disclosure, and Public Knowledge' (2020) 24 *Lewis & Clark Law Review* 611.

9 *Boddie v Connecticut* (1971) 401 US 371, 374.

> their affairs and definitely settle their differences in an orderly, predictable manner.[10]

Boddie centred on the role that courts play when public and private interests intersect in family life. In addition to households, courts are foundational to markets, as adjudication provides one mechanism for enforcing horizontal obligations among individuals and entities in contemporary societies. Paralleling Justice Harlan's account of why fees ought not to be a barrier to litigants is a UK decision, *R (in the Application of Unison) v Lord Chancellor*, rendered in 2017.[11] Writing the central opinion for the Supreme Court, Lord Reed found unlawful the high fees the government had imposed for use of its employment tribunals. As he put it:

> Every day in the courts and tribunals of this country, the names of people who brought cases in the past live on as shorthand for the legal rules and principles which their cases established. Their cases form the basis of the advice given to those whose cases are now before the courts, or who need to be advised as to the basis on which their claim might fairly be settled, or … that their case is hopeless. … But the value to society of the right of access to the courts is not confined to cases in which the courts decide questions of general importance. People and businesses need to know, on the one hand, that they will be able to enforce their rights if they have to do so, and, on the other hand, that if they fail to meet their obligations, there is likely to be a remedy against them. It is that knowledge which underpins everyday economic and social relations. That is so, notwithstanding that judicial enforcement of the law is not usually necessary, and notwithstanding that the resolution of disputes by other methods is often desirable.[12]

Turning to the question of inequality, Lord Reed insisted that 'the possibility of claims being brought by employees whose rights are infringed must exist, if employment relationships are to be based on respect' for the rights created by Parliament. Furthermore, even as resolutions often come through negotiation or mediation,

> those procedures can only work fairly and properly if they are backed up by the knowledge on both sides that a fair and just system of adjudication will be available if they fail. Otherwise, the party in the stronger bargaining position will always prevail.[13]

★★★

10 Ibid.

11 *R (in the Application of Unison) v Lord Chancellor* (2017) UKSC 51.

12 Ibid 70–71.

13 Ibid 72.

As these decisions reflect, courts have come to represent – and to present themselves as – venues of equality in which power redistribution is requisite to justice and hence to courts' own legitimacy. As political and social movements pushed democracies to make good on egalitarian commitments, they turned to courts to articulate rights of access and to materialise them in their facilities and structures.

These aspirations are reflected in the account provided by the Honourable Michael Black, who was Chief Justice of the Federal Court of Australia from 1991 to 2010 and was central to the construction of its 1999 Melbourne courthouse, which he saw as embodying 'light, transparency, access and equality'.[14] The effort to depart from the colonial court tradition is likewise vivid in the discussions by Elizabeth Grant, Martyn Hook, Julian Murphy, and Thalia Anthony. These two chapters examine the design of and the practices in the Kununurra Courthouse in northwestern Australia, the Port Augusta Court Complex, and other courthouses that aim to reflect commitments to Australia's Indigenous peoples.[15]

Part of the appeal of using courthouses as markers of this new egalitarian facet of governments' persona is their ubiquity. The personalisation of adjudication stands in contrast to many other centralised government services. Tasks that historically have been associated with sovereignty – war-making, peace-making, taxing, and legislating – are remote from wide segments of the population because the activities occur offshore, are episodic, or are concentrated at the site where a legislature sits. In contrast, the institutions on which sovereigns have relied to monitor and control, which include courts, along with police, prosecution, and prisons – turn the abstraction of government into a material presence, personifying the state and demonstrating its capacity to offer certain kinds of goods and services that can have utilities for the private as well as the public sector. The interactions among participants in these venues provide springboards for the development of different norms bounding the relationship between the governed and the government.

In many eras, such rules had authorised autocratic power. Hierarchies of status rendered some individuals abused on the streets, marginalised in courts, and mistreated in prisons. In prior centuries, buildings and government officials embodied inhospitable and often oppressive control. But constitutional injunctions now frame those exchanges across an array of government services and (whether realised in practice or not) require trained officials – such as judges – to treat individuals (whether suspects, detainees, adults, or children who are litigants, witnesses, lawyers, jurors, or staff) with dignity. In addition to the hoped-for experiences of efficacy, public adjudicatory processes can (when they work as intended) contribute to democracy by demonstrating through real-time interactions the ability to provide equal and dignified treatment, decision-making committed to forms of

14 Michael Black, this volume, page 31.

15 Martyn Hook and Elizabeth Grant, this volume, page 11; Murphy, Grant and Anthony, this volume, page 75.

self-restraint and explanation, and revelation of the exercise of power in response to conflicting claims of right.

Thus, while courts have long been a venue for interaction of individuals with sovereign power, their current constitutional obligations are novel. When they function well, courts generate collective narratives of identity and obligation. 'Connective justice' is a phrase proffered to describe the efforts of ancient Egypt to bridge the worlds of humans and the gods, but the phrase could be transposed to capture the aspirations for courts operating in democratic political systems.[16] Judges are supposed to treat all with dignity and respect, and disputants are obliged to do the same towards their adversaries.

These egalitarian exchanges of mutual recognition make adjudication a democratic practice; third-party rights of access put the performance of these obligations before the public eye. Jeremy Bentham, the nineteenth-century theorist, called for 'publicity' to enable his imagined 'Public Opinion Tribunal' to form independent judgements about the quality of government actions.[17] While presiding over a trial, the judge is, to paraphrase Bentham, on trial. The information forced into the public realm by court processes then becomes part of iterative exchanges with other branches of government and social movements.

Courts' mandate to operate in public endows the audience – the public – with the ability and the authority of critique. Through participatory parity, public processes at once teach about democratic practices of norm development and offer the opportunity for popular input to produce changes in legal rights. The redundancy produced by litigants who raise parallel claims of rights enables debate about the underlying legal rules. The particular structural obligations of courts have the potential to produce, redistribute, and curb power in a fashion that is generative in democracies.

★★★

Yet this account is clouded by the painful experiences of users, evocatively captured in the image of Indigenous peoples understanding themselves as entering the 'door of despair'[18] when coming into courts. For many people around the world, courthouses have symbolised the power of law to enforce the oppressions of colonialism and of racial and gender hierarchies. An effort at redemption comes from new designs, predicated on collaborative engagement of communities and building authorities who, as exemplified in this book, have reconceived public spaces through an integration of indoor and outdoor areas. Norms of

16 See J G Manning, 'The Representation of Justice in Ancient Egypt' (2012) 24(1) *Yale Journal of Law & Humanities* 4.

17 See Jeremy Bentham, 'Of Publicity and Privacy, as Applied to Judicature in General, and to the Evidence in Particular' in *The Works of Jeremy Bentham*, ed John Bowring (William Tait, 1843) 351.

18 Hook and Grant, page 11.

access to justice are translated through a focus on providing users with a sense of personal comfort and security through procedures and building designs that accommodate people who, when in or out of courthouses, do not all experience physical space in the same way. The indoor/outdoor continuities and openness assume the physical security of those situated in these buildings. In contrast, in some jurisdictions such as the United States, a good deal of attention is focused on fixing and monitoring the boundaries of government buildings to prevent efforts to perpetrate violence on court staff and users.[19]

The experiences of non-professional participants – from juror to litigant – are the subject matter of the chapters by Kirsty Duncanson and Emma Henderson[20] and Annie Cossins and Emma Rowden.[21] Like the discussion of Indigenous peoples' relationships to courts, these authors look at courthouses as structures of control that can inflict trauma, and call into question configurations that are commonplace.

New technologies can be seen either as a facet of control or as a remedy. Anna Carline, Clare Gunby, and Jamie Murray analyse the discomfort of barristers with the turn to 'remote' testimony as the lawyers interviewed insisted on the need for the interpersonal intensity that courtrooms provide.[22] Annie Cossins and Emma Rowden consider the challenges of live proceedings for children who are asked to testify about sexual assault; the authors argue the utilities of remoteness.[23] A different perspective is offered by Carolyn McKay, who raises the spectre of remote proceedings 'conflating' prisons and courtrooms, as courthouses via video link become extensions of the carceral state and the encounter between individuals and the state is diffused.[24] This volume's chapters and Peter Rush's photo essay called refracting 'legal justice' make plain the tensions in the practices of courts as they currently exist, even as redemptive efforts are under way. As I write, the United States has been swept by protests against inequalities in which courts have played a significant role. A welter of fines, fees, and other legal assessments run across the civil, administrative, and criminal systems. The fee waiver regime that enabled Ms Boddie to come to court in 1971 still exists, but the reach of that decision has been narrowed.

Municipal, state, and federal governments impose a host of fees – for criminal defendants to be 'diverted' to drug treatment programmes, for individuals with traffic violations and for people in detention, charged in some places 'to pay to

19 See, for example, 'All Too Frequent Tragedies Demand Action to Improve Judicial Security, Judge tell Judicial Conference, United States Courts' <https://www.uscourts.gov/news/2020/09/15/all-too-frequent-tragedies-demand-action?utm_campaign=usc-news&utm_medium=email&utm_source=govdelivery>.

20 Kirsty Duncanson and Emma Henderson, page 107.

21 Annie Cossins and Emma Rowden, page 140.

22 Anna Carline, Clare Gunby and Jamie Murray, page 169.

23 Cossins and Rowden (n 21).

24 Carolyn McKay, page 191.

stay'.[25] Court-imposed debt saddles many families, and a 2015 US Department of Justice report made plain the racial discrimination that laced the fines imposed by the police and judges in Ferguson, Missouri.[26] While some courts have held unconstitutional certain fees, fines, bail, and other assessments because they were excessive or discriminatory, a vast array of such charges remain in place. In short, the failures of court systems – and the failure to equip adequately users – are vivid and commonplace.

Moreover, the devolution of adjudication and its outsourcing to private providers and the reconfiguration of court-based processes to prioritise settlement for both civil and criminal cases have undercut the occasions for public observation of and involvement in adjudication. In the federal courts of the United States, for example, while filings increased, trial rates dropped over the last few decades. In 2020, trials began in only one out of every hundred federal civil cases filed. 'Vanishing trials' is a shorthand that cuts across the civil and criminal dockets, and exists in state as well as federal courts in the United States and elsewhere.

Through the privatisation of processes inside courts and the outsourcing of adjudicatory functions to providers outside of courts, the public loses its opportunities to engage. Gone are what Jeremy Bentham called 'auditors' and the potential for his conception of a Tribunal of Public Opinion to function, for no one can evaluate the decision-makers and the disputants.[27] More apt for this century, gone is the potential for many conflicting 'public(s)', including some that are predatory, to interact with the processes they can observe and the decisions announced.[28]

These closures stymie the potential to debate – in deliberate or harsh terms, with information or misinformation – whether procedures and decision-makers are fair, how resources affect outcomes, whether similarly situated litigants are treated comparably, and why one would want to get into (or avoid) court. Instead, a private transaction has been substituted and, unlike public adjudication, control over the meaning of the claims made and the judgments rendered rests with the corporate provider of the service. Just as Michel Foucault mapped how governing powers, eager to maintain control, moved punishment practices

25 See, for example, Anna VanCleave et al. (eds), 'Ability to Pay' (2019) Arthur Liman Center for Public Interest Law Colloquium, <https://papers.ssrn.com/sol3/papers.cfm?abstract_id=3387647>; see also *Who Pays? Fines, Fees, Bail, and the Cost of Courts* (Arthur Liman Center for Public Interest Law, 2018); see also Judith Resnik and David Marcus, 'Inability to Pay: Court Debt Circa 2020' (2020) 98 *North Carolina Law Review* 361.

26 United States Department of Justice Civil Rights Division, *Investigation of the Ferguson Police Department* (4 March 2015).

27 See Bentham (n 17); see also Judith Resnik, 'Bring Back Bentham: Open Courts, "Terror Trials," and Public Sphere(s)' (2011) 5 *Law & Ethics of Human Rights* 226.

28 See Judith Resnik, 'The Functions of Publicity and of Privatization in Courts and their Replacements (from Jeremy Bentham to #MeToo and *Google* Spain)' in Burkhard Hess and Ana Koprivica (eds), *Open Justice: The Role of Courts in a Democratic Society* (Nomos, 2019), 177.

from public streets into closed prisons,[29] adjudication is at risk of being removed from public purview, which will render the exercise and consequences of public and private power harder to ascertain. The public and private sectors increasingly rely on practices that do not admit the need to show their processes to justify the exercise of authority.

Given the number of filings, the demand for more services, and the spate of architecturally important courthouses, the diminution in the aegis of adjudication and the incursions on courts' authority are at risk of being overlooked. Yet, while courts may be monumental in ambition and often in physical girth, their durability as active sites of public exchange before independent jurists should not be taken for granted. Like other venerable institutions developed in the eighteenth century, such as the postal service and the press, which serve in parallel fashion to disseminate information and to support democratic competency, courts are vulnerable.

The struggles and the failures of courts to make good on promises of fair treatment, which lace the chapters in this book, need to become part of the narrative of the progressive, albeit uneven and challenging, realisation of rights. The continuation of accessible courts for ordinary disputants who seek state dispute resolution assistance is far from assured. Rather, it requires, as it always has, a political commitment to sustain – even as they are reconfigured – the services that courts, and the governments of which they are a part, provide.

29 Michel Foucault, *Discipline and Punish: The Birth of the Prison*, tr Alan Sheridan (Vintage Books, 2nd ed, 1995).

INTRODUCTION

Kirsty Duncanson and Emma Henderson

Lives are compellingly altered by the work conducted within court buildings. The design of each courthouse impacts on the capacity of people to participate in the legal proceedings that dramatically transform their lives. Courtrooms are hierarchical 'sets', in which docks, partitions, fixed seating, and technology materially impose on the roles played by each participant in the room. Design innovations can render court buildings less intimidating, with more natural light, flatter floor levelling, greater visibility, and more connection to the outside world. The texture, size, colour, and ornamentation both outside and within court buildings trigger intensities of feeling in court users and those who pass through, giving meaning to law that reaches beyond the cerebrally considered to the embodied senses of authority, security, fear, dread, and alienation. Architecture impacts upon our experiences of the justice system and shapes community attitudes towards law.

This collection of essays interrogates the relationship between court architecture and social justice. Beginning with explorations of design generation, this collection critically reflects on processes of expert and community consultation for courthouse design and the power of architectural principles and typologies. The impact of such thoughtfully created architecture is analysed in essays investigating the relationships between specifically identified court users – Aboriginal and Torres Strait Islander peoples, members of a jury, and children delivering testimony – and the designed space. Ultimately, the significance of physical presence within courtrooms is examined.

This is an actively multidisciplinary compendium, with international and cross-disciplinary collaborations as well as single-authored contributions from scholars of architecture, law, criminology, legal studies, and anthropology; from practising lawyers, architects, visual artists, and a former Chief Justice of the Australian Federal Court. By bringing together scholars and practitioners from

DOI: 10.4324/9780429059858-1

diverse fields, a range of methodological approaches are implemented to present new insights into the relationship between architecture, design, and justice. Chapters include praxis; photography; reflections on process and decolonising practice; postcolonial, feminist, and poststructural analysis; and theory from critical legal scholarship, political science, criminology, literature, sociology, and architecture. *Courthouse Architecture, Design and Social Justice* provides tools for those engaged in creating, and reflecting on, ethical design, and building use.

Within the broader context of the relationship between architecture and justice outcomes, three central themes are identified. The first, 'Building justice', concerns process, and is considered via reflections on establishing design principles as part of a consultative committee and methodologies for ethical consultation and collaboration with communities historically marginalised and exploited by law. The second theme, 'Justice buildings', is more straightforwardly analytic, and is considered by exploring the textures and affects of built forms and the spaces between them, the disjuncture between design intention and use, and the impact of architecture and the design of space. The last theme, 'Justice outwith buildings', contemplates the very real significance of material presence or absence in courtroom spaces and what this might mean for justice.

'Building justice' opens our collection with 'Reimagining spaces for Indigenous justice: The architecture and design of the Kununurra Courthouse'. This first chapter is co-authored by Martyn Hook, Dean of RMIT's School of Architecture and Urban Design and director of iredale pedersen hook architects, a firm that worked with Miriwoong, Gajirrawoong, and Gidja communities and TAG Architects to create the award-winning Kununurra Courthouse in Western Australia, and prolific architectural anthropologist and criminologist Elizabeth Grant. Together they argue that there is an urgent need for new architectural typologies using principles from outside the 'Anglosphere' to right historical injustices for Indigenous Australians. Hook and Grant describe the process of reconceptualising heuristic pathways in the design and physical setting of a court and courthouse. Central to the design process for the Kununurra Courthouse was the integration of the genius loci, geomorphology, and art, in an effort to reposition the role of the courthouse in a place brutally marked by colonisation, and to create a place for equitable and fair dispute resolution. The authors argue that the design team, working with local Aboriginal communities, created a meaningful and relevant building which brought new relevance to the figure 'of the regional courthouse as a landmark civic building' that represents the local community and provides a centre for dispute resolution where Aboriginal communities can feel some ownership and trust in mainstream law.[1] Hook and Grant claim that the design at Kununurra demonstrates the shift away from the view of courts as oppressive and threatening spaces towards a future in which courts are open and accessible, where respect for Indigenous peoples and

1 Elizabeth Grant and Martyn Hook, this volume, page 30.

cultures is on public view and the possibility of fair and equal, even decolonising, justice can be imagined.

Chapter 2, 'The architecture of law courts: How concepts of justice – light, transparency, access, and equality – drove the design of new and renovated courthouses for federal courts in Australia', is also concerned with processes of architectural design. Former Australian Chief Justice Michael Black examines architectural concepts and representations of justice in the development of Commonwealth law court buildings in Melbourne, Adelaide, Hobart, and Sydney. Arguing that these projects demonstrate the importance of a dynamic interplay of ideas, ambitions, and professions, Black focuses on the central importance of architects' creative skills in translating ideas and ideals into the built form. Describing the complex negotiations involved in the design process for public buildings, the chapter shines a light on the competing and sometimes contradictory agendas of architects, public servants, project managers, surveyors, senior officers of the courts, and judicial members of the steering committees involved. Echoing some of the themes raised by Hook and Grant, this chapter highlights the shift in Australian court design from the earlier colonial statements of authority and importance to the late twentieth-century focus on access, transparency, and equality. Black's analysis of the use of natural light in courtroom design, an important feature in colonial courthouse design due to the lack of indoor lighting but now an important contemporary aesthetic feature invoking notions of transparency and access, and his consideration of the ways in which the external aspects of courthouses connect with their location and community, add to our understanding of the role of architecture in the representation of justice.

Capturing the weight, form, and aspect of some of the court buildings Black discusses, in 'Refractions of legal justice (Forensic Precinct Series 2)', critical legal scholar Peter Rush explores the liminal spaces of court precincts in Tokyo, London, Adelaide, Melbourne, Canberra, and Sydney. His photo essay invites the audience to reflect on the complexities and paradoxes of court building architecture, the place of courts in urban environments, the relationship of courts to Indigenous jurisdictions, police, and administrative boundaries. Rush's play of images and words prompts us to respond in thought and affect to the line, light, and space of justice architecture, outside and between court buildings. We use this work to transition into the second theme, 'Justice buildings'.

Following immediately in Chapter 4, 'Indigenous courthouse and courtroom design in Australia: Case studies, design paradigms and the issue of cultural agency', lawyer and legal scholar Julian Murphy, anthropologist Elizabeth Grant, and criminologist Thalia Anthony add to this exploration of court architecture with a detailed analysis of the already discussed Kununurra Courthouse and two further Australian court complexes. Picking up from the opening chapter, and drawing on multiple disciplines, these authors provide a fascinating overview of emerging design principles and paradigms in court design for Indigenous peoples, arguing that these justice-building projects offer the architectural and psychological terrain for symbolic and actual attempts at decolonisation. The Kununurra Courthouse provides a powerful example for optimism. Despite this, the authors suggest that design intentions and outcomes exist in a complex relationship with their intended community. The courthouse, however aesthetically pleasing and sympathetically designed, may be perceived to be asserting (or reasserting) the dominance and inflexibility of the Anglo-Australian criminal justice system. The chapter reflects on the irony of engaging Indigenous peoples in debates and discourses about courthouse and courtroom architecture when courts are the very institutions that have sanctioned the control of every aspect of Indigenous lives since invasion. Thus, an Aboriginal Elder, when asked about how he thought courthouse architecture might be improved, suggested: 'Why don't you just send them some matches to burn those places down?'[2] To what extent can even the most sympathetic and well-thought-out building ever really right such entrenched wrongs?

The provocative burden placed upon architecture to right wrongs, to better influence justice outcomes, frames the ensuing chapters of our book. These chapters explore encounters between court users and building structures, the implications of digital technology versus material presence in the trial; and even the removal of the business of law from courtrooms altogether. Each asks what the micro-effects of courtroom design are on the possibilities of justice.

In Chapter 5, 'Interpellation by design: Could court buildings influence jury decision-making?', criminologist and cultural legal theorist Kirsty Duncanson and critical legal scholar Emma Henderson (the editors of this volume) propose that court architecture hails jurors throughout an interpellative encounter that lasts the duration of a rape trial, encouraging each juror to implement rape-supportive schemas when processing the evidence they hear and the negotiations they make in deliberation. We argue that this conspires with myriad other bearers of patriarchal logic to compel juries to acquit those accused of sexual violence. We suggest that architecture and design are pieces of the complex puzzle that is the rape trial, conspiring to undermine survivor accounts while reinforcing rape-supportive ideology. The puzzle piece we offer is one in which jurors are hailed by the ideologically enchanted architecture of court buildings to recognise within themselves an ideal liberal subjecthood. We argue that each juror is thus encouraged to put aside their divergent identities in order to exercise liberal 'reason' and 'neutrality'. In this manner, we contend, jurors are interpellated by court buildings to use rape myth schemas to help them make sense of the overwhelming abundance of disorderly information put before them at trial. These schemas make it difficult to believe accounts of rape, thus contributing to high acquittal rates across much of the common law world.

Pre-eminent scholar in sexual assault law reform Professor Annie Cossins and prolific interdisciplinary court architecture scholar Emma Rowden argue that

2 Murphy, Grant and Anthony, this volume, page 106.

human behaviour is influenced not only by spatial structure but also by room size, room shape, and architectural materials, features, furnishings, and finishes. In Chapter 6, 'The child sexual assault trials: Reconceptualising the design of court spaces according to trauma-informed principles', Cossins and Rowden quote Charles Goodsell to suggest that an environment is a form of nonverbal communication whose messages may or may not be heard, depending on the 'motivations, judgments and culture' of those on the receiving end.[3] To that end, they demonstrate that the physical and social environment of the court setting is a stressful stimulus for a traumatised child. Cossins and Rowden contend that children who have suffered sexual assault might be better able to participate in adversarial trials if the design of courtrooms, courthouses, and the trial processes within them was more explicitly governed and informed by the principles of trauma-informed care. They propose a purpose-built 'child-courtroom' where the child is physically separated from the accused, the jury, and the public. Additionally, Cossins and Rowden argue that all personnel who have contact or interaction with traumatised victims should undertake specialised training in trauma-informed care.

Continuing the examination of the intersections between sexual violence, court architecture, and vulnerable trial participants, Chapter 7, '"And that's why street-wise complainants now always give evidence behind screens, live": Exploring the intensive affects of the courtroom', focuses on the 'implementation gap' between policy intentions and the actual use of video technology in rape trials. In this final part of the book, 'Justice outwith buildings', legal scholars Anna Carline and Jamie Murray, with criminologist Clare Gunby, draw on theories of 'affect' to examine how barristers continue to place significant emphasis upon the affective capacity of the complainant's body to move or influence the jury. The authors demonstrate that this understanding has directly impacted on prosecuting barrister willingness to engage with 'remote testimony' in order to protect survivors of sexual violence from further trauma. The barristers with whom Carline, Gunby, and Murray worked explained that, when prosecuting, they want the complainant to deliver their testimony live in the courtroom, where the jury can see the 'whites of their eyes'.[4] Consequently, Carline, Gunby, and Murray argue that policymakers need to appreciate the importance of the corporeal intensive affects that inform barristers' practice and shape the dynamics of the courtroom. The barristers interviewed for this work expressed their frustration at the continuous production of provisions and reforms by those who have little, if any, experience and knowledge of the everyday reality of courtroom dynamics.

The final contribution to the collection, 'Digital justice and video links: Connecting and conflating courtroom and carceral space', continues the

3 Charles T Goodsell, *The Social Meaning of Civic Space: Studying Political Authority through Architecture* (University Press of Kansas, 1988) 46; see Cossins and Rowden, this volume, page 153.

4 Carline, Gunby and Murray, this volume, page 181.

exploration of this theme of the challenges posed to justice by the absence of the body from the trial space. Visual artist and criminologist Carolyn McKay focuses on the increasing use of audiovisual technologies to connect public courtrooms with non-public sites of custody or detention. McKay argues that the conceptual expansion of courtroom space into prisons and police cells, and the converse – prisons and police cells conceptually intruding into courts – has serious implications for the administration of, and access to, justice. In the earlier chapters, authors suggest that architecture rends court spaces into public manifestations of the symbolic weight and majesty of the law, offering the possibilities of fairer justice and engagement with the communities in which they sit – or potentially limiting those possibilities. McKay asks the crucial question: What does transitioning from the terrestrial world to a digital environment, which networks with police cells and prisons, mean for those who must interact with courts as 'already in custody?' In comparing courtroom space with prison video-link space, McKay contends that the loss of the atmospherics, aesthetics, and architecture of court spaces has a dramatic impact on the ability of remote defendants to actively participate in their cases: Effectively, they are reduced to distanced and docile objects on whom justice is enacted. She argues for a critical engagement with how the transformed practices, procedures, and spatial relationships of digital justice spaces can be reconciled with procedural justice principles.

When read together, these chapters demonstrate the complex and contradictory relationship between architecture, court design, and the processes of justice. Much time and huge sums of public funds have been devoted over the centuries to these physical manifestations of the rule of law. Ultimately, the authors represented in this volume express optimism about the possibilities inherent in the better housing of justice, while at the same time demonstrating the limitations of design when accompanied by inadequate justice processes. Significantly, discernible throughout this volume is a repeated call for more critically aware research, education, and practice across the fields of architecture and law, and all those that intersect in the spaces within and outwith court buildings.

The journey of this volume has not been short; the contributors have faced numerous personal challenges, and then COVID-19. We, Emma and Kirsty, are indebted to the patience of each author. We also wish to note our appreciation to a number of people without whom this volume would not have been possible. This collection has its origins in the Spaces of Justice Symposium held at La Trobe University in Melbourne, Australia, in July 2017, at which a range of international scholars and practitioners of architecture, law, criminology, legal studies, and sociology gathered to discuss the intersection of courthouse design and social justice. The symposium formed part of the tenth anniversary celebrations of an incredible centre of justice innovation, the Neighbourhood Justice Centre, and was launched by that doyen of courtroom design critique, Professor Pat Carlen. The symposium would not have been possible without funding from the Transforming Human Societies research focus area and the Law School at La Trobe University. Finishing this book in the age of COVID-19 was made possible by funding from the Social Research Assistance Platform at La Trobe University.

The symposium led first to a 2019 special issue of the *Griffith Law Review*, in which design innovations in community justice centres and Indigenous courts were explored by incredible authors including Koori Justice Worker Kylie Smith; former magistrate of the Koori and Noonga Courts, Kate Auty; criminologists Pat Carlen, Harry Blagg, Mark Halsey, Melissa Val Palumbo, and Sarah Murray; and coordinator of the Court of the Future Network, Professor David Tait.[5] As the second publication issuing from the symposium, this book focuses more explicitly on court architecture.

We are grateful for the guidance provided by the editors at Routledge and their anonymous reviewers, at whose suggestion we reached beyond symposium participants to seek contributions. This suggestion led us to invite a contribution from Carolyn McKay. It also enabled us to bring together Annie Cossins and Emma Rowden (a symposium participant whose life has since seen an additional child and an international relocation) for their powerful cross-disciplinary collaboration. Thank you both for your trust in and patience with our academic match-making when you both had so much on your plates. While Peter Rush did not deliver a presentation at the symposium, he was there, asking the important questions that cut to the heart of the matter. We then hassled him into contributing his photo essay and are grateful for the richness of his contribution. We are also sincerely grateful to Elizabeth Grant, whose generous contributions in the face of personal difficulties have added immeasurably to the whole. Her work enabled us to include the architect's perspective on the Kununurra Courthouse and to reproduce the analysis of Indigenous Court buildings that she co-authored with Murphy and Anthony for her edited collection with Springer, *The Handbook of Contemporary Indigenous Architecture*. Anna Carline, Clare Gunby, and Jamie Murray, you were so efficient and timely, it was a delight to work with you. To the Honourable Justice Michael Black, your contribution provided such important insights and was delivered with such charm. Caroline McKay, you responded so quickly and powerfully to our invitation.

We believe this collection is a rich and nuanced addition to the literature on courthouse design and we are genuinely grateful both to our colleagues, and to the contributors, who persevered in truly difficult, and in some cases tragic, circumstances. Jamie Murray passed away in April 2020 and we honour his life and contribution to this collection. We extend our condolences to his partner and co-author Anna Carline and their good friend and co-author Clare Gunby.

We also need to sincerely thank our wonderful research assistant Isabello Bettoso, who is responsible for converting a wide variety of referencing styles

5 'The Space of Justice: Courtrooms, Innovation and Practice' (2019) 27(2) *Griffith Law Review*; the special issue contains contributions from Pat Carlen, Mark Halsey and Melissa de Vel-Palumbo, Kylie Smith, David Tait, Sarah Murray, and Harry Blagg, and Kate Auty, and the editors, Emma Henderson and Kirsty Duncanson.

in line with the AGLC, and the talented Julia Farrell, for her copyediting excellence. Emma and Kirsty offer each other genuine thanks for the enduring friendship, tolerance, exciting conversations, and attention to detail that made this whole thing possible. And finally, we thank Judith Resnik, a symposium participant who agreed to write a foreword in the midst of COVID-19 hitting the US, where she has been juggling her academic load with social justice work seeking the release of prisoners during the pandemic. We regard your commitment as a sign that this collection is important.

PART I
Building justice

1

REIMAGINING SPACES FOR INDIGENOUS JUSTICE

The architecture and design of the Kununurra Courthouse

Elizabeth Grant and Martyn Hook

Introduction

The design of buildings and environs for the fair and just delivery of Western forms of justice for Indigenous peoples is a new architectural domain. In this chapter, we discuss the background and design of the Kununurra Courthouse, a new courthouse designed and built in Kununurra, a town in northern Western Australia on the eastern extremity of the Kimberley region near the border of the Northern Territory.[1]

Courts have been part of a 'revolving door of despair' for generations of Australian Indigenous people. Historically, procedures occurring in courts have contributed little to decreasing the overrepresentation of Indigenous people in the criminal justice system. The physical nature of the Western court settings designed with layers of hierarchy and control devoid of Indigenous control, have not allowed Indigenous people to participate meaningfully and have contributed to greater numbers of Indigenous people being remanded or sentenced to custody.

This chapter is a collaboration bringing the first author's theoretical scholarship in the field of Indigenous architecture and placemaking together with the architectural theory scholarship and practice experience of the second author as an academic and a senior member of the design team for the Kimberley courthouse project. It should be stated from the outset that the authors, in line with the views of many others, see inherent issues arising from the design of courts,

1 Kununurra was created as a service centre for the construction of Lake Argyle, a large human-made freshwater reservoir created by damming the Ord River. Kununurra's population comprises some 7,500 permanent residents, growing to approximately 10,000 people in the 'dry' season, due to tourism. Thirty per cent of the population identify as being of Aboriginal descent, who are highly overrepresented in the criminal justice system.

DOI: 10.4324/9780429059858-3

courthouses, and other criminal justice projects for Indigenous users. The vexing question continually arises as to how architects and design practitioners are able to design to engage Indigenous peoples with Western legal systems, when these are the systems that have usurped Indigenous peoples from traditional lands, destroyed sacred sites, and been used almost universally to divide and conquer.[2]

Colonial Australia was formed on the falsehood of *terra nullius*, and an epistemological arrogance that deemed English law, and those who deliver it, as having definitive and 'true' knowledge. English law was used deliberately to divide and conquer and to disrupt the traditional law/lore and cultural practices of hundreds of Aboriginal Nations across Australia. The ongoing impacts of colonisation are apparent across Australia, manifested in the manner in which Aboriginal Australians are overrepresented in the criminal justice system and are prevented from sharing the socioeconomic outcomes enjoyed by many non-Indigenous Australians. The authors argue for the need for new architectural typologies using principles from outside the Anglosphere to unseat the Western nation-state and right historical injustices for Australian Aboriginal peoples.

In accepting the commission to design the Kununurra Courthouse, Iredale Pedersen Hook, in collaboration with TAG Architects, assumed the responsibility of working with the various stakeholders including Traditional Owners.[3] This chapter discusses the history, social context and aspirations of Traditional Owners and knowledge holders of Kununurra, the Miriwoong (alternative spellings Miriuwung or Miriwung) peoples and their aspirations to create architecture that publicly addresses historical injustices, brings Indigenous values and aspirations to the forefront of design, and challenges traditional courthouse architecture.[4] The chapter goes on to discuss the manner in which architecture may address Indigenous cultural, socio-spatial, and environmental needs to create an 'Aboriginal place' where justice could be delivered, and how post-colonial approaches have been applied to the architectural and landscape design for a courthouse. This has taken place within a range of legal developments occurring in Australia. These initiatives have included the development of Aboriginal courts, circle sentencing, and mediation processes, which involve Aboriginal people as key participants.[5] All of these developments have required unseating

2 While Indigenous traditional law/lore is still applied by people in some Australian First Nations, all Australian citizens are held to account by the substantive law of Australia, which is largely derived from the common law system of English law.

3 The briefing process was complex and included a variety of stakeholders including local business owners, the judiciary, Courts Administration, and other parties.

4 The Mirima Dawang Woorlab-gerring Language and Culture Centre encourages the use of the spelling 'Miriuwung' only when referring to the native title determination legislation and the body corporate's name, and encourages the use of 'Miriwoong' in all other situations. See Mirima Dawang Woorlab-gerring Language and Culture Centre, *A Note on Miriwoong Spelling* (Web Page, 2019) <http://mirima.org.au/a-note-regarding-miriwoong-spelling/>.

5 See, for example, John Tomaino, *Aboriginal (Nunga) Courts* (Office of Crime Statistics & Research, 2004); Mark Harris, 'From Australian Courts to Aboriginal Courts in Australia: Bridging the

the Western nation-state as the point of engagement, and reconceptualising heuristic pathways in the design and physical setting of the court and courthouse. Indigenous personal and community *pagi* and the unceded *demesne* of Traditional Owners have had to be considered to reconceive courthouses as places that deliver fair and equal justice. Critical to such developments are understanding histories, empowering Indigenous peoples, respecting Aboriginal peoples as the First Peoples of Australia, and allowing Indigenous people to lead the way in reconstructing and reimagining a fair and just justice system[6] to achieve full emancipation, and the assertion and reclamation of the rights of First Nation peoples.

The attempted subjugation of the Miriwoong and Gajerrong peoples

Major relocations of Aboriginal people in the Kimberley region occurred as people were 'moved' when Crown land was 'leased' to pastoralists. The resultant displacements meant that '[f]or most Aboriginal people living in this region, the period between the 1880s and the 1920s [was] a time of fear and chaos'.[7] From 1886, legislative frameworks regulating mobility, employment, and other forms of interactions with Europeans underpinned the relationship between Aboriginal peoples and pastoralists.[8] Police collaborated with station managers to coerce Aboriginal peoples to work on stations.[9] Aboriginal mobility was encouraged by station owners to fit with the seasonal cycles of the monsoonal climate, when their labour was not required. By the mid-1940s, Aboriginal people were living in ration camps on pastoral stations throughout the dry season. Work on the stations ceased during 'the wet', during which time Aboriginal people would move to bush camps and live in a 'traditional'[10] manner.[11]

Gap?' (2004) 16(1) *Current Issues in Criminal Justice* 26–41; Elena Marchetti and Kathleen Daly, *Indigenous Courts and Justice Practices in Australia: Trends & Issues in Crime and Criminal Justice No. 277* (Australian Institute of Criminology, 2004); Elena Marchetti, 'Indigenous Sentencing Courts: Towards a Theoretical and Jurisprudential Model' (2007) 29 *Sydney Law Review* 415; Emma Henderson and Kirsty Duncanson, 'The Space of Justice: Courtrooms, Innovation and Practice' (2018) 27(2) *Griffith Law Review* 173–175.

6 See Harry Blagg and Thalia Anthony, *Decolonising Criminology: Imagining Justice in a Postcolonial World* (Palgrave Macmillan, 2019).

7 Pamela Smith, 'Station Camps: Legislation, Labour Relations and Rations on Pastoral Leases in the Kimberley Region, Western Australia' (2000) 24 *Aboriginal History* 75–97.

8 Ruth Lane, 'History, Mobility and Land Use Interests of Aborigines and Farmers in the East Kimberley in North West Australia' in Pamela J. Stewart and Andrew Strathern (eds), *Landscape, Memory and History: Anthropological Perspectives* (Pluto Press, 2003) 136–165.

9 Deborah Bird Rose, *Hidden Histories: Black Stories from Victoria River Downs, Humbert River and Wave Hill Stations* (Aboriginal Studies Press, 1991); Bruce Shaw, *When the Dust Come in between: Aboriginal Viewpoints in the East Kimberley Prior to 1982* (Aboriginal Studies Press, 1992).

10 Mary Durack and Elizabeth Durack, 'All-About: The Story of a Black Community on Argyle Station, Kimberley' (1936) *The Bulletin*.

11 Lane (n 8).

The upheaval of Aboriginal people in the Eastern Kimberley region was amplified with the commencement of the Ord Irrigation Scheme.[12] Kununurra was built as the service centre for the scheme in 1960, with the construction of the Kununurra Diversion Dam across the Ord River, completed in 1963. Without consultation,[13] Country (*dawang*) belonging to the Miriwoong and Gajerrong peoples[14] was flooded. Already excluded from sites of cultural importance by the establishment of pastoral leaseholds, the construction of Lake Argyle, Australia's largest dam reservoir (covering an area of 741 square kilometres), Aboriginal people were further expelled from their Country, including sites of historical and cultural significance.[15] The establishment of Kununurra and the construction of Lake Argyle also coincided with structural changes in the pastoral industry that resulted in Aboriginal people leaving the stations[16] and moving to Kununurra. Most families initially camped around Lily Lagoon, and then moved into self-built houses in a designated reserve area on the town's fringe.[17] Tensions that had arisen due to exclusions from traditional lands grew as mining activity[18] expanded. Aboriginal people experienced ongoing colonial penetration and

12 The Traditional Owners of the East Kimberley include the people of the Balanggarra, Miriwoong Gajerrong, Yurriyangem Taam, Gooring, Malarngowem, Koonjie Elvire, Purnululu, Ngarrawanji, Uunguu, Wilinggin, Gajirrabeng, Gooniyandi Kija, Walmajarri Kwini, Jaru, and Tjurabalan groups.

13 Jessica McLean, 'From Dispossession to Compensation: A Political Ecology of the Ord Final Agreement as a Partial Success Story for Indigenous Traditional Owners' (2012) 43(4) *Australian Geographer* 339–355.

14 The collaboration between groups of the East Kimberley is underpinned by the regional Indigenous social institution called the *wirnan* (alternative spelling *wunan*). This is a system of reciprocal exchange among the landowning and ritual groups. Relationships are based on the Aboriginal spiritual ceremonial cycle and exchange of spiritual objects, and on the conferring of status in the Kimberley and part of the Northern Territory, tying groups of people and their traditional estates together through sacred narratives and initiation ceremonies. Elders also conceive of this as an economic relationship, legitimised by its spiritual basis, and use its principles in everyday life as an economic logic. The *wirnan* ties people and countries together across vast landscapes in significant binding relationships.

15 Herbert Cole Coombs (ed), *Land of Promises: Aborigines and Development in the East Kimberley* (Australian National University and Aboriginal Studies Press, 1989); Deborah Rose Bird and Anne Clarke, *Tracking Knowledge in Northern Australian Landscapes: Studies in Indigenous and Settler Ecological Knowledge Systems* (Brinkin, 1997); Helen Ross, 'The East Kimberley Impact Assessment Project' (1991) 16(4) *Interdisciplinary Science Reviews* 313–323; Tanya Vernes, 'Ord: Case Study for Inappropriate Development and Poor Planning' in Rosemary Hill, Kate Golson, Pat Lowe, Maria Mann, Sue Hayes, and Jane Blackwood (eds), *Kimberley Appropriate Economies Roundtable Forum Proceedings* (Australian Conservation Foundation, 2006) 53–58.

16 Cathie Clement, *Historical Notes Relevant to Impact Stories of the East Kimberley* (East Kimberley Impact Assessment Project, 1989); Ann McGrath, *Born in the Cattle: Aborigines in Cattle Country* (Allen & Unwin, 1987).

17 Later renamed Mirima Reserve and then Mirima.

18 This included activities such as the creation of Argyle Diamond Mine at Kalkalnyimin in 1979 and the Normandy Poseidon Bow River Diamond Mine in 1987, and the continued exploration and intensified mining exploration in the 1980s and 1990s. As a consequence, a number of infrastructure projects were undertaken, including the construction of a hydropower station at the base of the Argyle Dam, and the building of power lines to service mines and link grids.

serious impingements on Indigenous livelihoods.[19] All the while, pastoralists, irrigators, and then mining companies[20] made unilateral decisions about the land with neither consultation nor compensation.

Reinstating the rights of the Miriwoong and Gajerrong peoples

From the 1980s, Aboriginal people began to establish outstations on traditional lands in the Northern Territory[21] and Western Australia. In 1998, the Federal Court of Australia ruled that the Miriwoong and Gajerrong people be granted native title to land within both Western Australia and the Northern Territory. A subsequent appeal mounted by the Western Australian and Northern Territory governments found that a number of contemporary land uses were incompatible with the exercise of native title rights and that consequently Indigenous rights to much of the area had been extinguished.

Following a decade of protracted litigation, successful appeals in 2003 and 2006 returned to the Miriwoong and Gajerrong peoples the right to possess, occupy, use, and enjoy the land and waters of approximately 7,900 square kilometres in the East Kimberley region of the north of Western Australia and adjacent land in the Northern Territory.[22] The area claimed covered all Crown lands (including pastoral leaseholds, township areas, as well as lands subject to valid mining leases and an area set aside for the Ord River Irrigation Scheme). The native title rights held by the Miriwoong and Gajerrong peoples included:

- A right to possess, occupy, use, and enjoy the area;
- A right to make decisions about the use of the area;
- A right of access to the area;
- A right to control access by others;
- A right to use and enjoy the resources of the area;
- A right to control the use of resources by others;
- A right to trade in those resources;
- A right to receive a portion of resources taken by others;
- A right to maintain and protect important cultural sites;
- A right to maintain, protect, and prevent the misuse of cultural knowledge.[23]

19 Jessica McLean, 'Still Colonising the Ord River, Northern Australia: A Postcolonial Geography of the Spaces between Indigenous Peoples' and Settlers' Interests' (2014) 180(3) *The Geographical Journal* 198–210.

20 Richard Howitt, 'A Different Kimberley: Aboriginal Marginalisation and the Argyle Diamond Mine' (1989) 74(3) *Geography* 232–238.

21 The Miriwoong and Gajerrong lands extend to the east of the Ord Valley into the Northern Territory, where land rights have had a legal basis since the enactment of the *Aboriginal Land Rights (Northern Territory) Act 1976*.

22 See *Northern Territory v Lane 138 ALR 544* (1996).

23 Gary Meyers and Lisa Strelein, *The Content of Native Title: Questions for the Miriuwung Gajerrong Appeal* (Australian Institute of Aboriginal and Torres Strait Islander Studies, 2000).

The rights of the Miriwoong and Gajerrong peoples under the determination differ from other native title claims in that they are not limited to 'traditional' uses of the land. Simply stated, the Miriwoong and Gajerrong peoples have the right to the development of cultural practices that are not limited to what might be construed as 'traditional' or 'customary' pre-colonial cultural practices.[24] The determination is consistent with Indigenous perspectives on relationships to Country. The Miriwoong and Gajerrong peoples are not required to 'compartmentalise' relationships to the Country, nor fragment native title claims,[25] and the nature of the native title determination has removed the typical anthropological approach of adjudicating 'authentic indigeneity'.[26] This is of particular significance given the destructive nature of colonisation in the East Kimberley region, and the amount of cultural knowledge that was erased.[27] Post native title determination, the Miriwoong are undertaking language and cultural maintenance and revival projects to recover and preserve Indigenous knowledges. Understanding and accepting that culture is living, changing, and evolving was critical to the design of the Kununurra Courthouse.

The use of architecture to celebrate and reinforce cultural knowledges

The application of principles of Australian law provided the vehicle for the Miriwoong peoples to reclaim their land and begin to right historical injustices. The Miriwoong and Gajerrong peoples' native title determinations sit against a backdrop of other landmark cases such as *Mabo v Queensland (No 1 and 2)*.[28] Other legal precedents such as the *Native Title Act 1993 (Cth)* provided for the recognition and protection of native title by establishing ways in which dealings regarding native title proceed and by setting standards and mechanisms for determining claims. These landmark cases have reinstated Indigenous peoples' rights, but have also changed the materiality of many courthouses across Australia. As one example, at the High Court in Canberra, where landmark legal cases are heard, artworks reflecting the cultural development of the nation (including

24 Kim Barber and Hilary Rumley, *Gunanurang (Kununurra) Big River, Aboriginal Cultural Values of the Ord River and Wetlands* (Western Australian Water and Rivers Commission, 2003).

25 Peter Yu, 'Possibilities for Regional Agreements in the Kimberley in the Wake of the Miriuwung Gajerrong Decision' (1999) 4(21) *Indigenous Law Bulletin* 24.

26 For more discussion on this important point see, for example, Tess Lea, 'Contemporary Anthropologies of Indigenous Australia' (2012) 41 *Annual Review of Anthropology* 187.

27 For example, Miriwoong is classified as a critically endangered language with few fluent speakers.

28 These provided legal precedent for the recognition of Indigenous peoples' rights in Australia by reviewing the implications of Australia's settled status, applying the principle of non-discrimination in the enjoyment of property rights, explaining the operation of the Crown's sovereign radical title, recognising native title and the source of rights in Indigenous law and custom, and asserting the power of the state to extinguish native title rights.

Aboriginal and Torres Strait Islander artwork) are prominently displayed. Other court and courthouse projects have considered how to conceptualise spaces and places for Indigenous users, and to increase Indigenous peoples' access to a system that is fair and just.[29]

The Miriwoong people, in maintaining cultural traditions, define themselves by their relationships to each other and to the landscape. These relationships are said to originate in a sacred past called the *Ngarranggarni*, a term that encompasses the time when ancestral beings created society and the natural world, including the principles of the social world that the Miriwoong people regard as their laws and customs. Indigenous belief systems are underpinned by understandings that ancestral beings created the social institutions that govern kinship, descent, the land tenure system, and the features of the natural and supernatural world. These forms of social organisation include the descent-based landowning corporations referred to as *dawang* (traditional estates). The *dawang*, as well as the owners of the estates, the *dawawang*, are related to each other in a number of ways according to these traditions. Thus, it was appropriate that Country (*dawang*) became the foci for the design.

Genius loci

Without knowledge of Country (*dawang*), Indigenous people's capacity to learn, understand, and live by Aboriginal knowledge systems will be lost. The knowledge systems weave together relationships between cultural values, belief systems, social structures, and traditions and cultural practices.[30] A community and individual understanding of one's knowledge systems is important in defining social capital and enabling communities to adapt to change, and for communities and individuals to become resilient and thrive.

In the first instance, the Kununurra Courthouse celebrates the Miriwoong people's stoic victory in regaining control over their land through native title. Place-based cultural knowledge was explored throughout the design of the courthouse, with the architects working with Traditional Owners who chose culturally significant landforms as design triggers. The building is sited with three axes: Thegoowiyeng (Kelly's Knob), Mirima National Park (Hidden Valley), and the distant landscape (see Figure 1.1).

29 See, for example, Elizabeth Grant, 'Port Augusta Courts' (2009) 98(5) *Architecture Australia* 86–90; Thalia Anthony and Elizabeth Grant, 'Courthouse Design Principles to Dignify Spaces for Indigenous Users: Preliminary Observations' (2016) 8 *International Journal for Court Administration* 43; Lawrence Nield and Andrea Nield, 'New Kununurra Courthouse' (2015) 104(3) *Architecture Australia* 80–87; Julian Murphy, Elizabeth Grant and Thalia Anthony, 'Indigenous Courthouse and Courtroom Design in Australia: Case Studies, Design Paradigms and the Issue of Cultural Agency' in Elizabeth Grant, Kelly Greenop, Albert L. Refiti and Daniel J. Glenn (eds), *The Handbook of Contemporary Indigenous Architecture* (Springer, 2018) 495–525.

30 These knowledge systems are applied in various ways – in ritual, economic, and social practices, and in the control, use, and management of land, resources, and environments.

FIGURE 1.1 Drawing of the development where the courthouse was sited to three axes. (Drawing: Adrian Iredale: Iredale Pedersen Hook)

FIGURE 1.2 The form of the courthouse echoing Thegoowiyeng (Kelly's Knob). (Photograph: Peter Bennetts)

The form of the Kununurra Courthouse draws on the geomorphology of the region, with the roofline emulating Thegoowiyeng (Kelly's Knob) (see Figure 1.2). Thegoowiyeng rises 190 metres above the surrounding plain and is visible from Kununurra. It is a culturally significant place for the Miriwoong people, as the Ngarranggarni site of the night pigeon. Thegoowiyeng (and the landforms of the Mirima National Park (Hidden Valley)) has provided shelter, a permanent water supply through rockpools, and an abundance of rock wallabies and other food sources to the Miriwoong people. As well as being a creation site, it is also a place associated with Aboriginal social history. Older Indigenous people hold fond memories of camping there during the pastoral period, and of visiting the site to gather together and escape the heat. It is a place where *wirnan* (reciprocal exchange) is ongoing. The formations were produced from sediments deposited by creeks and wind-blown sand about 300 million years ago. The fragile orange sandstone sedimentary rocks are protected by a thin layer of black-grey algae and lichens that resist the weathering. The colour palette used for the courthouse's roof imitates the thin grey protective coating on Thegoowiyeng's sedimentary rocks and emphasises the materiality unique to Kununurra.[31] While creating a dialogue with adjacent Country, the roof height is carefully controlled to relate to neighbouring buildings.[32] On the north-western façade, the roof form folds down with large panels perforated with an image of Lake Kununurra, providing a sunscreen that limits the direct sun and brings privacy to the judicial chambers and mediation suite. On the south-eastern façade a large brise-soleil follows the form of the roof, protecting the glass while changing the scale of the interior to create both communal and intimate spaces.

Reconceptualising the role of the courthouse

The East Kimberley region is a place where Aboriginal people have a strong connection to culture and Country, and Indigenous languages and practices have survived. Aboriginal organisations note that there are economic and social opportunities, but many Aboriginal people in the region remain in the grip of welfare dependency and suffer the effects of entrenched poverty, including poor health, substance misuse, mental health issues, homelessness, incarceration, fetal alcohol spectrum disorder, self-harm, and alarming rates of suicide. A backbone organisation, Binarri-binyja yarrawoo, was formed to lead the empowerment of Aboriginal people and facilitate reform for the East Kimberley region. Binarri-binyja yarrawoo states that:

> Our youth are full of promise and many of our people have fervent aspirations to take control of their lives, to build a future without reliance on Government. We as leaders of our community cannot stand by and watch this continue. Being poor and dying young will no longer be the story of our people.[33]

31 The roof also references the colour of the seed pods of the Gerdewoon (boab tree).

32 Nield and Nield (n 29) 80.

33 Binarri-binyja yarrawoo (BBY), *Empowered Communities* (2019, Web Page) <https://empoweredcommunities.org.au/our-regions/east-kimberley-3/>.

The emphasis for this and other projects is on building human capability, stressing that Aboriginal people must drive decision-making, and be accountable for the outcomes.

Given this framework, churning Aboriginal people through the criminal justice system is no longer acceptable. While youth offending rates, violent offences against the person, alcohol-related offences, and appearances of Aboriginal people before the courts in Kununurra[34] are exceptionally high, local Aboriginal organisations do not see the criminal justice interventions as useful or effective, advocating for programmatic responses to address the risk and protective factors impacting people. The deep-seated intergenerational nature of the factors contributing to the behaviours that result in involvement in the criminal justice system is seen to require a committed, long-term community-level response.[35] Using this model requires physical spaces for meaningful human exchanges and programme delivery, and for promoting the role of the courthouse as a place of fair and just dispute resolution.

Siting to create a place for equitable and fair dispute resolution

There has been a deliberate shift away from oppressive and authoritarian court design with the creation of non-threatening spaces. While traditional courthouse architecture manifests itself in enclosure, the Kununurra Courthouse is designed to be an open and accessible part of the community infrastructure. This has been achieved by using a design schema that includes careful siting, consideration of Aboriginal socio-spatial preferences, and designing the building to a human scale with connectivity to the external surroundings.

The courthouse is located on the corner of Coolibah Drive and Messmate Way, Kununurra. The building sits on the site of the former 1970s courthouse, which was built alongside the police station facing Coolibah Drive. The frontage of the courthouse was rotated to face Messmate Way,[36] to visually dissociate court activities from those of the police. A section of road reserve was co-opted, to extend the public spaces around the building. As a result of the rotation, the courthouse faces a building used by Aboriginal organisations and is closely connected to shops, other community infrastructure, and services. Existing trees were retained for shade, the area was grassed, and bespoke seating (designed to reflect the architecture) was installed to create a welcoming and useable threshold and civic space (see Figure 1.3).

34 Binarri-Binyja Yarrawoo Aboriginal Corporation, *Evidence Brief: Kununurra Youth Diversion* (2018, Web Page) <https://static1.squarespace.com/static/5a73dac1d0e62826b7a7521c/t/5c173c202b6a28e46b76f2b8/1545026617260/1Kununurra+YJ+Brief+Final+.pdf>.

35 Ibid.

36 External sunshades are installed on the Messmate Way elevation to reduce heat to the building and to further dissociate the building from the adjacent police station.

FIGURE 1.3 External view of entrance and outside area designed as a public space. (Photograph: Peter Bennetts)

The frontage increases public amenity and allows large groups of people using the courthouse to wait outside. This design was a planning response to counter the common issues arising from courthouses being sited to street frontages. For Aboriginal people and others, the experience of using court facilities is often emotionally charged; tempers can fray and disagreements can occur as people are forced to come into contact with other individuals and families in conflict. In some instances, this results in police arrests (such as during Aboriginal Court sitting days), when large numbers of Aboriginal people are required to congregate.[37] The inclusion of an outside area also fits with Aboriginal socio-spatial behaviour around courts. Aboriginal families/groups may choose to gather outside a courthouse en masse as a demonstration of support, dissent, or anger while a case[38] is heard. Typically, when a family member is involved, one or two people attend the court hearing and report progress back to the group. Groups

37 See Grant (n 29) for a discussion of the Port Augusta region and court use.

38 Especially in cases where a term of imprisonment may be imposed.

often congregate for long periods, and so, particularly as case outcomes vary, unconstrained spaces where emotions can be displayed without interference from outsiders are necessary. The design of the outside areas also allows court staff to visually supervise people occupying these areas, and to provide culturally appropriate support and intervention if required.

Internal schematics

Rethinking the role of the courts and of the importance of appropriate architecture began in the mid to late 1980s. Concerns to make justice relevant to all users has led to the consideration of many aspects of the courthouse experience, including the need for actual and perceptual access to the outdoors and fresh air, the need for privacy to deal with administration matters, how and where people wait for others and to appear in a trial or hearing, and the need to be able to gather – and these considerations have all informed the design of the Kununurra Courthouse. The parti adopted has changed from internal square floor plan models to the open-to-outdoors models with developed and useable threshold and interstitial spaces. Contemporary court architecture demands investment in design thinking to create calm and dignified environments that ameliorate disturbing experiences for users. Scale manipulation to modulate between institutional presence and personal comfort, greater acoustic performance, clear wayfinding, and the integration and use of positive distractions to create calming environments are all critical. The Kununurra Courthouse has the qualities of a contemporary court architecture. It is airy, full of natural light, and has good wayfinding, access to the outdoors, and meaningful views out of interior spaces such as courtrooms and jury deliberation rooms.

Courthouses require a secure public entrance and entries are often traditionally abrupt, funnelling the user from the exterior into the courthouse with little transition. The Kununurra Courthouse was designed using interstitial spaces that allow users to linger outside and that provide a gentle transition into the building/building's interiors. This has been achieved through using the same surface materials (local stone) on the exterior paths and in the foyer area. The entrance is clearly apparent and can be observed from the exterior areas, allowing people to delay their entrance to the building if they wish. The entrance area contains the security screening equipment stipulated in the briefs for all Australian courthouses. In contrast to the experience in many similar buildings, while being screened, people entering the Kununurra Courthouse have a view into the open foyer and beyond.

The volume and size of the public foyer (see Figure 1.4) is crucial to the design schematic and is much larger than outlined in the project brief. The area was conceived as an extension to the outside area and as a social space to allow people to gather in a variety of ways, resulting in a foyer ten times the size specified in the original brief. The stone-paved public foyer is lined with horizontal bands of natural timbers, using the same geomorphic design triggers used on the exterior

FIGURE 1.4 The foyer of the Kununurra Courthouse. (Photograph: Peter Bennetts)

of the building. The colour palette, selection of timbers (jarrah, Tasmanian ash, and blackwood) for the wall panels, zigzag seating, and the undulating peripheral walls reflect the local colour pallette and geomorphology, referencing the local orange sandstone sedimentary rocks and jagged rock formations (see Figure 1.5). Horizontal layers of timber panels replicate the stratigraphical profile, where fine layers of sandstone were laid by natural processes, one upon another, over 300 million years ago. The schema also respectfully acknowledges the longevity and depth of Indigenous cultures and knowledges. The building edges include continuous built-in timber seats of various configurations, enabling visitors to find a congruent space and to sit in groups or find a quiet place alone. The brise-soleil dialogues with the seating and visitors, framing views to the distant hills and local landscaping.

The glass frontage connects the internal and external areas and is accentuated by acoustic panels, offering acoustic privacy for the various activities taking place inside the building. The sun's position can be seen throughout the interior of the building providing ontological security. The design schematic is carried through into the magistrates and jury rooms and other facilities (including spaces for mediation, pre-trial conferences, a remote witness room, areas for jury deliberation, witnesses, victims of crime, and interview rooms).

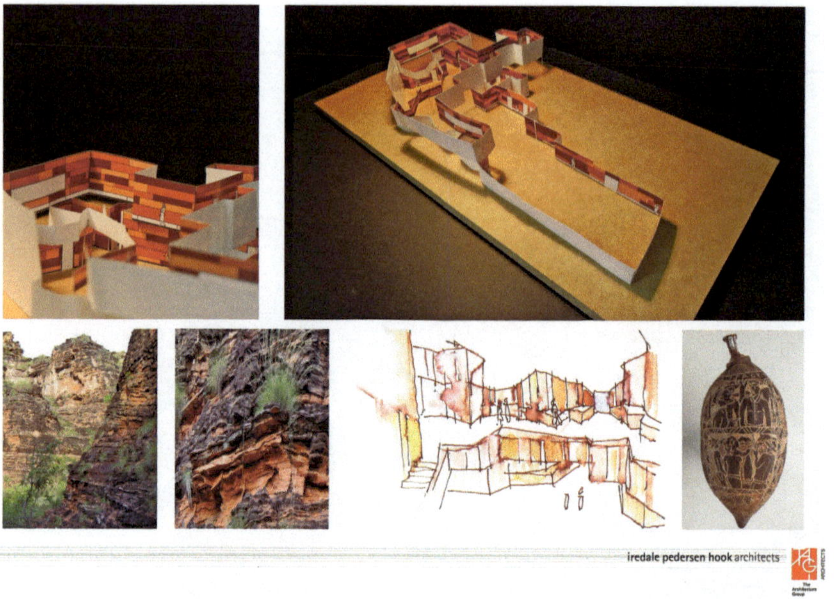

FIGURE 1.5 Internal schematic models pictured with the design drivers (landscape and boab seeds). (Image: Iredale Pedersen Hook)

Part of the design agenda was to allow people to move between internal and external spaces seamlessly. A secure external waiting space was devised, which extends from the main foyer to accommodate people as required. The secure courtyard includes artwork (discussed later in the chapter), shaded grass, and undulating built-in seating made from local stone (see Figure 1.6). The striated stone used for the seating repeats the references to the local geomorphology. While the courtyard is enclosed (on the roof lined with a fine wire mesh for security purposes), the roof is filtrated and open to the sky and weather. Being able to feel the sun and the wind on one's face has been known to contribute to greater ontological security of Indigenous people using institutional settings. It also provides an escape from air-conditioning, essential for the temperature extremes in Kununurra but a feature that some Aboriginal people dislike.

Every Australian courthouse has a court registry, where staff provide information about court matters and liaise with the public. As discussions conducted here are often sensitive and confidential (such as when applying for urgent apprehended violence orders, or registering a birth or death), the registry is screened and located beyond the view of the waiting areas. The acoustics and design of the registry were carefully considered to ensure people's safety and privacy and to minimise the stress for users.

FIGURE 1.6 Foyer showing seating, stone flooring, timber, and art panels. (Photograph: Peter Bennetts)

The integration of art

All of the public areas of the Kununurra Courthouse include artworks. Aboriginal people have been layering Western buildings with Indigenous signs, symbols, and motifs to create Aboriginal places since the 1970s, when Aboriginal organisations were set up in the self-determination era.[39] In the early 1980s, a significant development took place when the people of Yuendumu began transferring ochre ground paintings to canvas, and then to the doors of the Yuendumu School,[40] and created murals inside the Yuendumu Men's Museum.[41] The acts at Yuendumu were the beginning of the Western Desert

39 Elizabeth Grant and Kelly Greenop, 'Affirming and Reaffirming Indigenous Presence: Contemporary Aboriginal and Torres Strait Islander Community, Public and Institutional Architecture in Australia' in Elizabeth Grant, Kelly Greenop, Albert L. Refiti and Daniel J. Glenn (eds), *The Handbook of Contemporary Indigenous Architecture* (Springer, 2018) 57–105.

40 In 1983, five artists painted 30 school doors with Dreaming designs, negotiating the content with other Warlpiri men and women who also collectively owned the designs. Twenty-seven *Tjukurrpa* (Dreamings) were represented on the doors, referring to more than 200 sites in Warlpiri and Anmatyerre territory. (See Warlukurlangu Artists, *Kuruwarri: Yuendumu Doors* (Australian Institute of Aboriginal Studies, Canberra, 1987); Rex Butler, 'Before the Law: Reading the Yuendumu Doors with Eric Michaels' (1999) 41 *Eyeline* 28.

41 Carmichael Bethune and Apolline Kohen, 'The Forgotten Yuendumu Men's Museum Murals: Shedding New Light on the Progenitors of the Western Desert Art Movement' (2013) 1 *Australian Aboriginal Studies* 110.

Art Movement, and demonstrated that art could be used as an Indigenous placemaking tool. Many buildings display artworks as a way of making Indigenous voices heard, telling a story, defining a place, or marking a space as an Indigenous place. In Australian courthouse architecture, Indigenous art is often commissioned and exhibited to layer Western architecture with Indigenous signs, symbols, and motifs.[42] For the Kununurra Courthouse project, artworks were integrated into the design, and the artists became integral members of the design team.

Over 20 Aboriginal artists[43] from Miriwoong Country were involved in the project, commissioned through the Waringarri Aboriginal Arts Centre,[44] and their work is central to the design of the building. Through these works, the artists explored the themes of family using the process of *wirnan* (reciprocal exchange), demonstrating how lore and culture are passed from one generation to the next. These themes are central to Miriwoong existence. The Miriwoong people maintain a system of kinship that consists of eight named categories known as subsections or skins. Each person in the Miriwoong social envelope falls into one of these categories at birth and is related to others through a system of putative kinship ties represented by the subsection system and is, through birth, given responsibility for certain cultural knowledge. Five family groups (the Armstrong, Griffiths, Ningarmara, Mengil, and Malarvie families) from the Miriwoong and Djaru language groups produced the collaborative 'family boards' about kinship relationships to Country. Senior artists worked with children to create the series of artworks. The original artworks are displayed behind the registry counter and in the mediation and consulting rooms. The works were then interpreted as acoustic and glass panels, which are displayed outside the courtrooms and in the waiting areas. Woven through the fabric of the building, the original artworks produced by the family groups sit alongside digital interpretations.

Artists from other areas such as Warmun and Kalumburu were commissioned to provide additional work that reflects the *wirnan* occurring between Aboriginal groups in the East Kimberley region. Murrinh-Patha artist Bryan Murielle carved a bespoke timber handrail, which is positioned at the base of the stairs. It depicts two intertwined snakes, suggesting two systems of law/lore working side

42 One prominent exception to this is the Port Augusta Court Complex, which integrated Indigenous artists into the design team and used several Indigenous motifs as design generators for the courthouse. See Grant (n 29).

43 The artists involved were Agnes Armstrong, Armstrong Family, Alan Griffiths, Peggy Griffiths, Kittey Malarvie, Louise Malarvie, Judy Mengil, Gloria Mengil, Phyllis Ningarmara, Brenda Ningarmara, Minnie Lumai. Ben Ward Alan Griffiths, Griffiths Family, Judy Mengil, Mengil Family, Kitty Malarvie, Louise Malarvie, Malarvie Family, Ben Ward, Brian Muriell, Ningarmara Family, Rusty Peters, Freddy Timms, Mercy Fredericks, Peggy Patrick, Mabel Juli, Mary Teresa Tailor, and Minnie Lumai. The artwork was coordinated by Malcolm McGregor (Government of Western Australia Percentage for Art Program: Kununurra Courthouse, 2015).

44 See <https://www.waringarriarts.com.au/>.

by side.[45] Jaru artist Louise Malarvie's work *Nyamooli* ('Bush Soap')[46] is etched into glass panels located at the entrance, staircase, and in other public areas.

Research has shown that commissioning artists to work in design teams in large architectural projects results in increased cultural and two-way learnings. The Traditional Owners have a vision:

> We want for our children the same opportunities and choices other Australians expect for their children. We want them to succeed in mainstream Australia, achieving educational success, prospering in the economy, and living long and healthy lives. We want them to retain their distinct cultures and identities as peoples and to be recognised as Indigenous Australians.[47]

It is crucial that, to achieve this vision, Indigenous organisations and individuals be involved in civic developments such as this project. The economic importance of commissioning Aboriginal artists has also been highlighted by Waringarri Art Centre, who noted that such projects provide 'economic independence for local artists and their community' and opportunities for their work to reach wider audiences.[48]

As with any courthouse project in Australia, non-Indigenous readings of the space are also needed. Artist Jonathan (Jon) Tarry was commissioned to complete a sculptural piece for the secure courtyard. Tarry's piece alludes to the principle of 'balance' that underpins Australia's legal system. The artwork references the balancing rocks and geological forms of Mirima National Park and reiterates the geomorphic aspect of the architectural design.

Courtroom design

The Kununurra Courthouse includes both magistrates courtrooms and jury courtrooms. Both courtrooms are designed to be light and airy, with interiors lined with timber panels that conceal the security, recording, and teleconferencing technology, and the entrances to the 'back of house' circulation routes (that is, for custody, court officials, jury, and judiciary). In the planning process, the courts were offset to provide circulation routes that allow the judiciary to interact and move between the courts easily. The Western Australian Magistrates Courts deal with all lower court proceedings and are where all criminal proceedings start. The Magistrates

45 Leanne Collier, *Waringarri Art at the New Kununurra Courthouse* (Web Page, 2015) <http://desertriversea.com.au/blog/waringarri-art-at-the-new-kununurra-courthouse>.

46 Bush soap grows near swamps, rivers, and springs. During the dry season, the long pods split open, revealing the black seeds.

47 Binarri-binyja yarrawoo (BBY), *Empowered Communities* (2019, Web Page) <https://empoweredcommunities.org.au/our-vision>.

48 Kathy Cummins, Waringarri Aboriginal Arts.

Court in Kununurra also hears civil matters and family court matters, and may operate as an Aboriginal community court, a tenancy tribunal, a children's court, or operate as a mediation area. In terms of criminal matters, the role of magistrates courthouses across Australia is changing. Rather than being places for trials and hearings, they are increasingly becoming places for social interventions, with the application of therapeutic and restorative justice being used to address the factors leading to criminality. As such, the design of magistrates courts has changed and the design for Kununurra needed to reflect this.

The Magistrates Court at Kununurra is an open space, furnished with moveable furniture to allow the room to be reordered to host formal or informal hearings. It has a window fitted with an external screen facing Coolibah Drive that allows views to the distance. The screen has a pragmatic function in shielding the windows of the courtroom (and the offices of the judiciary and administration) from view, reducing heat load and preventing rain from hitting the façade. The perforated screen can be manipulated to provide various views and to adjust the shading. It is embedded with a graphic of Lake Kununurra (the flooded section of the Ord River valley formerly known as Carlton Reach). At night the screen is lit, emphasising the civic function of the building and providing an example of architectural excellence in the remote town.[49]

The jury courtroom (see Figure 1.7) accommodates the District Court, which deals with serious criminal offences that must be tried before a judge and jury or a judge sitting alone. In its civil jurisdiction, the court deals with commercial and debt recovery matters and personal injury claims. The District Court also has appellant jurisdiction for civil matters on appeal from the Magistrates Court and appeals in respect to awards for criminal injuries. The Western Australian District Court has 30 judges who are based in Perth, who travel on circuit to regional and remote areas on a regular basis.

The principles of therapeutic jurisprudence have not been widely embraced by the District and Supreme Courts across Australia. This is reflected in the design of the jury courtroom, which is the most formal room in the building and contains many of the elements of traditional courtroom design. The jury courtroom is, however, a contemporary design. It is similarly airy to the Magistrates Court, with neutral materials and discreet fittings (interestingly, including a relatively unobtrusive coat of arms). A clerestory window is situated above the judge's position – a design feature that occurred in consultation with Traditional Owners, drawing on the critical importance of viewing the sky in traditional law/lore practice. Through this consultation, it was determined that if the sky could be viewed behind the judge, then the two systems of law could be symbolically tied together.

The jury courtroom is located beneath the highest part of the roof line, producing a form that echoes the shape of the adjacent landforms. The high ceiling

49 This function is also a safety measure as court officials and the judiciary can work after dark without being observed from the road.

FIGURE 1.7 The jury courtroom within the Kununurra Courthouse complex. (Photograph: Peter Bennetts)

enhances spatial quality in providing unobstructed views for all participants, creating a 'civic' aesthetic and a court that exudes considerable gravitas. The impact of this on the outcomes for Indigenous participants is yet to be measured.

Conclusion

Indigenous peoples in the Kimberley region have had a long history of exposure to attempted subjugation, with the criminal justice system employed as one method to control people and remove their rights. In line with the aspirations of the Traditional Owners and other members of Indigenous communities, the design of the Kununurra Courthouse was intended as a place for orderly dispute resolution, and for the delivery of fair and appropriate justice. The architecture of the Kununurra Courthouse sends a clear message that the judiciary values Indigenous peoples and cultures, and that measures delivered in the courthouse will be fair and just. At this point in time, in the absence of post-occupancy evaluation, it remains unclear whether the new courthouse is furthering justice for Indigenous users and leading to the empowerment of Indigenous people in the region. It is important that such evaluations are completed as the role of architecture in this genre needs to be better understood.

The Kununurra Courthouse is a significant development in Australian courthouse architecture. Developing spaces for justice that incorporate narratives of Country, complex meanings, and Indigenous knowledges is a relatively new domain. Such design is important, as without knowledge of Country, Indigenous people's capacity to learn, understand, and live by Aboriginal knowledge systems will be lost. Community and individual understandings of one's knowledge systems are important in defining social capital and the ability of communities to adapt to change, and for communities and individuals to become resilient and thrive.

The complexities of design, overlaid with the complexities of the justice system and its application in relation to Indigenous peoples, and how that is to be manifested through architecture, still constitute an area requiring further exploration. There is much work to be done. This includes investigating the design impact of court custody on the physical and psychological wellbeing of Indigenous peoples and others; universal access; the nature and use of separate circulation routes; developing environments to meet the needs of Indigenous judiciary, lawyers, and employees of the court; and the planning and design of spaces that reduce conflict for divergent parties and lessen the trauma of court appearances for children, victims, and families. Further work is likely to enable greater reimaginings of court architecture to allow Australian Indigenous people to further assert and reclaim their rights, to right historical injustices, and to create more inclusive civic places and spaces.

Civic buildings should be places where citizens feel safe and welcomed, where they can grow and learn, and where they can strengthen their community ties. The design of the Kununurra Courthouse reintroduces the value of the regional courthouse as a landmark civic building that represents the local community. This is public architecture that provides positive readings of Indigenous histories and knowledges, and conveys, to the population at large, the value of Indigenous peoples and cultures.

Acknowledgements

The authors would like to acknowledge the assistance of Finn Pedersen, Adrian Iredale, and John Fien in the preparation of this chapter.

2

THE ARCHITECTURE OF LAW COURTS

How concepts of justice – light, transparency, access, and equality – drove the design of new and renovated courthouses for federal courts in Australia[1]

The Hon Michael Black[2]

Introduction

Courthouses are buildings of the highest importance in a community and to a nation. As well as being places in which the rule of law finds tangible expression, these buildings have enduring significance as architectural representations and symbols of the place of law, and the rule of law, in the life of the nation.

That is why, in the early 1990s, it was seen by judges as vitally important that the proposed, and much needed, Commonwealth law courts in Melbourne should not be located in a converted office building or, worse, in fitted-out floors of such a building. In Adelaide too, where the Federal Court did occupy two floors of an office building, a purpose-built courthouse for it and the Family Court was seen as essential. It was also highly desirable that the High Court of Australia should have suitable Commonwealth premises in all the state capitals so that it would not have to rely upon the Supreme Courts when sitting in capitals other than Sydney or Melbourne.

1 The chapter is written from the perspective of the Federal Court of Australia. The High Court has its own courtroom, registry, and other facilities in the Commonwealth Law Courts in Melbourne and Sydney and sits in the Roma Mitchell Commonwealth Law Courts in Adelaide when on circuit there. The Family Court and the Federal Circuit Court have separate courtrooms, registries, and other facilities in the Melbourne, Adelaide, and Hobart courthouses.

2 Chief Justice of the Federal Court of Australia from 1991 to 2010. The author has a longstanding interest in court architecture. As a barrister he became familiar with courthouses throughout Australia, particularly the principal courthouses of the Commonwealth, the states, and the territories. As a judge he sat in all the Federal Court's courthouses and many of those of the territories and as a guest on the bench in courts in Canada, New Zealand, the United Kingdom, the United States, and the Asia-Pacific Region.

DOI: 10.4324/9780429059858-4

The issue was, however, very much larger than the poor symbolism of a court being accommodated permanently in one or more office buildings; it was about how contemporary concepts and ideals of justice should find architectural expression.

This chapter examines, in a historical context, how those concepts and ideals drove the design of new courthouses in Melbourne and Adelaide, the redevelopment of an important courtroom in Hobart and the refurbishment of the Federal Court's section of Law Courts Building in Sydney. It has as its focus the Federal Court's accommodation, its design challenges and their solutions. A comprehensive description of the buildings has not been attempted,[3] nor has the complexity of the choices faced by the architects in achieving the design aims been examined in any detail. The architectural firms and the principal architects have been named but the buildings are of course the outcome of the creative work of hundreds of people, including the project managers, contractors, tradespeople, and building workers on the job.[4]

Courthouses in colonial times

Speaking very generally, from early colonial times until the last two or three decades of the twentieth century, whilst court buildings in Australia reflected the importance and authority of the law, the principal courthouses in the state capitals and larger regional cities and towns appeared to say less about other fundamentals, such as access to justice and the concerns the law should have for the individuals who, for whatever reason, might have to attend a court. In many instances it would seem, too, that the courthouse had a substantial role as a representation of the importance of the city or town it was built to serve.

The authority of the law was often asserted by the use of classical or other formal design elements. In the capital cities and principal regional cities the courthouses were generally large and impressive and they remain outstanding examples of the public architecture of their time.[5] The Supreme Court of Victoria (1884), with a dome suggestive – though by no means a copy – of the dome of the Four Courts in Dublin,[6] is the largest and one of the most impressive examples, but there are others in every state.

3 Much information, including images, is available online on the websites of the architects and on other sites, including some of the court websites. There is also a large online collection of images of Australian courthouse from colonial times to the present.

4 The buildings are described in the online sites of the architects and elsewhere online. More comprehensive acknowledgements were made in the author's addresses at the ceremonial sittings for the openings of the buildings.

5 For the early courthouses of Victoria, see Michael Challinger, *Historic Court Houses of Victoria* (Palisade Press, 2001) and of New South Wales, see Peter Bridges, *Historic Court Houses of New South Wales* (Hale & Iremonger, 1986). Many of these buildings are heritage listed.

6 Underlining, for many, the Irish strands in the heritage of the legal profession in Victoria and particularly that of the Victorian Bar.

The beautiful library of the Supreme Court of Victoria must surely be one of the finest secular interior spaces in Australia. It is a space of tranquillity that invites scholarship and speaks of the learning that underpins the common law. The external faces that the court building, and others of its era, turn to the public speak, however, very differently. Whilst the Supreme Court building is unquestionably dignified, elegantly proportioned, and assertive of the power and importance of the law, it may also be seen to enclose – contrary to the ethos of the Court it houses – a special world that is not readily accessible to the public and is perhaps remote from it. In this respect it stands in contrast to the modern County Court building, directly opposite.[7]

The perceived need in the colonial era for an architectural statement of authority varied in strength with time and place but, generally, the emphasis seems to have been on authority and importance rather than access, transparency, or equality. Indeed, the familiar figure of Justice, holding scales in one hand and a sword in the other, may have said more about justice than the buildings in front of which she stood.[8]

The smaller country courthouses should be excluded from these generalisations. Whilst they often displayed, on a smaller scale, some of the classical features and formality of their city and regional counterparts, many of them appeared to have a closer connection with their communities. Whether that connection had its source in the architecture of the courthouse and its smaller scale or in the nature of the community it served, or both, is a subject that invites exploration. Certainly, the author's memory of observing, as very junior counsel, wise justice being delivered in a small country courthouse, in deep winter, Mallee roots burning silently in the open fireplace of the single courtroom, provokes many thoughts about justice, intimacy in architecture, and the ultimate origins of some of the fine roots of our common law.

Early courthouses with abundant natural light

The colonial courthouses – large and small – generally had the benefit of abundant natural light, usually from large windows set high in the side walls of the courtroom. This arrangement of the windows worked well since it enabled elements such as the jury box to be placed in the lower half of the space and made for an orderly and efficient courtroom. In smaller country courthouses it also allowed for a single level of registry spaces and other ancillary rooms to be placed adjacent to the main courtroom or directly behind it, forming a T-shape. It was an arrangement for which a classical façade was well suited.

7 Daryl Jackson Architects, Lyons and SKM Architects, architects in association (2002).

8 For an exceptional consideration of the iconography of justice and of art and architecture in the law, considered in a global (including Australian) and historical context, see Judith Resnik and Dennis Curtis, *Representing Justice: Invention, Controversy, and Rights in City-States and Democratic Courtrooms* (Yale University Press, 2011).

With natural light and adequate space, the early courthouses could provide calm, well-lit courtrooms for judicial proceedings including, importantly, trials by jury; although, where opaque glass was used (and some notable examples come to mind), the benefits of the sight of the sky and clouds were unnecessarily denied.

Natural light disappears, but re-emerges in temporary courtrooms

Australian courthouses of a later era, now lit by electricity, often had greatly reduced access to natural light. The large windows of an earlier age were no longer necessary for illumination and the courtroom spaces became more enclosed. The courtrooms of some of the courthouses built in the 1950s and 1960s, and even later, had no external windows at all; the former County Court in William Street, Melbourne (1965), was an example.[9]

When, in the early 1990s, it was proposed on behalf of the Federal Court of Australia that justice might be better served and represented in courtrooms that related to the outside world, with natural light and even views of the world outside the courtroom, it was objected that this would invite constant distraction. This risk was said to negate any benefits, themselves disputed, of conducting the important work of the courts in spaces in which the natural rhythms of the light and shade of the passing day and of the changing seasons could be seen and felt.

There was, however, powerful contemporary evidence to the contrary. In the 1960s and 70s, and into the 1980s, significant judicial and quasi-judicial proceedings were being conducted in spaces that not only had natural light but views of the world outside as well. They were on floors in office buildings, leased to state and federal governments to house courts. In some instances, most notably in the premises occupied by the Commonwealth Conciliation and Arbitration Commission in William Street, Sydney, the views from the hearing rooms over Sydney Harbour were indeed potential distractions, as were the views of the Swan River from the courtrooms of the Federal Court's 'temporary'[10] premises in an office building in Perth. Nevertheless, just as in a courtroom without windows, proceedings were in fact conducted without interruption or discernible distraction.

The design of the important 1976 Law Courts Building in Phillip Street, Sydney,[11] on a site also offering superb views of Sydney Harbour, was evidently not influenced by the experience of hearings in nearby William Street. Despite the merits of Law Courts Building and a design that was in many respects ground-breaking, its courtrooms had virtually no natural light.

9 Now the William Cooper Justice Centre. It now has a substantially rearranged interior and access to natural light and external views.

10 For some 16 years.

11 Architects, McConnell Smith and Johnson, Sydney.

The attraction of a different approach was, however, suggested by the practice of some judges of having the external doors to their courtrooms left open, expanding the lines of sight beyond the courtroom and bringing in a little of the natural light from the windows in the lobbies and corridors.

May 1980: The High Court building points to light and access, and to the future

The new building for the High Court of Australia in Canberra, opened in May 1980,[12] whilst clearly reflecting the independence, importance and authority of Australia's highest court, pointed in an entirely different direction to the courthouses of earlier times; it pointed to the future. Its huge public areas were flooded with light. Any memories of the reticence in colonial times to have high ceilings and large internal spaces were swept aside. So, too, were memories of domes, spires, and the classical revival. The building was and remains remarkable for its space, its embrace of light, and its relationship to the world around it. As others have remarked, the building is very much Australian in its embrace of light and space.

From an advocate's viewpoint, it is a building that one can come to admire from the inside first – from the experience of walking through the great spaces with their abundant daylight and then into the principal courtroom and standing at its lectern.[13] Here is a space perfectly conceived for close intellectual engagement.

Whilst Court 1 does not offer views of the outside world to the advocates or to the public, it is partially illuminated by shafts of light entering the courtroom from a tall, high, narrow window at the west end of the judicial bench. Courtroom 2 goes further; it has a row of windows at waist level on the west (National Library) side.

Although it is categorised as an outstanding example of 'late Brutalist modern' architecture,[14] to the general reader this description of the building does not seem apt to reflect the building's relationship to its site, its use and embrace of light, and its embrace of the visiting public.[15]

The Commonwealth's court construction programme evolves

The experiences of advocates appearing in the new High Court and before courts and tribunals conducting hearings in adapted office buildings with windows and

12 Architects, Edwards Madigan Torzillo and Briggs, Sydney.

13 The author was privileged to be one of a small group of counsel taken on a tour of the building by the Chief Justice, The Rt Hon Sir Garfield Barwick, on the evening before its opening on 26 May 1980 by Her Majesty, The Queen. Chief Justice Barwick had been closely involved in the project and his observations were very illuminating.

14 See 'The Building', *High Court of Australia* (Webpage, 2010) <http://www.hcourt.gov.au/about/the-building>. See also the history podcast via the same site.

15 Perhaps following the precedent of Law Courts Building, the new High Court had a café that was open to both the profession and the public.

views of city, sea, clouds, and sky formed the background against which the Commonwealth's court construction programme was to evolve. After the opening of Law Courts Building and the subsequent construction of Commonwealth courthouses in Hobart and Canberra in the mid-1980s, and in Perth and Brisbane in the early 1990s, it remained to complete the programme by building courthouses in Melbourne and Adelaide.[16]

The Commonwealth Law Courts project for Melbourne

Fifteen years after its establishment, the Federal Court in Melbourne was still located 'temporarily' in two buildings: the superb and historically important, but then-rundown, High Court[17] and in 451 Bourke Street, directly opposite. The Family Court's situation was worse; it occupied several floors of Marland House, a large office building in Bourke Street then on the edge of Melbourne's rapidly evolving legal precinct. In Adelaide, both courts occupied congested space in an office building in Grenfell Street, colloquially known as the 'black stump'.

In late 1994, after a period of much uncertainty about funding for the project, the Commonwealth determined that the construction of a purpose-built Commonwealth Law Courts in Melbourne would proceed. The possibility of converting an office building, which had been seriously entertained[18] but stoutly resisted, was finally put to rest. Although concerns about funding remained, and the budget was always tight, it should be put on record that the successive Attorneys-General and senior officials with responsibility for this and subsequent court projects had no preconceptions about the design, were supportive of the concepts as they emerged, and never stood in the way of innovation.

Design concepts evolve

Broad concepts for a new courthouse in Melbourne were developed by a steering committee, convened and chaired by a Deputy Secretary of the Attorney-General's Department, on which the four courts[19] that would occupy the building were represented. Moreover, as it was put at the time, this steering committee was actually allowed to steer, although strictly within the channel of never-to-be-crossed budget markers. Whilst the committee's contributions

16 An exciting plan for a tropical federal courthouse in Darwin did not proceed.

17 The High Court of Australia building, 1925, designed by the first Chief Architect for the Commonwealth, John Smith Murdoch, in Stripped Classical style and extended in 1935 to the design of Horace John McKennal with the addition of a second story, was partly restored and renovated in 1991–1992 under the supervision of the Australian Heritage Commission. It was placed on the National Heritage List in 2007.

18 Though not by the Attorney-General.

19 The High Court, Federal Court, Family Court, and the newly established Industrial Relations Court. The Federal Court was represented by the author as Chief Justice and by Justices Heerey and Ryan, the latter having a dual capacity.

were encouraged and given substantial weight, the budget limits were not open for discussion.

From the outset, it had been proposed[20] on behalf of the Federal Court that the new courthouse should reflect the importance of the system of justice to the community and that, *consistently*, the new building should be attractive to those who were to use it and should encourage the public to observe the workings of the system of justice in the courts of the Commonwealth. The reflection of this importance was now to take on a very different character.

It was said that, to achieve these ends, the building should be 'full of light and that particular attention should be given to the use of interior space as a powerful design element'.[21] It was submitted that light should be a strong characteristic of the building, and that the courtrooms should have natural light and take advantage of the external views available from the site. It was also said that 'the foyer' should embody a design philosophy of light and space and, whilst having 'appropriate dignity', should not be threatening and 'should invite the public to witness the work of the courts'.[22]

The importance of collegiality was well understood by the judges and it was proposed that the design should encourage the interaction of members of the Court and that judges and their staff should be accommodated on their own floors.

It was also submitted that works of art, for which a (small) percentage of the budget for Commonwealth public buildings was set aside, should be part of the building and not 'mere additions' afterwards.[23]

March 1995: The great 'live-in' project consultation

In early 1995, the architects for the project were appointed and joined the steering committee, which had been closely consulted and involved in the appointment process.

By now, some of the earlier broad ideas had been developed and others had emerged. As well as being a building that would invite the public to enter, it was now also considered that the courthouse should be 'egalitarian' and that the external views and light should be for the benefit of everyone: Parties, witnesses, lawyers, court staff, and judges alike.

To take the project forward in a way that would allow for all suggested design ideas and concepts to be considered and for the fundamental requirements to be set, the Attorney-General's Department took consultation in such matters to a new level by proposing a two-day live-in workshop. It was to be attended by

20 'User requirement brief' submitted by the Federal Court to the Attorney-General in October 1991.

21 Ibid.

22 Ibid.

23 Ibid.

the architects, representatives of the Department of Finance and Administration, a representative of the Attorney-General's Department, the project managers, quantity surveyors, Principal Registrars and other senior officers of the courts, and the judicial members of the steering committee.

The workshop was held on the weekend of 22–23 March 1995 in a hotel in the Dandenong Ranges, and over the course of the first day there was an extensive exchange of ideas about the project, illuminated by the observations and proposals of the architects and the aims and perspectives of the numerous participants. The progress of the workshop was led by a professional facilitator and the conclusions reached were recorded on numerous sheets of texta-engrossed[24] butcher's paper, hung around the walls of the large conference room.

At the end of the day, however, serious concerns had emerged that the aims of the project could not be met within its strictly limited budget and the mood is recalled as being gloomy. It was a big project, with big aims, on a difficult site and with a tight budget.

The architects did not join the other participants for dinner and instead worked alone into the night to confront the issues that had emerged. They worked on, developing concept plans for a building that would embody, as well as all the functional fundamentals, the characteristics and qualities, such as light, access, and transparency, sought by the meeting but at a cost that would not exceed the budget.

When the meeting reconvened after breakfast the next morning the architects presented and explained the outline plans they had produced overnight. The new plans were a remarkable reflection of the previous day's ambitions and discussions; they foreshadowed, essentially, the building as it was ultimately constructed. The plans were adopted with acclamation.

The consensus of design aims that had been reached, and which now found expression in the plans, were for a courthouse that would, within the constraints of the budget and the overriding requirements of security and functionality:

- Reflect the importance of the system of justice *but also* its transparency and accessibility;
- Be full of light and have external views;
- Be dignified but not intimidating;
- Invite the public into the building to see their system of justice at work;
- Be egalitarian such that all the users and occupants would have access to natural light, views, and facilities;
- Contain works of art that would be part of the building, not additions to it afterwards;
- Be Australian in concept and materials;
- Be energy efficient and ecologically sound.

24 A texta is a felt-tip pen.

1999: Owen Dixon Commonwealth Law Courts, Melbourne[25]

The L-shaped site had presented substantial challenges in the design of a large and complex courthouse. Part of the site was occupied by the Flagstaff underground railway station, with its busy public entrance and large external ventilation ducts. Opportunities for views and abundant natural light were limited on the lower levels by a tall office building to the immediate west and a substantial office block built to nearly half of the site's eastern boundary. Secure judicial access to every courtroom, usually provided by long enclosed corridors and in older courthouses sometimes from the level above, presented another challenge.

When the Melbourne building was opened in March 1999 it was apparent that these and the many other challenges had been addressed. The building was indeed flooded with light, having as a central element 'a long gallery stretching from Latrobe Street to Little Lonsdale Street' with 'natural light [that] permeates the main central volume from all aspects via extensive glazed facades and elliptical skylights – supporting the desired notions of openness and clarity'.[26] Moreover, whilst the building, through its form, size, signage, and entrance, did speak of justice and its importance, it also spoke architecturally of transparent and accessible justice.

A visitor approaches the building from its substantial forecourt on William Street. The forecourt, with its double row of pleached trees[27] to the south, its generous space, and its long water terrace to the north, provides a calm and dignified entrance to the courthouse and reflects many of the design aims for the building, including transparency. Moreover, as its architects have rightly said, public institutions such as courts have a clear responsibility to contribute to the wellbeing of the communities they serve, and in that respect the forecourt also provides a safe and comfortable public space – a space as much for the city as it is for the courts. The forecourt also speaks of the courts' connection with Melbourne, a connection affirmed by the Melbourne-grey colours of the materials chosen for parts of the exterior and the arrangements of elements of the exterior.

Moving through the forecourt towards the public entrance, the huge ventilation ducts for the underground railway, clad now with dark blue enamelled panels, have become part of the architecture of the courthouse.

Nearby, the large, pivoting horizontal door of the public entrance presents a pattern of enamelled panels in colours reflecting, according to the door's architect[28] (whose view we must surely accept), the palette of the great Sienese artist of

25 Tim Shannon, Paul Katsieris, Anna Müller, Brian Felgate, and Donald Holt, Architects, Hassell Studio, Melbourne.

26 'Commonwealth Law Courts', *Hassell Studio* (Web Page, 2019) <https://www.hassellstudio.com/en/cms-projects/detail/commonwealth-law-courts>.

27 Reminiscent of their use in Paris. At one point replaced with inappropriate lollipop-like substitutes, these important trees have now (2018) been replaced, appropriately pruned, and maintained, and again contribute to the architectural aims of the building.

28 Paul Katsieris, Architect.

the late thirteenth and early fourteenth centuries, Duccio di Buoninsegna. The author asserts it to be one of the finest doors of any public building in Australia and a work of art in itself. It is also the central element of a larger entrance structure which is also faced with enamelled panels.

Unsurprisingly, the door and its surrounds, including the water terrace, is the background that camera crews and producers frequently select for the on-site reporting of newsworthy proceedings in the building. Entrances to courthouses have now become part of the daily face of the justice presented to the public on the television news; the Great Door and the water-terraced forecourt of the Commonwealth Law Courts in Melbourne are exemplars in this respect.

Once the water terrace and the trees of the forecourt have led the visitor to the Great Door, an entrance corridor of glass[29] now invites entry to a high, light-flooded atrium from which there are views of the Flagstaff Gardens to the north and the heritage-protected Royal Mint and the tall buildings of the city to the west. The pleached trees, readily visible from the interior, provide a soft foreground to the view of the city and contribute to a feeling of calm.

The sense of space a visitor immediately feels upon entering the atrium is enhanced by its contraction, by a barely perceptible 3°, from the point of entry at its north end to its marginally narrower southern end.

One of the great achievements of the Melbourne building is that, as one of its architects has said, it progressively reveals itself as the visitor moves from the forecourt through the entrance into the atrium and then to the courts. There is an element of procession and a sense of being guided – led perhaps – to a destination; not in any formal or didactic way but in a way that is reassuring and conducive to calm.

Further into the building, still on the ground floor, the ideal that it should contain works of art that form part of the building emerges to fine effect in a wall of curved metal panels by the artist John Young. Other works that can be considered part of the building include a sculptural spiral staircase in concrete leading from the floor of the atrium to the court level above and the adjacent tubular sculpture by Robert Owen extending to the full height of the eastern wall.

Consistent with the design requirement for equal access, the workplaces of the registry staff and of the judicial staff have natural light and external views.

The constraints of the site made it very difficult to give natural light and external views to all the courtrooms. For the courtrooms at the northern end of the building this was readily achieved with windows facing north over the Flagstaff Gardens and west towards Latrobe Street, but providing views for the other Federal Court courtrooms on the western side – the side closely flanked by a tall building – was indeed challenging. The solution made use of mirrors, fixed in external 'mirror niches'; set at 45°, the mirrors reflect the view of the Flagstaff

29 Also a security checkpoint since September 2001.

Gardens across the judicial corridor and into the courtrooms through windows designed and placed for that purpose. The privacy of the corridor is maintained by using a window glass that becomes temporarily opaque when a sensor in the corridor detects the approach of a person.

In the southern part of the atrium there is another example of two apparently distinct design aims driving a creative solution. At this point, the adjacent office buildings prevent any direct access to natural light from the sides; instead, light enters the building from above through four 'light cannon' – deep oval cavities, set at a gentle angle from the vertical, somehow suggestive of the raked funnels of an early steamship. No mere skylights, these are beautiful objects, with a harmony of shape, size, angle, and purpose. Within the intent of the design objectives, they are indeed works of art.

Court 1 of the Federal Court, the courtroom in which appeals are heard and ceremonial sittings of the Court are held, also contains examples of the interaction of design aims and here, too, works of art and artistic craftsmanship form part of a building that has natural light and external views in abundance.

The entrance to Court 1 is notable for the large bronze door fixtures by sculptor Rodney Broad, inspired by the form of the white waratah and bearing the coat of arms of the Commonwealth. The courtroom's distinctive bronze coat of arms was also designed and made by Broad. A series of abstract paintings by Aida Tomescu appear as panels in the south wall.

On the bar table rests the lectern – a central element in an appellate courtroom – designed by Damien Wright and crafted by him from mineralised river red gum.[30] The wood is from a tree that grew between 8,000 and 10,000 years ago on a bank of the River Murray at the eastern edge of Yorta Yorta country. It was mineralised and darkened in colour by a process involving thousands of years of submersion; it is the wood of an ancient land.[31]

Court 1 also speaks of access. Unless a principal courtroom is very large there will be occasions when it cannot seat everyone. Commonly this occurs on important public occasions such as the swearing-in of a newly appointed judge or a judicial farewell, but it also happens when a court hears cases of exceptional public interest.

A video screen in an adjacent courtroom is a poor substitute for physical presence and so at the public entrance to Court 1, next to the large ceiling-height entrance door, what appears to be a wooden panel forming part of the rear wall is in fact another door. The panel, even wider than the main courtroom entrance door, can be opened to expand the public space of the courtroom. The facility

30 *Eucalyptus camaldulensis.*

31 For a history of the discovery and use of mineralised *E. camaldulensis*, an explanation of the process of mineralisation, and an account of its later use by Damien Wright to make the centre table in the County Koori Court in Morwell, Victoria, see Gideon Haigh, 'The Pursuit of Usable Beauty, Damien Wright and His Table', *The Monthly* (online, April 2009), <https://www.themonthly.com.au/issue/2009/march/1244094220/gideon-haigh/pursuit-usable-beauty>.

has been used to advantage on many occasions and a similar arrangement was later adopted for Court 1 in Adelaide and in the rebuilt Court 1 in Hobart.

Finally, the windows of Court 1, with their outlook to the Flagstaff Gardens offering an ample source of natural light, reveal another innovation, present throughout the building – many of the glazing panels are etched with lines of words. Noting that 'words form the language of the law', the architects had proposed that the courthouse should be 'veiled with words'. There was no precedent, for although the courtrooms of the Italian Republic remind and reassure that '*La legge è uguale per tutti*' and the courthouses of the French Republic proclaim '*Liberté, Égalité et Fraternité*', these noble words do not 'veil' their courthouses.[32]

The words that veil the Melbourne courthouse – as lines of words and phrases rather than sentences – are taken from the first three chapters of the Constitution: Chapter I, which established the Parliament; Chapter II, which provides for the Executive Government; and Chapter III, titled 'The Judicature', which established the High Court of Australia and empowers the Parliament to create other federal courts. Chapter III was the source of the Parliament's power to create the Federal Court of Australia. The structure and content of Chapters I, II, and III attest to the separation of powers, one of the foundations of the rule of law in Australia, symbolically reflected in the veil of words.

Pausing at this point before turning to the Adelaide, Hobart, and Sydney projects,[33] it is important to emphasise that, from the Federal Court's perspective at that time, the new building in Melbourne was to be for a court of essentially civil jurisdiction. Whilst careful provision was made for secure and private rooms[34] for witnesses, there are additional important considerations[35] for court buildings in which issues involving physical and mental violence and abuse are routinely determined.

Dame Roma Mitchell Commonwealth Law Courts, Adelaide, 2006

The Melbourne project was followed by the project for the construction of the Dame Roma Mitchell Commonwealth Law Court in Adelaide.[36] Again there was a carefully structured process of consultation about the design objectives, the highlight of which was a very successful two-day workshop involving all

32 The portico of the Supreme Court of the United States bears the words: 'Justice the guardian of liberty'. The front page of the website of the Supreme Court of Victoria states: 'The Supreme Court of Victoria safeguards and maintains the rule of law to ensure equal justice for all'.

33 The Nigel Bowen Commonwealth Law Courts Building in Childers Street, Canberra, was renovated in 2005 with the aim, amongst others, of introducing natural light to the principal Federal Court courtroom and elsewhere.

34 Themselves an interesting and powerful design element within the atrium, with their conceptual roots in Greek villages.

35 Some now mandated in Victoria and elsewhere.

36 Mariano De Duonni and Mark Coventry, Architects, Hassell Studio, Adelaide.

interested parties, including of course the judges and court administrators. The workshop was held at Victor Harbor and was similar in many respects to that conducted in the Dandenong Ranges for the Melbourne building. Here also, it was agreed that the building should have abundant light, external views, access, and space; and this too was to be an egalitarian building, designed with the needs of all users at the forefront: Practitioners, litigants, witnesses, staff, and judges. And it was to be sensitive and responsive to its important location in Angas Street, in full view of Victoria Square, in the heart of the city and its legal precinct.[37]

The building was completed in early 2006 and, like the Melbourne courthouse, has an entrance flanked by a water terrace, opening to a very high and spacious atrium. The first atrium, with its 27-metre central column, is one of two, each filled with natural light. Here too, the building gradually reveals itself from the point of entry.

The objective of providing courtrooms and public spaces with abundant natural light and external views was again a driver of the design. In Adelaide, the innovative solution to the problem of secure judicial corridors restricting access to natural light was to go vertical – judicial access is by 'vertical judicial corridors' comprising three small lifts for judges and their staff. There was nothing new about secure judicial lifts; the innovation was to provide three of them, instead of the usual secure corridors, to give almost direct access to each courtroom on each level.

In the result, every courtroom has natural light and external views. The chambers of the judges and their staff and the offices and workplaces of the registry were also afforded natural light and external views, although, regrettably, some now (in 2019) have been blocked by a new apartment building.

To take the natural light and views objective further than in Melbourne, all the corridors in the Adelaide building were designed to have a window at each end, again bringing more natural light to public spaces and, importantly, workspaces. The virtue of this approach, particularly in relation to workplaces and public areas, is apparent when any such building is compared with one that has enclosed interior corridors.

The courthouse has strong connections with Adelaide and with South Australia. The materials and colours used for the exterior were chosen to reflect the colours of the Adelaide Hills and Plains and to relate to them. There is also an intended reference, through colour, to Colonel Light's garden city plan, perhaps emphasised by the fact, revealed in a copy of his plan on display inside, that the courthouse is in a zone set aside for public purposes.

The design of Court 1, the courtroom in which the High Court of Australia sits when in Adelaide and the principal courtroom of the Federal Court at other

37 The Court is on a site set aside for public purposes in Colonel Light's visionary 1837 plan for Adelaide.

times, is especially noteworthy for its innovation, its embrace of light, and its powerful sense of connection.

Court 1 and six other courtrooms, including an Indigenous courtroom with a central round table, are within a tapered copper-clad ellipse, known as 'the Opal', which relates through its colour and patina to the city, its trees and green spaces beyond. The Opal also speaks of another connection; its axis points directly to the traditional meeting place of the Kaurna people in Victoria Square.

With connections and outstanding artistic craftsmanship both in mind, special attention was given to the interior of Court 1. As well as connection from the alignment of the Opal, and the broader outlook to Victoria Square and to the sea, connection comes from the river red gum, *Eucalyptus camaldulensis*, of which the judicial bench, the associates' bench, and the bar table are made. The wood was milled and crafted[38] within sight of the courthouse from an ancient river red gum in the Coonawarra. The tree, which had become hollow and had lost its crown long ago, had been felled by the wind.

In the language of the Kaurna people of Adelaide and the Adelaide Plains, the river red gum is *karra* and is of great cultural significance and connection. *Karra* is also a tree of great ecological significance in the Murray–Darling Basin. Connection through *karra* is also present elsewhere in the building through two works commissioned by the Federal Court. One of them, a large work in nine parts by Nici Cumpston, is in the main lift lobby and is passed by every visitor. It provokes reflection upon the very well-known *Evening Shadows, Backwater of the Murray, South Australia*[39] in the Art Gallery of South Australia. The other *karra* work, which hangs near Court 1, is a botanical drawing by Gilbert RM Dashorst. *Karra* and the furnishings and fit-out of Court 1 were aspects of a special project for excellence for the principal courtroom, requiring the diversion of funds, to which the Department of Finance agreed.

Elsewhere in the building, art speaks of the rule of law. *Continuum*, a commissioned sculptural work by Warren Langley, comprises three installations. Each is on a separate floor and represents a different theme associated with the rule of law. One of the works contains an unattributed inscription:

> The law is the unbroken thread of precedent guiding a path with a responsible origin and a comprehensible destination. It enfolds and protects. Because the rule of law exists we believe that tomorrow will be better than today.

The design criteria for the Melbourne and Adelaide buildings, and later for the Sydney rebuilding project, aimed to foster the collegiate nature of the courts by providing inviting connections between the secure judicial areas. Improving on

38 By Gray Hawk, Hawk Design, Adelaide.
39 Henry James Johnstone, Painter, London, 1880.

Melbourne, where the two levels of judges' chambers are connected by a single narrow staircase, in Adelaide they are linked by a broad stairway, with abundant natural light, continuing to a third level to link with the Court's library. The result is an excellent example of architecture encouraging connection and collegiality.

And finally, in another example of architecture furthering the objective of access, the courthouse was designed with a café. Entered from outside the secure areas, the café has always been popular with litigants, witnesses, and the profession. In their own way, such facilities support the many-faceted ideal of access.

Edward Braddon Commonwealth Law Courts, Hobart: Natural light for Court 1, 2008

The positive experiences with natural light, external views, and other design concepts for the Melbourne and Adelaide courthouses prompted a project, completed in mid-2008, to rebuild one of the two courtrooms in the Federal Court portion of the Commonwealth Law Courts in Davey Street, Hobart.

The Hobart courthouse incorporates the external walls and the form and fenestration pattern of a Victorian Regency building that has its origins in the 1840s and was for many years the Trades Hall,[40] with an outstanding modern building constructed in the early 1980s. The courthouse, which has Commonwealth and Tasmanian heritage listing, respects the notable streetscape of Davey Street of which the former Trades Hall remains a dominant element.[41]

One of the courtrooms was built as a jury courtroom, but in contrast to the Federal Court's other Hobart courtroom, which has natural light from windows overlooking Jennings Lane and the adjacent Real Tennis Club court, it had no windows.

The design brief for the redevelopment of the jury courtroom aimed, as with the Melbourne and Adelaide projects, for a reflection of the ideals of light, access and visibility. To achieve these aims the substantial jury box – in which no jury had ever sat – was removed, enabling the axis of the courtroom to be changed to allow for windows on the Davey Street frontage, opposite the bench. These windows now fill the courtroom with light and give views towards St David's Park and its trees, and Salamanca Place. Improved access, and with it natural light, comes from a rebuilt foyer outside Court 1 into which, as in the Melbourne and Adelaide courthouses, the courtroom can be opened.

The design was developed by the architects[42] with the aim, embraced by the Court, of linking justice and transparency to a distinctly Tasmanian courtroom. This they achieved by its windows and the use of Tasmanian timbers: Huon pine, celery top pine, and Tasmanian oak. Unique amongst the courthouses of

40 From about 1924 until the 1970s.

41 Architects, Philp Lighton, Tasmania.

42 Tim Penny, Architect, Philp Lighton, Tasmania.

the world, the tops of the judicial and associates' benches are made of solid Huon pine with facings of bookended birds-eye Huon pine. The coat of arms above the bench, from the original courtroom, is also of Huon pine.

The success of the linkage with place was reflected in an observation made in the address by the President of the Law Society of Tasmania at the opening ceremony on 6 August 2008. Having referred to the use of Tasmanian timber and craftsmanship, he said: 'the extensive window at the rear of the court has been added, symbolic of the transparency of the court and linking it to the Tasmanian community generally'.[43]

In the Hobart courtroom, as in other Federal Court courthouses, the design of the courtroom clock was part of the architect's brief. A clock is an important object in a place where proceedings should run to time and it should be seen as an architectural component – but with the footnote that when counsel or a judge glance at the clock, they do not necessarily want to know the time.

With an eye to the future when the Federal Court may well have a substantial criminal jurisdiction in indictable federal matters with a constitutional requirement for trial by jury, a demountable jury box was built as part of the project. The other jury facilities remain and the jury box can readily be assembled.

Law Courts Building, Sydney: 2011 refurbishment[44]

Law Courts Building in Phillip Street, Sydney,[45] in the heart of Australia's first legal precinct, was built to satisfy an urgent need for accommodation for the Supreme Court of New South Wales and for the courts of the Commonwealth. Completed at about the time that the Federal Court of Australia was established, Law Courts Building housed the new court, which had its inaugural sitting on 7 February 1977 in Court 21A.

In his speech at the opening of Law Courts Building a few months earlier, the Attorney-General for New South Wales, Mr Walker, had noted that the building had been designed to avoid people being 'scared out of their wits' when going to court and that the new courtrooms would create a 'more humane atmosphere', and this was undoubtedly true.[46] As well, the public areas had natural light and external views and there was a café for the public and the profession on the twelfth floor with an outstanding outlook.[47] Nevertheless, none of the

43 Federal Court of Australia, *Opening of the Refurbished Court No. 1 Hobart* [Transcript] 6 August 2008, (Auscript Australasia Pty Ltd, Brisbane, 2008).

44 Architects for the refurbishment: Group GSA, Melbourne, and Hassell Studio, Melbourne, with the particular involvement of Hassell's former chairman, Tim Shannon, in the project for Court 1.

45 Architects, McConnell Smith and Johnson, Sydney.

46 Attorney-General Frank Walker (NSW), speech at opening of Law Courts Building, Sydney, 1 February 1977, quoted in '"Humane" Courtrooms Opened by Premier', *The Sydney Morning Herald* (2 February 1977) para 33.

47 Eventually, as the precinct changed, it ceased operation, as did the café at the High Court in Canberra.

courtrooms or the witness and interview rooms had any external views or natural light.

For technical, safety, and environmental reasons which had become apparent by the time the Melbourne courthouse was completed, and required urgent attention when the Adelaide courthouse was opened, Law Courts Building needed to be refurbished. This provided an opportunity, taken by all the courts, to make changes and improvements.

In planning for the refurbishment of the Federal Court's floors of Law Courts Building, the concepts developed in the Melbourne, Adelaide, and Hobart projects were powerful influences. Once again, there was substantial judicial consultation and input.

The refurbishment, which began in 2007, was a lengthy, extensive, and costly project involving much disruption. The work in the Federal Court areas was not completed until 2011.

As well as attending to the environmental and other concerns, the work transformed the Federal Court's floors. Whereas, previously, none of the Federal Court's 14 courtrooms in Sydney had natural light, all but five now had windows and access to abundant natural light and external views.

For the registry and judicial support staff, recreation and lunch facilities, facing north with views to the Opera House and the Harbour, had been provided on each of its six floors. As before, most of the administrative and judicial support staff also had workplaces with natural light and views.

The public still had natural light and views; the relocated waiting lobbies had windows and most of the internal corridors in the public areas had windows at each end. Importantly, the mediation facilities, which were built as part of the project, had natural light and external views.

One of the substantial challenges facing the architects in redesigning the interior of the Federal Court's floors (and facing the builders in executing the changes) was to relocate courtrooms to the outer walls of the building to give direct access to the existing windows. In one notable instance, in what is now Court 18D, there were no existing windows on the north wall and no practical external access by scaffolding or otherwise to the north side of the eighteenth level. Court 18D nevertheless has windows, which were fitted, and the external openings for them made, entirely from within. The architects' determination that the design objective of natural light should be achieved had inspired, here too, a solution to the difficulty.

As in Adelaide, ample stairways now connect all the floors upon which there are judicial chambers, again emphasising the potential of design to foster collegiality in a court.

An important aim of the project was to build a new principal courtroom for the Federal Court. The new Court 1 was designed with several objects in mind. The first was to provide a principal courtroom of appropriate capacity for the hearing of appeals, for the ceremonial sittings that all courts have from time to time, and for the conduct of substantial multi-party litigation.

The second object was to build a courtroom that was capable of conversion into a space for public lectures and seminars on legal topics. The third object was to create a courtroom that would reflect the design philosophies of light and access now evident in the Federal Court's other buildings. And the fourth was to create, in achieving the first three, a courtroom of artistic excellence.

All these objects were achieved. Court 1 has two levels and can seat 200. It has proved very suitable for the hearing of substantial cases and for ceremonial sittings its judicial bench can seat all the members of the Court. It has external views and substantial natural light.

The suitability of Court 1 for public lectures and seminars on legal topics has been demonstrated many times, especially by its use by the Australian Academy of Law. A notable utility for these purposes is the capacity to convert the seating configuration from that of courtroom with parallel rows of seats to a U-shaped configuration more suitable for seminars and lectures.

By an ingenious and elegant design, when the lectern is turned away from the bench to face an audience for a lecture, its pivot point adjusts so that the correct distance of the lectern from the speaker is maintained.

As noted earlier, it is important that courthouses, and ideally their courtrooms, have a connection with their community and Court 1 has strong connections with Sydney. Most obviously, the connection is through the views of Hyde Park and the not-so-distant Botany Bay, but there is also connection through the design and materials of the bench, bar table, and witness box.

These courtroom fundamentals, the work of Simon Zablotsky and his team, were created from timber taken from a single blackwood tree and, with a nod to history, blackwood from the dismantled Court 21A, the Federal Court's first ceremonial court, was used for the base of the bar table. The design reflects, especially through the shape and rib-based structure of the bar table, the strata of the rock upon which Sydney rests and the city's maritime heritage.

The connection with Sydney's maritime heritage – appropriate for a court of admiralty jurisdiction – is also suggested by the very large and beautiful shallow object suspended from the ceiling. Designed and installed to reflect sound as an element in the courtroom's acoustic design, the reflector was created in Sydney by a firm whose composite structures include the hulls of yachts, with which its shape has a strong resonance.

Possibly unique in concept, the coat of arms was cast in lead crystal by artist Lis Cahill.

Conclusion

The four courthouse projects considered in this chapter were, between them, in progress for nearly 20 years. They have much in common and say much about the creative process – a process as fundamental to the law, its administration, its development, and its reform, as it is to architecture. The three courthouses and the Hobart courtroom reflect shared ideas and ideals about law and justice and reflect, architecturally, the symbolic affinity between light and justice. Each speaks also of access to justice and the rule of law. The success of these projects for public buildings demonstrates the importance of a dynamic interplay of ideas, ambitions, and professions and the central importance of the creative skill of architects in translating ideas and ideals – often abstract – into the built form.

Courts and the nation: A postscript

This chapter began with a statement about the importance of courthouses in a community and to a nation. The reference was to courthouses generally but the recent observations of the retiring Chief Justice of New Zealand, the Rt Hon Dame Sian Elias, at her valedictory sitting in the Supreme Court in Wellington[48] draw attention to the exceptional significance of the architecture of the courthouse of a nation's highest court.

Dame Sian was the first Chief Justice of the Supreme Court of New Zealand, a court that formally came into existence on 1 January 2004, replacing the Judicial Committee of the Privy Council as New Zealand's final court of appeal. Sitting in the courthouse built for the newly established Supreme Court and opened in 2010, the Chief Justice said of the courtroom:

> It is not one of our historic courtrooms, which still echo with the footfalls of the past. It is not a place built to convey the majesty and power of the law or to command obedience. It is not indelibly stained with sad episodes in our history where doors have been shut and hopes dashed. It is instead a place built to express the hope of justice through law and the confidence that a new Court will administer the laws in this country with knowledge of its own history and traditions.[49]

Notwithstanding the differences in history and constitutional context, Her Honour's observations are a reminder of the exceptional importance of the architecture of the High Court of Australia as the building created in modern times, in the nation's capital, for Australia's highest court and final court of appeal.[50] Chief Justice Elias's remarks also prompt the reflection that it was in a case heard and determined in the High Court in its new principal courthouse, *Mabo v Queensland (No 2)*,[51] that the common law of Australia[52] was seen to

48 8 March 2019.

49 Supreme Court of Wellington, *Valedictory Sitting for the Chief Justice, the Rt. Hon. Dame Sian Elias* [Transcript] 8 March 2019.

50 In all relevant respects since the passing of the several Australia Acts in 1986.

51 [1992] HCA 23, 175 CLR 1.

52 The judicial use of the term in *Mabo v Queensland (No 2)* was notable. Earlier usage was very rare: see *R v Sharkey* (1957) 79 CLR 121 at 163 per Webb J.

recognise fundamental aspects of Australia's history that, here too, had been shut out in the past.[53]

Bibliography

Articles/books/reports

Bridges, Peter, *Historic Court Houses of New South Wales* (Hale & Iremonger, 1986)

Challinger, Michael, *Historic Court Houses of Victoria* (Palisade Press, 2001)

Haigh, Gideon, 'The Pursuit of Usable Beauty: Damien Wright and His Table', *The Monthly* (online, April 2009), <https://www.themonthly.com.au/issue/2009/march/1244094220/gideon-haigh/pursuit-usable-beauty>

Resnik, Judith and Dennis Curtis, *Representing Justice: Invention, Controversy, and Rights in City-States and Democratic Courtrooms* (Yale University Press, 2011)

Cases

Mabo v Queensland (No 2) [1992] HCA 23, 175 CLR 1.

Wik Peoples v State of Queensland & Ors [1996] HCA 40; (1996) 187 CLR

R v Sharkey (1957) 79 CLR 1

Other

'Commonwealth Law Courts', *Hassell Studio* (Webpage, 2019) <https://www.hassellstudio.com/en/cms-projects/detail/commonwealth-law-courts>

Federal Court of Australia, *Opening of the Refurbished Court No1. Hobart* [Transcript] 6 August 2008, (Auscript Australasia Pty Ltd, Brisbane, 2008)

Supreme Court of Wellington, *Valedictory Sitting for the Chief Justice, the Rt. Hon. Dame Sian Elias* [Transcript] 8 March 2019

'"Humane" Courtrooms Opened by Premier', *The Sydney Morning Herald* (2 February 1977) para 33.

'The Building', *High Court of Australia* (Webpage, 2010) <http://www.hcourt.gov.au/about/the-building>

53 It was of course here that *Wik Peoples v State of Queensland & Ors* [1996] HCA 40; (1996) 187 CLR and other landmark cases about native title were argued and decided.

PART II

Justice buildings

3

REFRACTIONS OF LEGAL JUSTICE (FORENSIC PRECINCT, SERIES 2)

Peter D Rush

A forensic precinct gives form and attaches the conduct of legal justice to a place. The photographs in this series refract a number of such attachments and traverse several places in Australia, Japan, and England. They are associated with cities and city-spaces: Melbourne, Sydney, Adelaide, Canberra, Tokyo, London.

The affective force of the common law, its home so to speak, is housed between the City of Westminster and the City of London in the legal precinct formed by the Inns of Court and the Royal Court of Justice. The Sydney legal precinct is most often associated with Phillip Street at the north end of Hyde Park, but warps itself around the park and extends to the southern end of Elizabeth Street. Some displacement has taken place with the recent relocation of law firm offices to the tall towers of Barangaroo. Parramatta also maintains a legal precinct, and was given impetus by the more recent installation of the 'Justice Precinct'. In Adelaide, a legal precinct is gathered around Victoria Square and Reconciliation Plaza; with legal offices in the wide streets at the southern end behind the courts. Canberra is marked by two legal precincts: The Parliamentary Zone houses the High Court of Australia on the shore of Lake Burley Griffin; but there is also the city legal precinct on London Circuit, which backs onto City Hill, one of the points of the Parliamentary Triangle in Burley Griffins' plan for the city of Canberra. Parts of the city legal precinct are being reconstructed, or at least renovated. In Tokyo, the legal precinct is found in Kasumigaseki, seven metres above sea level. It is associated with the 'government sector', somewhat like the High Court of Australia within the Parliamentary Zone. The Melbourne legal precinct was perhaps the first in Australia to take form and attach itself to a place, and to do so with consequences for the national understanding of law. All these forensic precincts are inscribed by local, state, federal, domestic, and international jurisdictions. They are also cross-hatched by the administrative divisions of a police jurisdiction.

DOI: 10.4324/9780429059858-6

Aboriginal jurisdictions are marked, and sometimes acknowledged on a plaque adorning a court entrance, with flags or through public artworks. A forensic precinct exhibits centrifugal and centripetal tendencies, despite its etymology. It is girt by laws, as it were.

The photographs assembled here, like forms of law, are not illustrations or documents, although they retrace the declarations and interrogatories of a state of affairs. They are not presented as a lawscape, nor as chronotopes, nor as an archive. They are less general and more institutional, heterogeneous, and punctual. They are a visual assemblage. The photographs work in series by the condensations of detail, by juxtaposition, and by association with the density of public places, people, and images. Attached to place, they commune with official and unofficial lives lived with law.

Forensic Precinct, Series 2 continues a project initiated with a short film that, through montage and narrative, followed the place of public art and law in a settler city.[1] A subsequent photographic essay remarked the distinctiveness of the forensic precinct as a juridical form and attended to its laneways.[2] The current and second series curates a fourfold concern with *refractions* of legal justice: the insistence of and encounter with an Indigenous presence, the legibility that comes with reflecting surfaces, the force and forms of water, as well as a renewed jurisprudence of place. Each engages with architectural and urban types that give human character – symbolic and imaginary, as much as traumatic – to the building of law and the justice of place.

1 Peter D Rush. *Thick Skin*, 2002. Available at https://vimeo.com/73176355

2 Peter Rush, 'The Forensic Precinct: Notes on the Public Address of Law' (2016) 20 *Law Text Culture* 216.

FIGURE 3.1 'Forecourt'. (© Peter D Rush)

FIGURE 3.2 'Flows beneath'. (© Peter D Rush)

FIGURE 3.3 'Field'. (© Peter D Rush)

FIGURE 3.4 'Sightlines'. (© Peter D Rush)

FIGURE 3.5 'Background'. (© Peter D Rush)

FIGURE 3.6 'Aedification'. (© Peter D Rush)

FIGURE 3.7 'Folding grounds'. (© Peter D Rush)

FIGURE 3.8 'The dry'. (© Peter D Rush)

FIGURE 3.9 'Font'. (© Peter D Rush)

FIGURE 3.10 'Australian Hall, Day of Mourning, 26 January 1938'. (© Peter D Rush)

FIGURE 3.11 'Justice without prejudice'. (© Peter D Rush)

FIGURE 3.12 'On Lake Burley Griffin'. (© Peter D Rush)

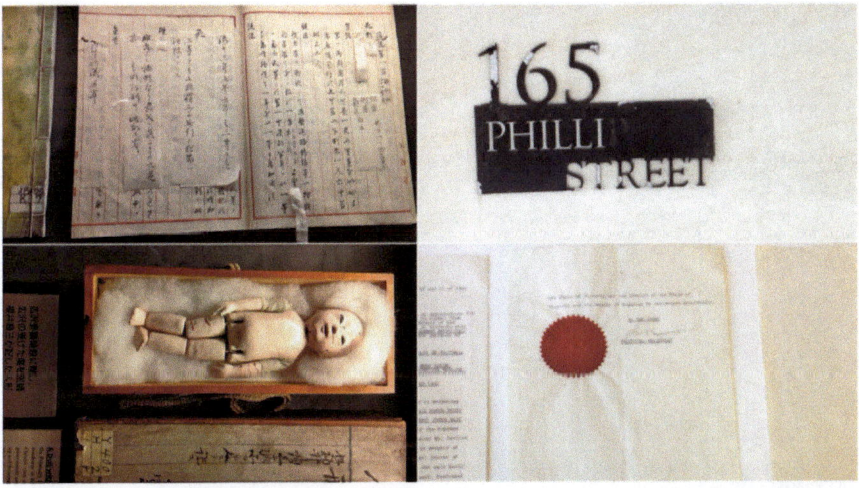

FIGURE 3.13 'Cabinet of traces'. (© Peter D Rush)

FIGURE 3.14 'Colonial colonnade'. (© Peter D Rush)

FIGURE 3.15 'Kasumigaseki, 7m above sea level'. (© Peter D Rush)

FIGURE 3.16 'Reflections'. (© Peter D Rush)

FIGURE 3.17 'Under reconstruction'. (© Peter D Rush)

FIGURE 3.18 'Untitled'. (© Peter D Rush)

FIGURE 3.19 'Myth'. (© Peter D Rush)

FIGURE 3.20 '透明性 + 光, transparency + light'. (© Peter D Rush)

4

INDIGENOUS COURTHOUSE AND COURTROOM DESIGN IN AUSTRALIA

Case studies, design paradigms, and the issue of cultural agency[1]

Julian R Murphy, Elizabeth Grant, and Thalia Anthony

Introduction

If it is true that public buildings 'reflect the beliefs, priorities and aspirations of a people',[2] what do Australia's public buildings say about Australians? More specifically, what does the design of Australia's courthouses say about the beliefs, priorities, aspirations, and agency of Australian people and in particular, Aboriginal and Torres Strait Islander peoples? Around the world, the design of courthouses (and the courtrooms within them) has become a powerful medium through which to convey a vision of justice and cultural agency to Indigenous peoples. South Africa's Constitutional Court sits on the site of a prison that held activists during apartheid, and its design symbolises South Africa's post-apartheid search for reconciliation. Communicating reconciliation and transparency were paramount in the design, and the courtroom incorporates windows to reinforce its theme of transparency, allowing passers-by to observe proceedings. In Wellington, Aotearoa New Zealand, design of the exterior of the Supreme Courthouse references significant cultural icons for Māori (see Figure 4.1).[3] The design of the courtroom is semi-spherical in shape lined with a tessellation of

1 A version of this chapter was originally published as 'Indigenous Courthouse and Courtroom Design in Australia: Case Studies, Design Paradigms and the Issue of Cultural Agency' in Julian R Murphy, Elizabeth Grant and Thalia Anthony (eds) *The Handbook of Contemporary Indigenous Architecture* (Springer, 2018) 495–525. Republished with permission.

2 Lewis Powell, 'Foreword' in John Peters and Margaret Peters (eds) *Virginia's Historic Courthouses* (University Press of Virginia, 1995).

3 Imogen Beynon, 'Structuring Justice' (Conference Paper, The Third Justice Environments Conference Court Architecture Exhibition, 20–22 May 2010) 59.

DOI: 10.4324/9780429059858-7

FIGURE 4.1 The Supreme Court of New Zealand complex in Wellington, Aotearoa New Zealand. Architects Warren and Mahoney wrapped the building in a complex eight-metre-high bronze screen referencing Rata and Pohutukawa trees in a design strongly influenced by Māori concepts (b). In the centre of the building is the orb-shaped courtroom finished in panels of silver beech timber (a). (Photographs: Warren and Mahoney Architects)

2,294 silver beech panels, the result evoking the cone of the Kauri tree, considered to be the chief of trees.[4]

These symbolic architectural gestures derive from a belief in the communicative force of architecture, and from an understanding that the courthouse and courtrooms are the canvas upon which societal priorities as to law and justice are writ large. These design precedents note the importance of correcting past wrongs and demonstrating respect for the Indigenous peoples of those countries.

In Australia, commissioning bodies and architects have been considering ways courthouses and courtrooms can be designed to: (1) symbolically and physically acknowledge Australian Aboriginal and Torres Strait Islander peoples as the First Peoples of Australia; (2) rectify past wrongs; (3) increase Indigenous participation; (4) allow Aboriginal peoples to engage meaningfully with court processes; (5) reduce the stress felt by Indigenous users; and (6) promote Indigenous 'ownership' of courthouses and courtrooms. This chapter examines the design outcomes for three Australian courthouse developments of national and international significance; Port Augusta (South Australia), and Kununurra and Kalgoorlie court complexes (Western Australia).

Courthouse and courtroom architecture in Australia

Historically, the law of settler Australia operated to the detriment of Aboriginal people and, accordingly, the symbolic and practical functions of the courthouse were not moulded to their benefit. Throughout Australia's European settlement history, Indigenous people have been excluded from meaningful mention in the Constitution;[5] denied franchise until the latter part of the twentieth century;[6] refused legal recognition of their land;[7] and disadvantaged before the criminal law.[8] Indigenous people were denied equal wages for equal work,[9] and suffered myriad other systematic legal disadvantages.[10]

The significance of the foregoing is that, for Indigenous people, historically, the courthouse and the courtroom have been neither a symbol of a legitimate or desirable legal system nor a forum for enforcing one's rights. Inversely,

4 Ibid 54–55. For more information on the Supreme Court of New Zealand; see Matthew T Watson, 'Representing Justice: Architecture and the New Zealand Supreme Court' (Master's Thesis, Victoria University of Wellington, 2012).

5 Larissa Behrendt, Chris Cunneen and Terry Libesman, *Indigenous Relations in Australia* (Oxford University Press, 2009) 257–265.

6 Ibid 26–27.

7 See for example *Cooper v Stuart* (1889) 14 App Cas 286 [291]–[292]; Kent McNeil, 'Racial Discrimination and Unilateral Extinguishment of Native Title (1996) 1 *Australian Indigenous Law Reporter* 181.

8 Behrendt, Cunneen and Libesman (n 4) 24–25, 45, 113–136.

9 Chris Cunneen and Juan Tauri, *Indigenous Criminology* (University of Chicago Press, 2015).

10 See John Chesterman and Brian Galligan, *Citizens without Rights: Aborigines and Australian Citizenship* (Cambridge University Press, 1997); Bain Attwood and Andrew Markus (eds), *The Struggle for Aboriginal Rights: A Documentary History* (Allen & Unwin, 1999).

FIGURE 4.2 'Judgement by his Peers' (1978) by Aboriginal artist, Gordon Syron is a satirical comment on a white imperialistic system of justice branded onto Indigenous Australians. It is a system based on a lie: Australia never was *terra nullius* (empty land). The painting uses role reversal to highlight how legal systems can be unjust: the judge and jury are black but the accused is white. (Painting: Gordon Syron)

courthouses are an unwelcome reminder of the law's indifference and outright hostility to Indigenous rights (see Figure 4.2).

Historically, courthouses in the British Empire borrowed heavily from English architectural design with the effect of cementing an adversarial system.[11] Research has identified the alienating effect of courthouses and courtrooms on Indigenous Australians due to, inter alia, their colonial details,[12] their structural layering calculated to confer power to the (almost always non-Indigenous) judicial officer,[13] and their imposition of a foreign structure on a local landscape.[14]

11 Norman W Spaulding, 'The Enclosure of Justice: Courthouse Architecture, Due Process, and the Dead Metaphor of Trial (2012) 24(1) *Yale Journal of Law & the Humanities* 311.

12 Richard Mohr, 'Enduring Signs and Obscure Meanings: Contested Coats of Arms in Australian Jurisdictions' in Anne Wagner, Tracey Summerfield and Farid Benevides (eds) *Contemporary Issues of the Semiotics of Law* (Hart Publishing, 2003) 180–195.

13 Elena Marchetti, 'Australian Indigenous Sentencing Courts: Restoring Culture in the Sentencing Court Process' in Jane Bolitho, Jasmine Bruce and Gail Mason (eds) *Restorative Justice and Emerging Practice* (Sydney Institute of Criminology, 2012) 111.

14 Elizabeth Grant, 'Port Augusta Courts' (2009) 98(5) *Architecture Australia* 86, 86–90 ('Port Augusta Courts'); Thalia Anthony and Elizabeth Grant, 'Courthouse Design Principles to

This can have an adverse effect on Indigenous peoples' confidence in the judicial process,[15] contribute to discomfort in courthouse and courtroom settings,[16] and exacerbate experiences of disadvantage in the legal system.[17]

To the extent that Australia wants to apologise for, undo, redress, and reverse the wrongs of the past, the courthouse and the courtroom offer an architectural and psychological terrain for symbolic and actual attempts at decolonisation.[18]

Many courthouses in towns and cities around Australia have attempted to recognise Aboriginal and Torres Strait Islander peoples through the incorporation of artworks. There is often an uneasy juxtaposition between the courthouse architecture and artworks. The High Court of Australia is the Supreme Court in the Australian court hierarchy. The building (completed 1980) is an example of late modern Brutalist architecture (architects Edwards Madigan Torzillo and Briggs (EMTB)) (see Figure 4.3). The monumental building featuring bold geometric shapes and raw massed concrete is home to an art collection that, it has been stated, 'should reflect the traditions, symbolism and practice of the law'.[19] Aangkum woman, Rosella Namok from the Cape York Peninsula in far north Queensland, won the 2003 High Court Centenary Art Prize. Her work entitled 'Now we all got to go by same laws' is a large-scale nine-panel work depicting traditional law overlaid by contemporary law which hangs in one of the public halls. Namok described her work:

> When I look in the middle … it's hard, hard for me to think, to talk 'proper English'. Look inside middle … before time … then go look, go outside … that's Australia today. Inside middle … before time … there was strong law. People … they would know what way they belong … it was really strong those days … strong … tradition … culture … people … country … law. Strong and straight … everyone knew it … everyone followed it. Then other people came from all over the world … every place different … got own laws … own culture. Today now … we all got to go by same laws … but … that traditional law … it's still there underneath.[20]

Dignify Spaces for Indigenous Users: Preliminary Observations' (2016) 8(1) *International Journal for Court Administration* 43.

15 Marchetti (n 13).

16 Chris Cunneen and Melanie Schwartz, 'Civil and Family Law Needs of Indigenous People' (2009) 32(3) *University of New South Wales Law Journal* 725, 725.

17 The discrimination facing Indigenous people in the legal system has been identified in both its criminal and civil processes. For example, see the *Royal Commission into Aboriginal Deaths in Custody National Report* (Final Report, April 1991) vols 1–5; see Cunneen and Schwartz (n 16) 726–727.

18 Judith Resnik and Dennis Curtis, *Representing Justice: Invention, Controversy and Rights in City-States and Democratic Courtrooms* (Yale University Press, 2011) 372.

19 'Artworks of the High Court', *Artworks of the High Court* (Web Page, 2010) <http://www.hcourt.gov.au/artworks>. 'Artworks of the High Court'.

20 Rosella Namok, 'Today now … we all got to go by same laws', *Other Law-Themed Artworks* (Web Page, 2010) <https://www.hcourt.gov.au/artworks/other-law-themed-artworks/today-now-we-all-got-to-go-by-same-laws>.

FIGURE 4.3 High Court of Australia, Canberra (a), which displays Rosella Namok's work entitled: 'Now we all got to go by the same laws' (b). (Photograph (a) Elizabeth Grant, (b) High Court of Australia)

Artworks displayed in other Australian courthouses are not so quick to provide messages about the need for Aboriginal and Torres Strait Islander peoples to observe and acquiesce to Western systems of Law. Within the Northern Territory's neo-colonial building designed by architects Peter Doig, Ron Findlay, Roger Linklater, and Susie Cole[21] that houses the Supreme Court (where 80 per cent of those appearing before courts identify as being of Indigenous descent)[22]

21 The design for Supreme Court building in Darwin included a mosaic for the forecourt designed by Warlpiri artist Norah Nelson Napaljarri in the first instance; see Margo Birnberg and Janusz B Kreczmanski, *Aboriginal Artist Dictionary of Biographies: Australian Western, Central Desert and Kimberley Region* (J.B. Publishing, 2004) 209.

22 Australian Bureau of Statistics, '2016 Census Shows Growing Aboriginal and Torres Strait Islander Population' (Media Release 075/2017, 27 June 2017) <http://www.abs.gov.au/ausstats

there is an extensive collection of Indigenous artworks.[23] Courts administration and others have sought works that bring Indigenous perspectives in the courthouse, an act which in itself has not been without concern for Indigenous communities, as it might place Indigenous secret and/or sacred knowledge on public display.[24] Other artworks show Indigenous rights being asserted under Western law and illustrate legal battles fought in the Supreme Court. One such legal case *Milpurrurru v Indofurn Pty Ltd*[25] (informally known as the *Carpets Case*) involved the work of Aboriginal artists which had been transferred without permission to carpets manufactured in Vietnam. The legal decision extended recognition of Aboriginal intellectual property rights in the creative arts and one of the carpets, a reproduction of Tim Leura Tjapaltjarri's *Kooralia*, is on display.[26] While the inclusion of such artworks layers the courthouses with signs and symbols, and signifies the presence of Indigenous peoples in the Australian legal landscape, the often odd juxtapositions of the artworks against the colonial architecture of courthouses does little from an architecture perspective to acknowledge Aboriginal and Torres Strait Islander peoples as equal players in the Australian legal process.

The first formal architectural responses to designing courtrooms to better accommodate the needs of Aboriginal peoples came through the initiatives now known across Australia as Indigenous Sentencing Courts. Indigenous Sentencing Courts arose for the reasons outlined by Magistrate Chris Vass. He noted:

> there was enormous dissatisfaction with the court system as it was. There was a lack of trust. A lot of frustration about not having their say in court ... they felt lawyers were not putting their story across as they wanted.[27]

/abs@.nsf/mediareleasesbyReleaseDate/02D50FAA9987D6B7CA25814800087E03?OpenDocument>.

23 A number of courthouses around Australia hold large collections of Aboriginal art and artefacts and could be seen as operating as informal Indigenous keeping houses; see Elizabeth Grant and Kelly Greenop, 'Affirming and Reaffirming Indigenous Presence: Contemporary Aboriginal and Torres Strait Islander Community, Public and Institutional Architecture in Australia' in Elizabeth Grant, Kelly Greenop, Albert L Refiti and Daniel J Glenn (eds) *The Handbook of Contemporary Indigenous Architecture* (Springer, 2018).

24 The aforementioned 55m2 (592 ft2) mosaic by Norah Nelson Napaljarri entitled *Yiwarra Jukurrpa* (Milky Way Dreaming) (1990–1901) became the subject of dispute (and traditional litigation) within the artist's community. Both its subject matter and innovative style caused some degree of discord amongst senior law men and women at Yuendumu – see Anita Angel, 'Art and Law: Things that Endure' (2000) 122(6) *Balance: Journal of the Northern Territory Law Society* 12, 12–13 – which was in time, resolved. It is now displayed inside the building to allow viewing from above. Pedestrian access is not allowed across the artwork.

25 (1994) 30 IPR 209.

26 Toni Bauman, Samantha Wells and Julie Therese Wells, *Aboriginal Darwin: A Guide to Exploring Important Sites of the Past & Present* (Aboriginal Studies Press, 2006).

27 Vass quoted in Jennifer Powell, 'The Nunga Court: A Descriptive Study of Aboriginal Sentencing Day' (Honours Thesis, The University of Melbourne, 2001).

Legislative changes were made to allow the establishment of the first Aboriginal (Nunga) courts in South Australia in 1999. There were minimal physical changes to the courtroom to accommodate Nunga Court in the early days. Magistrates, guided by Aboriginal Elders sitting either side of them, sat around the bar table with all of the parties concerned. Dr Kate Auty, who presided as a Magistrate over Indigenous Sentencing Courts in Victoria and Western Australia, further developed and facilitated a consultative and collaborative approach as the concept of Indigenous Sentencing Courts spread to other jurisdictions.

Alongside the jurisprudential methods was the practice of giving Indigenous participants the authority to change the physical configuration of existing courtrooms, thereby facilitating some Indigenous occupation and cultural agency of judicial spaces.[28] Jones, paraphrasing Professor David Tait, noted that Indigenous Sentencing Courts may provide 'a space which, through the creative use of symbolism, mediates between memory and tradition and anticipation of a future of hope'.[29]

Large numbers of Indigenous people come into contact with Australia's legal system, particularly as defendants or victims in the criminal context.[30] Beyond the Indigenous Sentencing Courts (which only deal with Indigenous people who have pleaded guilty to an offence), Aboriginal peoples' experiences are often marred by the physical environment of the courthouse. The Judicial Council on Cultural Diversity in their report entitled 'The Path to Justice: Aboriginal and Torres Strait Islander Women's Experience of the Courts' described:

> how intimidating it was for Aboriginal and Torres Strait Islander women to arrive at court. [and] … the remote courts are often very small, and victims and perpetrators are often in close physical proximity for many hours. Stakeholders described overcrowded waiting rooms, people lined up standing in corridors and corners, sitting on the steps and outside areas. Women were frightened being so close to their partners [who were often perpetrators and who] sometimes arrived with family members who could behave in an intimidating fashion.[31]

Stakeholders involved in that study noted that the courthouse and courtroom were terrifying for women and felt much could be done to 'humanise' them.[32] Cunneen et al. have stated methods of rendering these court engagements more

28 Kate Auty, 'Room with a View: Courtrooms and Culture (2009) 98(5) *Architecture Australia* 49, 49–50. See also Marchetti (n 13).

29 Diane Jones, 'Historic Courts: Between Civic Memory and a Future of Hope (2009) 98(5) *Architecture Australia* 58, 58–59.

30 See generally 'Artworks of the High Court' (n 19); Thalia Anthony, *Indigenous People, Crime and Punishment* (Routledge, 2013); Harry Blagg, *Crime, Aboriginality and the Decolonisation of Justice* (Federation Press, 2nd ed, 2016).

31 Judicial Council on Cultural Diversity, *Path to Justice: Aboriginal and Torres Strait Islander Women's Experience of the Courts* (Judicial Council on Cultural Diversity, 2016) 26.

32 Ibid.

productive and meaningful, and less oppressive and intimidating.[33] The lived reality of the Australian experience is that Indigenous people disproportionately appear in courts on criminal and child protection matters. This is especially true of regional courts in Western Australia, South Australia, the Northern Territory, and far north Queensland.

The question then becomes *how* courthouses and courtrooms in such places might be designed so as to incorporate and include Indigenous needs and aspirations with traditional court functions. The next part of this chapter discusses the emerging design principles and paradigms for courthouse and courtroom design for Indigenous people, drawing later from three projects at locations where Indigenous peoples constitute a significant proportion of court users.

Design approaches and paradigms

Courthouse complexes at Port Augusta, Kununurra, and Kalgoorlie were designed against the backdrop of a growing body of research and practice from the fields of environmental psychology, architecture, and placemaking, specific to an emerging contemporary architecture for, with, and by Australian Aboriginal and Torres Strait Islander peoples. Each project has (consciously and/or unconsciously) drawn from certain design approaches, paradigms, and precedents from contemporary Australian Indigenous architecture.

One common approach to designing for Indigenous users is to consider the 'fit' between the behaviours and environmental preferences. This approach focuses on the need for congruency between the environment and cultural behaviours and socio-spatial needs of the users. It is underpinned by environmental psychology, in particular, the stress paradigm, under which environments are seen to act as stress-modulating devices.[34] Preferences for particular environments can, thus, be interpreted in terms of stress reduction with poorly designed environments leading users to experience high degrees of stress with resultant impacts on their physical and psychological wellbeing. Gifford et al. state:

> The users' personal factors and cultural background and the physical aspects of the setting (stressors and amenities) are presumed to influence the way people think about certain environments.[35]

33 Chris Cunneen et al., *Penal Culture and Hyperincarceration: The Revival of the Prison* (Routledge, 2013) 144–146; Philip Kirke, *The Shelter of Law: Designing with Communities for a Culture of Natural Justice* (Friend Books, 2009) 49–50 ('*The Shelter of Law*').

34 See Gary W Evans (ed), *Environmental Stress* (CUP Archive, 1984); Gary W Evans and Janetta M McCoy, 'When Buildings Don't Work: The Role of Architecture in Human Health' (1998) 18(1) *Journal of Environmental Psychology* 85; Sheldon Cohen et al., *Behavior, Health, and Environmental Stress* (Springer, 2013).

35 Robert Gifford, Linda Steg and Joseph Reser, 'Environmental Psychology' in Paul R Martin, Fanny M Cheung, Michael C Knowles, Michael Kyrios, J Bruce Overmier and Josè M Prieto (eds), *IAAP Handbook of Applied Psychology* (Wiley-Blackwell, 2011) 451.

Indigenous people have differing and varying complex cultural, socio-spatial, and environmental needs for built environments and there is a growing amount of evidence-based research drawing from fields of housing, community, public, and institutional architecture.[36] Understanding and translating the culturally specific responses has the capacity to produce environments which better 'fit' the needs of individuals and groups and minimise the adverse effects commonly caused by poorly designed environments.[37] In addition to evidence-based research, further information regarding specific environmental needs of a particular group of Indigenous users and their preferences is often gleaned by architects (proficiently or otherwise) in consultation processes. Some projects have included an architectural anthropologist on the design team and/or the preparation of specific briefs outlining the Indigenous considerations for a specific project.

Another approach has come from the field of placemaking, a multi-faceted approach to the planning, design, and management of public spaces. The knowledge that colonisation has involved the 'imposition of western spatiality and a denial of Indigenous spatial understandings'[38] has led to discourses on the importance of placemaking as a way of asserting Indigenous 'ownership' and reasserting Indigenous presence.[39] Memmott and Long describe the creation of an Indigenous place:

36 See for example Paul Memmott, 'From the Curry to the Weal: Aboriginal Town Camps and Compounds of the Western Back-Blocks' (1996) 7(1) *Fabrications* 1; Cathy Keys, 'Defining Single Aboriginal Women's Housing Needs in Central Australia: Dealing with Issues of Culture, Gender and Environment (1996) 1(1) *Architectural Theory Review* 69; Cathy Keys, 'Unearthing Ethno-Architectural Types (1997) 54–55 *Transition* 20; Elizabeth M Grant, 'Towards Safer and More Congruent Prison Environments for Aboriginal Prisoners: A South Australian Study' (PhD Dissertation, The University of Adelaide, 2008); Elizabeth Grant, 'An International Overview of the Initiatives to Accommodate Indigenous Prisoners' in Yvonne Jewkes, Jamie Bennett and Ben Crewe (eds), *Handbook on* Prisons (Routledge, 2nd ed., 2016); Paul Memmott and Cathy Keys, 'Translating the Design of Behaviour Settings for Aboriginal Well-Being' (Conference Paper, Society of Architectural Historians, Australia and New Zealand (SAHANZ) Annual Conference, 2–5 July 2014); Paul Memmott and Cathy Keys, 'Redefining Architecture to Accommodate Cultural Difference: Designing for Cultural Sustainability' (2015) 58(4) *Architectural Science Review* 278; Paul Memmott and Cathy Keys, 'The Emergence of an Architectural Anthropology in Aboriginal Australia: The work of the Aboriginal Environments Research Centre (2017) 21(2) *Architectural Theory Review* 1; Grant and Greenop (n 23).

37 This approach has been termed the cultural design paradigm in the housing setting. Go-Sam writes:

> 'The cultural design paradigm uses models of culturally distinct behaviour to inform definitions of Aboriginal housing needs. Its premise is that to competently design appropriate residential accommodation for Aboriginal people who have traditionally-oriented lifestyles, architects must understand the nature of those lifestyles'; Carroll Go-Sam, 'Working with and against Indigenous Design Paradigms' (2008) 97(5) *Architecture Australia* 53, 53.

38 Emily Potter, 'Introduction: Making Indigenous Place in the Australian City' (2012) 15(2) *Postcolonial Studies* 131, 134.

39 See for example Anoma Pieris, 'Occupying the Centre: Indigenous Presence in the Australian Capital City' (2012) 15(2) *Postcolonial Studies* 221; Anoma Pieris, *Indigenous Cultural Centers and*

> A place can be partly or wholly created by enacting special types of behaviour at a particular piece of environment … A place can also be created by the association of knowledge properties such as concepts, past events, legends, names, ideals, or memories.[40]

Architects have often attempted to enculturate courthouses by incorporating Indigenous signs and symbols[41] through the inclusion of artwork or within the architecture or landscape architecture of a project, thereby reinforcing the value of Aboriginal cultures and knowledge systems[42] and asserting or reasserting Indigenous peoples' presence. Approaches can be simple, such as hanging an Aboriginal artwork and displaying Aboriginal and Torres Strait Islander flags in a courtroom,[43] or more complex, like the endeavours seen in the following case studies where Indigenous culture/s and identity form the basis of the architectural design.

Such a great number of projects from various genres have employed it, that a contemporary architectural aesthetic/s for projects for Australian Aboriginal users has/have been defined to some degree. The typologies tend to be (1) the use of natural materials and curvilinear forms employing colours from the surrounding natural landscape, or (2) designs at a domestic scale featuring lightweight materials, or (3) reflecting the landscape in the form of the building. Across all these typologies, aspects of the local Aboriginal culture/s and oral histories may be referenced in the design, and the development of sympathetic landscape design using Indigenous planting is generally completed as part of the

Museums: An Illustrated International Survey (Rowman & Littlefield Publishers, 2016); Anoma Pieris et al., *Indigenous Place: Contemporary Buildings, Landmarks and Places of Significance in South East Australia and Beyond* (Melbourne School of Design, 2014); Janet McGaw and Anoma Pieris, *Assembling the Centre: Architecture for Indigenous Cultures, Australia and Beyond* (Routledge, 1st ed, 2014).

40 Paul Memmott and Stephen Long, 'Place Theory and Place Maintenance in Indigenous Australia' (2002) 20(1) *Urban Policy and Research* 39, 39.

41 While there has been some debate about who is authorised to express Aboriginality through the incorporating of signs and symbols into architecture. See Mathilde Lochert, 'Mediating Aboriginal Architecture' (1997) 54 *Transition* 8; Kim Dovey, 'Myth and Media: Constructing Aboriginal Architecture' (2000) 54(1) *Journal of Architectural Education* 2, and there have been concerns about appropriate use; see Paul Memmott and Joseph Reser, 'Design Concepts and Processes for Public Aboriginal Architecture' (2000) 55–56 *PaPER* 69. However employing this approach is common.

42 Elizabeth Grant, Michael Colbung and Ian Green, *Architecture for Aboriginal Children and Families: A Post Occupancy Evaluation of the Taikurrendi, Gabmididi Manoo and Ngura Yadurirn Aboriginal Children and Family Centres* (The University of Adelaide, 2015).

43 Judge Paul Grant, President of the Children's Court of Victoria notes that: '[c]ourtrooms used for [Children's] Koori Courts have been adapted for the court's particular processes. Aboriginal artworks are on the walls and the Australian, Aboriginal and the Torres Strait Islander flags displayed'; Judge Paul Grant, 'The Children's Koori Court in Victoria' *Children's Court of Victoria* (Paper, September 2009) 6 <https://www.childrenscourt.vic.gov.au/sites/default/files/Prato_presentation_final.pdf>.

building. These typologies are accepted and embraced by many Aboriginal and non-Aboriginal people across Australia while rejected by others.[44] In discussing each of the case studies the application of these design approaches and paradigms becomes evident.

Case study 1: The Port Augusta Court Complex

The first Australian courthouse designed predominantly for Indigenous users was constructed in Port Augusta, South Australia, in 2008.[45] The former courthouse had been located on the main street and Indigenous people would gather on the street (kerbside consultations between lawyers and their clients were accepted as a matter of course) with larger groups congregating in a nearby public square. The lack of safe waiting spaces created the potential for conflict between the families of different parties to legal proceedings, especially victims and defendants. In planning for the new courthouse, a site was requisitioned from the railway yards, adjacent to the Port Augusta central business district.[46]

The project architect, Denis Harrison, decided that any design for a new court complex needed to take into account: The way Indigenous people gather and use public space, the complexities and importance of the place, and the varied cultural and socio-spatial needs of different user groups and organisations. In order to achieve this, the design team (Department for Transport, Energy and Infrastructure (DTEI) with project architect Denis Harrison; project team Paul Drabsch, Ian Abbott, Brian Carr; interior designer DesignInc; landscape designer Viesturs Cielens design) worked closely with Indigenous and non-Indigenous stakeholders.[47]

The location dictated the design. Grant said the site 'commands distant views of the culturally important Flinders Ranges with shorter views to the Minburie Ranges and Spencer Gulf',[48] and, accordingly, the building was oriented to emphasise those views. Ochres used in traditional ceremonies in the local area defined the colour palette for the building's exterior. The complex was constructed of a combination of lightweight materials in order to be non-intimidating and large areas of glass were used to allow visual connection with the outdoors (see Figure 4.4).

The axis of the building lies along the street frontage with consideration given to the manner in which Indigenous people use and perceive space. A series of long, low, sand dunes were formed around the building to reflect the local landscapes. Between the mounds, mass plantings direct visitors along pathways, while allowing privacy and views under the canopy zones. An open shelter has

44 Grant and Greenop (n 23).
45 Grant, 'Port Augusta Courts' (n 14).
46 Ibid 86.
47 Ibid.
48 Ibid 87.

FIGURE 4.4 Exterior, Port Augusta Courthouse. (Photograph: Georgie Sharp)

been erected adjacent to the court waiting area. It is a multi-functional structure intended to be used as an outdoor court space, a consultation and/or waiting area. Seats in the shelter and around the exterior of the site are three-dimensional translations of the Indigenous depictions of *yuus* (Pitjantjatjara: windbreaks) and *wurlies* (Pitjantjatjara: shelters). The seating allows two or three people to sit as a group; however, where people are located in different seats, the layout also permits the practice of socio-spatial behaviours (i.e. the avoidance of eye contact, necessary in Western Desert and Central Australian Aboriginal cultures) (see Figure 4.5).

The approach to the building is unique in its incorporation of Indigenous law (lore) for wayfinding (orientation) purposes. As has been described elsewhere:

> Visitors arriving at the street frontage are led along the main pathway where a depiction of Arkurru, the powerful and feared, bearded Spirit Serpent of the Flinders Ranges Dreaming lies. Arkurru's head sits under the front verandah with his beard protruding as geometric shapes from under the verandah screens. His elliptical eye appears as a pattern in the cement and nearby a high cone shape symbolises his tail breaking the ground outside the building. The presence of Arkurru acts as a symbol and a guide which leads people to the main entrance.[49]

49 Ibid 89.

FIGURE 4.5 Internal (a) and external (b) waiting areas, Port Augusta Courthouse. The external waiting area has the capacity to function as an outdoor courtroom but has not been used for that purpose. (Photographs: Georgie Sharp)

At the entrance to the court complex, another path allows users to deviate from the main route, should they sense conflict in the public or entrance areas or wish to collect their thoughts or wait outside. The entrance directs visitors into a double-height circular foyer with extensive glazing offering long-range views and continuing the strong relationship between the interior and exterior of the building (see Figure 4.5). The design employs a legible organisational system and numerous wayfinding mechanisms such as depictions of Akurru's path and other images denoting his path pointing to the doors of each of the courtrooms (see Figure 4.6).

The complex has three courtrooms opening from the (circular) foyer: A jury courtroom, a Magistrates Aboriginal courtroom, and a multi-purpose courtroom. Each courtroom has an adjacent courtyard developed to provide visual relief and to allow people to stay connected to the external environment. The Magistrates Aboriginal Courtroom also doubles as an Indigenous Sentencing or Conferencing Courtroom. Parties meet around a central table to discuss the

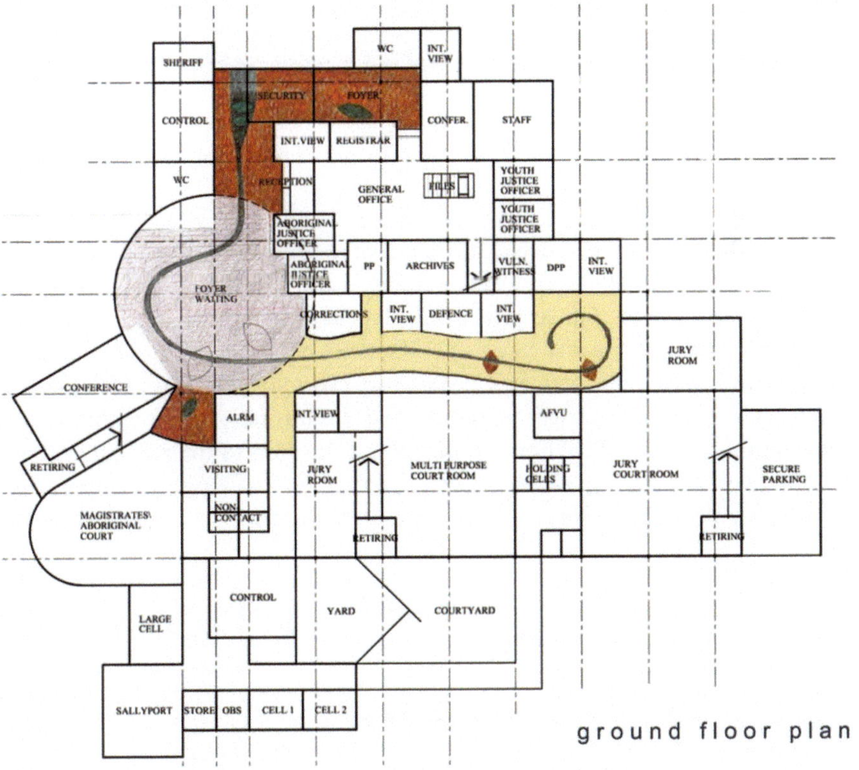

FIGURE 4.6 Plan, Port Augusta Courthouse. The presence of Arkurra, the Spirit Serpent of the Flinders Ranges acts as a wayfinding mechanism to lead people to the main entrance and through the building. (Drawing: Denis Harrison)

FIGURE 4.7 Port Augusta Courthouse: Aboriginal Sentencing Court. Note the screens with motifs to enclose the space are not down in this image. (Photograph: Elizabeth Grant)

offence, offender, and sentence. The design of the Indigenous courtroom at Port Augusta – with windows, retractable screens,[50] and a round table – departs from the conventional rectangular courtroom layout (see Figure 4.7).[51] Five slump glass panels framing one window depict the story of Seven Sisters Dreaming – an Indigenous legend with messages about observance of moral and social codes.[52] Signs and symbols are used to imbue and enculturate the courthouse with Indigenous culture and to impart Indigenous meanings to the judicial system.

The Port Augusta development was the first Australian project designed to incorporate the needs of Indigenous users across the entire courthouse complex.

50 The retractable screens are a technological solution to conceal the dock, the bench, the witness box/remote screen, and other accoutrements of the traditional court; Elizabeth Grant, Emma Rowden and Mira Taitz, 'Evaluating the Cultural Responsiveness of the Design of an Aboriginal Court Complex for Aboriginal Users: Post Occupancy Evaluation of the Port Augusta Court Complex' (Conference Paper, Australian and New Zealand Society of Criminology (ANZSOC) Conference, 28–30 September 2011).

51 Note: The Magistrates Aboriginal Courtroom at Port Augusta contains a dock, despite architects attempting to negotiate for its exclusion; see Interview with Denis Harrison (Elizabeth Grant, Interview, 4 March 2002).

52 Elizabeth Grant, *Whyalla Aboriginal Children and Family Centre: Indigenous Design Considerations. Report to Department of Transport, Energy and Infrastructure* (Report, 2011) 35.

The connections between the interior and exterior of the building are strong and allow users to stay (in part) connected with Country.[53] Views to the exterior are possible from most internal spaces. Individuals and groups can choose to wait outside in different spaces, large and scattered enough to allow the continuation of Aboriginal avoidance practices[54] and to let people escape from possible conflictual situations and maintain one's safety and dignity. People outside can be clearly observed by staff and can also see into the waiting area. Grant et al. made observations of Indigenous family groups from remote areas.[55] They observed that one or two people from larger groups attended the hearing whilst the remainder of the group waited outside as support. The visual connections between the waiting area and the outside shelter allowed people to observe what was occurring from a distance.

However, there are a number of impediments to Indigenous peoples' engagement with the space, especially in the Magistrates Aboriginal Courtroom, which may be construed to be genuflection to institutional priorities. For instance, there has been an obtrusive inclusion of technology on the oval table (see Figure 4.7), which disrupts the openness of the roundtable discussion in Indigenous Sentencing Courts. There is also a cumbersome almost unusable pull-down lever to reveal the Indigenous artwork. Finally, there is a partially enclosed 'glass dock' in the courtroom, which was installed contrary to the original design. Some parties have reported that the presence of the dock in the courtroom conveys a negative message of the continuing disempowerment of Indigenous peoples.

Furthermore, there are anecdotal reports that the Indigenous courtroom may not function effectively due to the layout of the room, given the above issues as well as the compression of functional areas into one end, making circulation around the courtroom difficult. This contradicts the design principles underpinning Indigenous Sentencing Courts where all court participants sit around a table to deliberate on issues. Other shortcomings have emerged in the functional layout of the courthouse design, such as the position of the toilets, the lack of capacity to separate vulnerable people (e.g. children, witnesses, and victims), and the absence of sightlines in the holding cells.

The design of the Port Augusta courthouse and courtrooms is worthy of further investigation in terms of how they are used as well as Indigenous users' perception of whether the complex meets their socio-spatial needs, responds to their beliefs as Indigenous people, and is conducive to connecting court users to Country. This may not only inform the ways future courthouse design can respond to and respect Indigenous users, but may also provide a rationale for modifications to the existing Port Augusta courthouse.

53 'Country' is a place of belonging and connection for Indigenous Australians that extends beyond the meaning that non-Indigenous Australians attach to land.

54 Aboriginal avoidance practices refer to those relationships in traditional Aboriginal society where certain people are required to avoid others in their family or clan as a mark of respect.

55 Grant, Rowden and Taitz (n 50).

Case study 2: The Kalgoorlie Courts Project

The State Government of Western Australia set out to design a major contemporary court complex in Kalgoorlie in 2007. The project encompassed the renovation of the Kalgoorlie Warden's Court and Post Office, as well as an upgrade of the adjacent police lockup and the construction of new buildings (architects Hassell in collaboration with Graham Brawn, Lin Kilpatrick, and Kevin Palassis).[56] The ceremonial superior courtrooms were located in the old building to capitalise on its existing historical spaces, while the new building houses the Magistrates Court. In order to make it relevant to Indigenous users, one of the major design challenges was reconciling the physical and cultural requirements of a contemporary courthouse with the constraints of nineteenth-century colonial buildings.[57]

From the outset, the design of the courthouse sought to incorporate cultural expressions and accommodate the diverse needs of Indigenous users into its design, such needs being ascertained through consultation with an Indigenous Reference Group. The group suggested the inclusion of multiple access routes to facilitate Indigenous peoples' observation of avoidance practices and to reduce contact between conflicting parties.[58] The forecourt is accessible from two directions and provides a central point from which both wings of the complex may be accessed.

In view of the need for Indigenous users to have close connections to exterior environments, such spaces assumed a critical role in the project. The design allows people to maintain a view of their social and outdoor environment[59] and is organised around a linear landscaped courtyard spine. Tilt-up glass doors bordering the entire length of the public gallery of the new building visually and physically create an indoor–outdoor connection. The separation of the old and new buildings allows the greater part of the outdoor area to be a secure zone, defined and contained by the two parallel wings of the complex (see Figure 4.8). The fully glazed elevated courtyard of the new building is accompanied by large folding wall panels, which enable both the public domain and the courtrooms to dissolve into landscaped outdoor areas. The complex features four courtrooms (with provision to expand to five when required) and mediation, registry, and other support facilities.[60]

The three courtrooms of the Magistrates Court are on ground level and accessible from the secure central courtyard. This allows a large number of people

56 Philip Kirke, 'Kalgoorlie Courts Project' (2009) 98(5) *Architecture Australia* 71, 71 ('Kalgoorlie Courts Project').

57 Philip James Kirke, 'Culture-Based Justice Architecture: Building Community Wellbeing through Deeper Cultural Engagement' (Working Paper No 10/2010, Justice & Development Working Paper Series) 28–29.

58 Kirke, 'Kalgoorlie Courts Project' (n 56).

59 Ibid.

60 Anthony and Grant (n 14).

FIGURE 4.8 Kalgoorlie Courthouse: Tilt-up glass doors allow connection to the exterior. (Photograph: Hassell)

to wait immediately outside their scheduled courtroom in the enclosed public waiting area, or in the fresh air. The direct proximity of an outdoor waiting area to each court simplifies the process of locating and calling people scheduled to appear. It also obviates the problematic practice of announcing names over public address systems. Each of the courtrooms in the Magistrates Court is connected to a private courtyard to allow proceedings to take place with direct access to fresh air, light, and visual connection to an autochthonous garden.

Indigenous art has also been incorporated into the design. The interior colour scheme comprises colours reflecting the surrounding landscape. Artworks by Indigenous artists were incorporated providing insights on Indigenous life in the region. In the public waiting area, large sculptures have been installed and in the central courtyard a sculpture depicting a split circular form alludes to the fusion of old and new – a concept embodied by the courthouse itself (see Figure 4.9).

The Kalgoorlie Community Court – an Indigenous Sentencing Court[61] – was established to promote 'a sense of Aboriginal ownership of the justice process'.[62] According to one evaluation report, the Community Court provides

61 In 2015, the Kalgoorlie-Boulder Indigenous Sentencing Community Court lost government funding; however, it continues to operate without a dedicated budget.

62 Heather Aquilina et al., *Evaluation of the Aboriginal Sentencing Court of Kalgoorlie* (Final Report, 16 October 2009) 1.

FIGURE 4.9 Kalgoorlie Courthouse: Sculptural pieces in the forecourt. (Photograph: Hassell)

a 'courtroom sentencing experience and environment that is more relevant and less intimidating to Aboriginal people' through its provision of culturally relevant advice to magistrates and by assisting the 'accused in understanding court process'.[63] The newly designed complex allows Indigenous Elders to play their integral role of contributing cultural knowledge and understandings in the Community Court sentencing process. To facilitate the panel discussions, an Elders' meeting room associated with the Community Court is located off the judicial circulation route.[64] The courtroom space itself has been designed to permit maximum flexibility in its modes of operation. A single elliptical table replaces the usual tables for legal counsel. While the table can still be used for traditional proceedings, it can also transform into a Community Court or conferencing table for mediation.

There were design changes that may have reduced the flexibility of the spaces and adversely affected users. Anthony and Grant noted that the 'community courtroom has a courtyard sufficiently large to allow proceedings to take place outside'[65] and the area was to include an opening wall along the public gallery. However, when built, the area included a fixed wall, which may create issues

63 Ibid.
64 Kirke, 'Kalgoorlie Courts Project' (n 56).
65 Anthony and Grant (n 14) 52.

in conducting a hearing in this area. It is likely that participants would not be actively engaged due to the constraints of the space. The architects also designed the holding cells purposefully with full-height windows overlooking native gardens. The State vetoed the installation of full-height windows, leaving the holding cells, as in the other two case studies, without a sightline to the external environment. This raises concerns as to the cultural safety of Indigenous persons in custody.[66]

The design of the Kalgoorlie Court Complex raises a number of critical questions. One wonders whether layering new Indigenous meanings onto these buildings suppresses messages of colonial dominance and injustice. Can one make colonial architecture meet the cultural and socio-spatial needs of Indigenous users by opening up or providing external areas? Do external areas without long-range views provide Indigenous users with a connection to place that can redefine the court complex as an Indigenous place?

Case study 3: Kununurra Courthouse

The third of the recent courthouse developments designed specifically with Indigenous court users in mind is situated in Kununurra in Western Australia (TAG Architects in association with Iredale Pedersen Hook Architects). A replacement court project was conceived because the original Kununurra courthouse was:

> inadequate to discharge the volume of judicial work undertaken … during the many weeks of the year in which the Supreme and District Courts [were] using the only court room in the building, the magistrate … performed court business in other public buildings.[67]

The inadequate accommodation at Kununurra made conducting court and court-related activities difficult. Vulnerable witnesses were forced to confront the accused person when arriving to give evidence due to poor circulation patterns in the building.[68] There was no office space for visiting judges and their staff. The courthouse is adjacent to the police station, where people may be remanded prior to appearing

66 By contrast, the new courthouse in Coffs Harbour, New South Wales (within the Coffs Harbour Justice Precinct; PTW Architects in collaboration with the National Aboriginal Design Agency) was designed with windows in the holding cells. These windows allowed for sight to the external environment. However, police raised risk-mitigation issues that forced designers to increase the height of the window to above the height of juvenile offenders; see Emma Rowden and Diane Jones, 'Design, Dignity and Due Process: The Construction of the Coffs Harbour Courthouse' (2015) 14(2) *Law, Culture and the Humanities* 317, 16.

67 The Hon Wayne Martin, 'Law Week – September 2009 Opening Address "The State of Justice – 2009"' (Speech, Supreme Court of Western Australia, 14 September 2009) <https://www.supremecourt.wa.gov.au/_files/Law_Week_Address_14_Sept_09.pdf> 7.

68 Ibid.

FIGURE 4.10 Kununurra Courthouse: Exterior. (Photograph: Peter Bennetts)

in court for their bail application to be heard. The Law Reform Commission of Western Australia had criticised the colocation of courthouses with police stations because it conveys to Indigenous users the message that the police and courts are part of the same hegemonic apparatus.[69] In this development, the proximity of the courthouse to the police station needs to be assessed on its own merits as they are both located (along with the shopping centre) along a route which delivers community services in a hub, thus increasing their accessibility.

An Indigenous Community Reference Group was established in 2011 to bring the views of the Indigenous community to the project and design team. Members gave input on various aspects of the building including public areas within the complex, internal design elements, and public art. The design, colours, and material finishes were chosen to reflect the local cultures and surrounding landscape. The two-storey courthouse, framed with steel and concrete, was opened in 2014. It is fabricated from a mixture of precast concrete panels, stone, and metal cladding, and covered by a metal roof (see Figure 4.10).

TAG Architects in association with Iredale Pedersen Hook Architects designed the building to enable people to have strong connections to the external environment, to remain connected to place, and to experience the external environment from inside the building. With the building oriented for maximum use of natural light, there is a reduced reliance on artificial lighting. The windows also permit a view to the horizon and distant ranges from the courtrooms, potentially subverting the traditionally isolating nature of courtrooms. The design profile of the roof mirrors the outline of the distant ranges and creates large volumes in the interior spaces. Natural materials such as timbers are used throughout the building to connect with the external stonework, which is interspersed with glass panels.

69 Law Reform Commission of Western Australia, *Court Perspectives: Architecture, Psychology and Law Reform in Western Australia* (Report, 1999) 307.

Some socio-spatial needs of Indigenous people are reflected in the design of the courthouse. Waiting areas were informally planned to allow people to wait as individuals, as small family units, or to congregate in larger groups. Screens were used to provide a degree of privacy to people waiting and to defuse potential conflict between users. A secure external courtyard was provided to allow people to wait outside before entering a courtroom.

Indigenous artists from the East Kimberley region of Western Australia were engaged to create artworks under the theme of 'law and culture'. The artworks take many forms, from sculpture and painting, to designs integrated into the fabric of the building to share knowledge about Country. For example, a carved timber handrail at the base of the stairs depicts two intertwined snakes, suggesting two systems of law, working harmoniously. In the enclosed courtyard, a sculpture alludes to principles of 'balance' underpinning the legal system. The artworks also depict the landscape and geological forms characteristic of the region to provide a sense of place; for example, the main entry houses a glass print design of *Nyamooli*, a bush soap that grows near water. Perforated aluminium screening along the western side of the exterior of the building provides shading and portrays a landscape scene of nearby Lake Argyle. However, artwork is not displayed in the courtrooms, where its impact on the court users' experience of the legal process might arguably be most required or most influential.[70]

The new Kununurra Courthouse is an imposing presence in the local landscape. Constructed of heavy materials (i.e. concrete, stone cladding, and steel), there is a risk that the courthouse may be perceived by some Indigenous members of the community to be asserting (and reasserting) the dominance and inflexibility of the Anglo-Australian criminal justice system.

Emerging cultural and socio-spatial principles for courthouse design for Indigenous peoples

As previously outlined, a large body of literature reiterates the importance of acknowledging the diversity of Indigenous users and language groups. Architectural design needs to be responsive to the cultural and socio-spatial requirements of the users and the group/s. In addition, some of the practitioners for these projects have a great deal of experience in working with and for Indigenous clients and users. For example, Iredale Pedersen Hook with TAG Architects have undertaken and completed multiple projects for Indigenous clients[71] and the willingness of the architects to engage is an indicator that they are keen observers of how Indigenous peoples use space and aspire to make places.

70 Lawrence Nield and Andrew Nield, 'Local Rules: New Kununurra Courthouse' (2015) 104(3) *Architecture Australia* 80.

71 See 'Kununurra Courthouse', *Iredale Pedersen Hook* (Web Page) <http://iredalepedersenhook.com/?portfolio=kununurra-courthouse>.

It is possible to extract from the literature and the precedents discussed, some emerging principles of courthouse design for Indigenous people. In the hope that these principles might provide a premise for recasting some of the assumptions behind orthodox courthouse design, what follows is an attempt to articulate these newly emergent principles. It must be remembered, however, that each and every project will require adaptation of the principles to ensure the design process is responsive to the spatial priorities of the local Indigenous community.

Provision for heterogeneous Indigenous groups and spatial avoidance practices

Many Indigenous cultures require individuals to avoid contact or close proximity with other individuals. Kirke describes the real implications of these beliefs for courthouse design:

> Aboriginal cultures seem to have included an understanding of particular relationships that may be prone to tensions and are pre-emptively restricted by injunctions on contact. The most common of these is the relationship between son-in-law and mother-in-law. There are numerous instances of our courts system causing conflict in Aboriginal society, for example by unwittingly imposing upon a woman the necessity to testify as a witness in a case concerning a son-in-law. Even the matter of people (of a kinship type governed by avoidance relationships) having to sit in close proximity in waiting rooms will at the very least cause distress, if not trigger actual punishment under customary law to be reckoned with when they return to their respective communities.[72]

Courthouses designed for Aboriginal peoples adhering to avoidance behaviours need spatially distinct waiting areas and courtroom galleries as well as separate entries to the courthouse and courtrooms, where possible. The Kalgoorlie, Port Augusta, and Kununurra courthouses have, to various degrees, achieved these aims.

Recognising that Indigenous court users may wish to gather as distinct social groups, courthouse and courtrooms designs must accommodate such preferences and avoid mandating one common meeting area. There should be sufficient spaces for physical separation to allow conflicting parties, victims, perpetrators, and vulnerable witnesses to be located away and out of sight from each other with acoustic privacy.

This consideration should also apply to the organisation and placement of amenities, as well as public area access and egress. Any rooms, spaces, or communal areas that are intended for the joint use of men and women must be

72 Kirke, 'Kalgoorlie Courts Project' (n 56) 73.

planned with separate entry/exit points to allow for sustained avoidance behaviours where applicable. Apertures in doors can afford some transparency to occupants, allowing new entrants to be recognised prior to physical colocation upon entry or exit.

Interpenetration of indoor and outdoor space

Kirke uses the phrase 'inside-out architecture' to encapsulate this form of architectural thinking. He writes:

> At its heart, the design has inverted usual architectural thinking by making the outdoor spaces the central organising principle of the whole project. In making these outdoor spaces work appropriately and comfortably for traditionally orientated Aboriginal people … the built elements have derived their form and qualities.[73]

This approach is based on research showing that most people are more relaxed and focused in naturally lit spaces with a direct relationship to the outdoors. One might imagine this may be particularly true for Indigenous people from remote communities.

In the recent past, court design only went so far as to allow natural light into the courtroom, the fear being that it would be too distracting or impermissibly voyeuristic to allow noise, air, smells, and views from outside into the courtroom. The architect of the Brisbane Supreme and District Court felt bound by this tradition in his design of that precinct, asserting:

> We knew from our research and from the expressed desire of judges that courtrooms with an external aspect and with natural light give better trial outcomes. People are more relaxed and are able to concentrate for longer periods of time in healthy, day-lit spaces with a direct relationship to the outside world … [But] [i]t is simply not acceptable to have a courtroom where direct sunlight enters the court, where people outside can see into the court, or where external sound can enter the court. The inside-outside relationship is really a one-way relationship.[74]

This is no longer the consensus position, as commissioning bodies and architects begin to acknowledge the 'need for *actual* and *perceptual* access to the outdoors and fresh air'.[75] Innovative courtrooms are now being built in ways that

73 Ibid.

74 John Hockings, 'Brisbane Supreme and District Court' (2009) 102(2) *Architecture Australia* 65, 67.

75 Graham Brawn, 'The Changing Face of Justice: The Architecture of the Australian Courthouse' (2009) 98(5) *Architecture Australia* 39, 40. Emphasis added by authors.

erase traditional spatial hierarchies by physically melding indoor and outdoor spaces, preferring natural light, affording views of the surrounding landscape, and allowing the sounds and smells of the outdoors into the courtroom itself.

The above-mentioned Kalgoorlie courthouse in its design intent was the most ambitious of all Australian courthouses in its melding of indoor and outdoor space. In the new building, each courtroom has an attached outdoor courtyard offering visual respite from the proceedings inside. Just as importantly, the holding cells for offenders in custody were to have access to this same landscaped courtyard. This design feature was included in response to requests from the local Indigenous legal service[76] but unfortunately this did not occur. The design anticipated that court proceedings might take place in the courtyard itself, and the adjoining wall of the courtroom is articulated to allow it to be folded up, so as to transform the court into a hybrid indoor–outdoor hearing space.[77] Alas, again these design features did not eventuate. Equally radical was the design of Kununurra Court complex's outdoor court space. Essentially a paved area with a quadrilateral shade structure that is open to the elements on all four sides, the space represents perhaps the most complete sloughing off of the historical baggage of preconceived ideas about what a court ought to look like.[78]

Visual connection to Country

Another shared feature of courthouses designed for Indigenous court users is the pre-eminence afforded to views of the surrounding landscape. Historically, outlooks from the courtroom were prohibited, being thought to distract and detract from the intensity of the proceedings within. Accordingly, enclosed spaces in courts (including in waiting areas, courtrooms, jury rooms, and holding cells) tend to prohibit sightlines to the external environment. However, such sightlines are essential to enabling Indigenous users to maintain cultural connections to Country.[79] The notion of Country is central to Indigenous ontology and epistemology, which is distinct from Western notions of land. Country informs Indigenous relationships between the individual and the group, as well as the broader world. Country is associated with knowledge such as Indigenous laws (lore), past events, legends, and cultural ideals.[80] Indigenous connection and reconnection with place has important implications for Indigenous self-governance,

76 Kirke, 'Kalgoorlie Courts Projects' (n 56) 75.

77 Ibid 74.

78 Grant, 'Port Augusta Courts' (n 14) 90.

79 The importance of sightlines for Indigenous Australians is discussed in Elizabeth Grant and Paul Memmott, 'The Case for Single Cells and Alternative Ways of Viewing Custodial Accommodation for Australian Aboriginal Peoples' (2008) 10(3) *The Flinders Journal of Law Reform* 631, 644; Rowden and Jones (n 66) 15; Joseph Reser, 'The Design of Safe and Humane Police Cells' in David Biles and David McDonald (eds), *Deaths in Custody Australia: 1980–1989* (Australian Institute of Criminology, 1992) 147, 191.

80 Memmott and Long (n 40) 39.

wellbeing, and healing[81] and assists Indigenous people to reclaim and assert their relationships to Country. Therefore, maintaining sightlines to Country is more likely to improve Indigenous users' sense of safety and wellbeing.

In more recent times, windows in courtrooms are seen as important sources of visual relief and essential to making courts perceptually and psychologically accessible.[82] The importance of Country to many Indigenous people means that views of the outdoors take on a special significance in the design of courthouses and courtrooms. Where possible, the orientation of the building and its outdoor spaces should provide a view of the horizon to maximise users' access to the external natural environment and allow Indigenous users to feel the sun on their face if they choose.[83] A number of writers and architects have noted the importance of establishing sightlines from courtrooms to the landscape and flora outside.[84] Kirke has written: '[t]he ultimate reference – the land itself – [should] be visible wherever possible, the silent and ever-present context of all the events of the court and of community'.[85] As was mentioned above, the Kununurra Court complex was designed with the Indigenous connection to Country in mind, with the result that the whole building and windows within it are orientated to afford views of the dramatic sandstone and conglomerate mountains in the distance.[86]

Natural light

Another priority shared by the small set of courthouses primarily catering for Indigenous users is the utilisation of natural light. Natural light, or 'sun ingress', has not always been privileged in courthouse design.[87] Traditional Anglo-centric courthouse architecture employed muted lighting from multiple sources to evoke a solemn chiaroscuro effect redolent of candlelit churches. That position has changed and, with a growing appreciation of the benefits of natural light for wellbeing, particularly for Aboriginal people, windows and skylights often now feature in courtroom design. In a happy coincidence of practical and symbolic function, natural light is today also regarded as a desirable element in court architecture for the reason that it represents truth and transparency in the legal system. In Ipswich, Queensland, a town with a high rate of Indigenous contact

81 Blagg (n 30).

82 The Pine Rivers Courthouse, in Queensland, designed by Guymer Bailey Architects, provides an exemplary transparent court frontage; Beynon (n 3) 40–43.

83 Grant, 'Port Augusta Courts' (n 14).

84 See Elizabeth Grant and Thalia Anthony, 'Kununurra Courthouse', *Australian Design Review* (Webpage, 2015) <https://www.australiandesignreview.com/architecture/kununurra-courthouse/>; Anthony and Grant (n 14).

85 Kirke, *The Shelter of Law* (n 33).

86 Grant and Anthony (n 84).

87 See for example Don Hardenbergh, Robert Tobin and Chang-Ming Yeh, *The Courthouse: A Planning and Design Guide for Court Facilities* (National Center for State Courts, 1991) 47–49.

with the police, the local police watch house, designed by ABM Cox Rayner, has natural skylights.[88] The courthouse at Port Augusta, which received a collaborative design award for the architects' consultation with the local Indigenous community, includes large expanses of glazing which spread a diffuse natural light over the interior.[89]

Ventilation: Sounds and smells

Perhaps most innovative are the buildings beginning to permit sounds and smells from the outdoors into the previously insulated sanctum of the courtroom. The Neighbourhood Justice Precinct in Collingwood, Melbourne, not only allows for views into the courtroom but permits some outside noise to filter in.[90] The Lyons designed Parramatta Trial Courts Building in Sydney, New South Wales, utilises natural ventilation, as does the Billard Leece Partnership's upgrade to the Supreme Court of Victoria building and FMSA's Moorabbin Justice Centre, also in Victoria.[91] While the buildings just referred to were not designed exclusively for Indigenous users, they exhibit the same intent to interweave indoor and outdoor spaces. These buildings might be seen as offering an innovative medium for connecting indoor courtrooms to the outdoor environment, an innovation which may be used more frequently in courthouse and courtroom design for Indigenous users into the future.

Security and comfort for Indigenous court users

All spaces should allow Indigenous users an acceptable degree of personal control over their immediate environment with regard to natural ventilation, views, temperature, illumination, and privacy. Sightlines should also be drawn to non-private internal spaces to maintain visual contact with others and public space. As courthouses and courtrooms frequently lack views to the outside world, the design of spaces (waiting and meeting rooms and courtrooms) with views to open spaces or to courtyards is a significant shift in design. This is in response to Indigenous preferences for adequate sightlines from all spaces in their day-to-day activity pattern. Access around and within the building should be facilitated through the continuous flow of spaces and a series of wayfinding/orientation mechanisms that are comprehensible to a range of users. Access to facilities, such as a telephone (to arrange pickup or to contact family) and hearing technology for Indigenous people with hearing problems, serves to enhance Indigenous peoples' sense of safety.

88 Beynon (n 3) 25.
89 Grant, 'Port Augusta Courts' (n 14) 86, 90.
90 Jones (n 29) 97.
91 Beynon (n 3) 32–33, 37, 61.

Accommodation of Indigenous users living with disabilities and chronic health conditions

A significant portion of court users will be living with pre-existing physical (especially hearing and vision) impairments, cognitive and psychosocial conditions, health issues and/or chronic diseases. Courthouses and courtrooms should incorporate design features that make them accessible for people living with disabilities and chronic health conditions. For instance, acoustic design should accommodate people with hearing difficulties, and private spaces should be available to relieve the stress of people with anxiety and other psychosocial or mental health issues. In addition, sheltered hubs for public transport and passenger drop-off points next to the entrance of the courthouse are optimal. Designated parking spaces, such as those found outside courthouses for police and law enforcement authorities, should also be available to Indigenous users for easy access and to convey respect to different (and often difficult) experiences in the court process.[92]

Engaging Indigenous communities in the design process

Much of the literature on architecture for Indigenous communities discusses 'consultation', 'collaboration', and 'authorisation' as the basis of good design, but methodologies and definitions of what constitutes consultation are largely absent. Consultation is a generic term which is constrained in the design process by factors such as budget, time, expertise, location, and planning regulations. Many court officials and architects will take up the challenge of facilitating or being involved in consultation for projects, without understanding that this is a specialist field.

Consultation is not simply a matter of form; it must be meaningful. Alison Page, founder of the National Aboriginal Design Agency, explains why it is undesirable that consultation occurs as a discrete act undertaken after the design phase; rather, Page suggests, consultation is most meaningful when it occurs synchronously with design so that the knowledge gained from consultation can be incorporated effectively into the plans.[93] Kirke goes further; he contends that consultation should precede design such that the seed of the design germinates in early community consultations. Kirke, preferring the phraseology of 'collaboration' to consultation, writes:

> The most successful projects only come out of full collaboration. In our experience, collaboration means that the very earliest definition of a project

92 Grant, 'Port Augusta Courts' (n 14); Grant, Rowden and Taitz (n 50).

93 Allison Page, 'Living Spaces: Gurung Gunya: A New Dwelling in Margo' in Sylvia Kleinert, Margo Neale and Robyne Bancroft (eds), *The Oxford Companion to Aboriginal Art and Culture* (Oxford University Press, 2000) 423.

> should take place with the community, not presented essentially defined with circumscribed areas for input.[94]

Kirke explains how this may require the architects to consult with community members to discuss their desires for the building and continue this consultative conversation subsequently as the plans take shape.[95] Undoubtedly, this level of consultation is an onerous obligation. One can anticipate objections that such efforts at consensus building would stymie the creativity of the architects themselves. In fact, the experience of architects who have adopted this process tends to the contrary. The development of relationships between architects and Aboriginal communities often appears to lead to rewarding experiences for the architects involved, and buildings adapted to the particular needs of their users, although at present such assessments are largely anecdotal and would benefit from empirical confirmation.

It is paramount that the design process is developed in partnership with the appropriate Indigenous stakeholders. The location, orientation, form, layout, scale, and the choices of materials and finishes of any courthouse construction or renovation project should be informed by local Indigenous preferences. Should cultural references, identity, and ancestral histories be embodied in the building, it is vital that consultation take place to ascertain that these are appropriate. Representations of cultural identity, history, and spirituality should provide connections between users, the place, Indigenous history, and Country. Equally, the input of Indigenous design professionals and Indigenous people who have experiences using courthouses should be encouraged to ensure that the court's new facilities reflect Indigenous needs for access to justice and cultural safety.

Conclusion: Towards cultural agency

The design of site-specific courts for Indigenous Australians has the capacity to embody new conceptions of public space, law, and justice; and shine light on the colonial subjectivity of historic courthouse design in Australia. Design paradigms and approaches to courthouse and courtroom architecture to meet the cultural, socio-spatial, and environmental needs of the Indigenous users are emerging. Ways to honour and acknowledge Country and Indigenous histories and knowledge systems and to provide a tangible statement that Indigenous Australians will be treated in a fair and equitable manner within the postcolonial legal system are more problematic. Findley argues for architecture that reverses control over the economic, political, and cultural aspirations of minority cultural groups and Indigenous peoples. Findley asks:

94 Kirke, *The Shelter of Law* (n 33) 64.
95 Ibid 36.

> How is it that the buildings we design can support the general trend toward more widespread cultural agency and spatial manifestation of peoples who have been systematically made invisible or excluded from representing themselves in the built world?[96]

Outcomes for courthouse and courtroom design that acknowledge Country, Indigenous Nations, traditional owners, and Indigenous knowledge systems are largely to be determined by procedural and legal substance rather than space. In locations such as Aotearoa New Zealand, the Treaty of Waitangi has led to a bicultural country with the status of Māori enshrined in law. In South Africa, The Truth and Reconciliation Commission was a court-like restorative justice body assembled after the abolition of apartheid. The changes in law led to courthouses and courtrooms which give Indigenous peoples cultural agency and ownership of the spaces and the procedures within them. Australian Indigenous peoples, however, have not yet had the benefit of such broad-reaching legal reform. The landmark 1986 report by the Law Reform Commission into the recognition of Indigenous customary laws resulted, at best, in piecemeal reform. More recently, Australia has begun moving, albeit haltingly, towards constitutional recognition of Indigenous rights whilst simultaneously exploring options for a treaty or treaties with First Nations peoples.[97] In a small but meaningful step, the Victorian Parliament introduced a legislative Bill with an Indigenous language title and preamble.[98] Despite these developments, however, Australian Indigenous peoples are still affected by a myriad of procedures and laws that disproportionately disadvantage them and the challenge of giving Indigenous Australians cultural agency in courthouse and courtroom design remains problematic.

The sad irony of engaging Australian Aboriginal and Torres Strait Islander peoples in debates and discourses about courthouse and courtroom architecture must be acknowledged. Courts are the very institutions that have sanctioned the control of every aspect of Australian Indigenous people's lives since colonisation and continue to do so. The brutalities inflicted on Indigenous people by settlers and colonial officials, the theft of land and children, and the imposition of Aboriginal Protection Acts that managed Indigenous lives through networks of 'protectors' was sanctioned by the courts. In the rare instance where injustices against Indigenous people came before courts, more often than not the legalisation of discrimination and dispossession meant the courts would not hear matters. Although Aboriginal and Torres Strait Islander peoples have had some of their rights restored through courts, one wonders about the ethics of attempting to co-opt Indigenous people into the architectural façade of what

96 Lisa Findley, *Building Change: Architecture, Politics and Cultural Agency* (Routledge, 2005) 33.

97 Megan Davis and Marcia Langton, *It's Our Country: Indigenous Arguments for Meaningful Constitutional Recognition and Reform* (Melbourne University Press, 2016); *Uluru Statement from the Heart*, Uluru, 23–26 May 2017 (Referendum Council).

98 Yarra River Protection (Wilip-gin Birrarung murron) Bill 2017 (Vic).

remains an essentially colonial legal system. When Grant, in conversation with an Aboriginal Elder, asked about how he thought the courthouse and courtroom architecture in Australia might be improved, he suggested: 'Why don't you just send them some matches to burn those places down?' Quite rightly, many Australian Aboriginal and Torres Islander peoples continue to see courthouses and courtrooms as Western institutions of power that need to be disassembled.

5

INTERPELLATION BY DESIGN

Could court buildings influence jury decision-making?

Kirsty Duncanson and Emma Henderson

Introduction

In this chapter we propose that the design of court buildings influences jurors during rape trials, encouraging them to adopt rape-supportive schemas to process the evidence they hear and to acquit those accused of sexual violence. Our purpose is not to argue that architecture is the central cause of low conviction rates. Rather, we suggest that architecture is yet another piece in the complex puzzle that is the rape trial, conspiring to undermine survivor accounts while reinforcing rape-supportive ideology. The puzzle piece we offer is one in which jurors are called on by the idiosyncratic, ideologically enchanted architecture of court buildings to recognise within themselves an ideal liberal subjecthood. We argue that this 'hail' encourages jurors to put aside their divergent identities to exercise liberal 'reason' and 'neutrality'. In this manner, we contend, jurors are interpellated by court buildings to use rape myth schemas to help them make sense of the overwhelming abundance of disorderly information put before them at trial. These schemas make it difficult to believe accounts of rape, thus contributing to high acquittal rates across much of the common law world.[1]

Our argument is at once simple and complex. There is a degree to which it is generally accepted that court architecture affects those who enter. The threat of law's violence, manifest in monumental entrances and dramatic hierarchies, still circulates through the popular imagination as necessary to make people speak

1 Kathleen Daly and Brigitte Bouhours, 'Rape and Attrition in the Legal Process: A Comparative Analysis of Five Countries' (2010) 39(1) *Crime and Justice* 56; Wendy Larcombe, 'Falling Rape Convictions: (Some) Feminist Aims and Measures of Rape Law' (2011) 19 *Feminist Legal Studies* 27.

DOI: 10.4324/9780429059858-8

the truth or obey the law.[2] Nonetheless, to suggest that these buildings might affect a jury and its decision-making is less easily digested.

For this reason, we have constructed an extended argument bringing together theory from philosophy, feminist legal critique, literature, architecture, and management studies. Our central argument relies on Althusser's theory of interpellation, which allows us to imagine jurors 'hailed' by agents of ideology to take up specific subject positions for the duration of trials. Scholars in management studies demonstrate that building design hails building users at the same time that it manipulates movement and positioning through space as 'emplacement'; as it resonates with cultural significance (ideology) as 'enchantment'; and as those building users interact with, use, and experience the space as 'enactment'. Critical race and gender architecture scholarship has enabled us to examine the ideology informing court construction, which imbues those buildings with semiotics of liberal ideals and assumptions. Feminist legal theorists have demonstrated similar ideology shaping the reform and implementation of law as liberal legal philosophy and revealed philosophy's reliance on, and maintenance of, rape as a theoretical foundation of democratic social order and valid law.[3] Meanwhile, narrative theory helps us understand how people process information. This work demonstrates how we rely on familiar frameworks of logic, narrative, or schemas. In a situation such as a trial, in which information is abundant and delivered without order or consistency, foundational cultural schemas provide implicit tools for those seeking to identify a singular truth and reach a binary verdict. We argue that the liberal ideological hail of court buildings offers jurors a preferred set of schemas to aid their task, such that they do not hear or do not retain counter-narratives, and thus are encouraged to reconstruct evidence according to narratives of consensual sex and to acquit those accused of sexual violence.

Of course, it is important to acknowledge that there are some convictions in rape trials, and that interpellation is not monolithic. Nor are people powerless dupes. In our elucidation of interpellation, we note that resistance is executed to smaller and greater degrees throughout society, with subtle and dramatic effects. However, it is also important to recognise the insidious power of interpellation (which is always at work) to encourage each person to recognise within themselves a subject position with which they do not fully identify, and to take on an ideology with which they may not agree, for a period of time. This

2 This assertion is based on anecdotal evidence from teaching law, criminology and legal studies, chatting to volunteers while undertaking court observation fieldwork, and interviews with barristers.

3 Ngaire Naffine, 'Possession: Erotic Law and the Law of Rape' (1994) 57 *Modern Law Review* 10, 24; Anél Boshoff, 'Woman as the Subject of (Family) Law' in Rosemary Hunter and Sharon Cowan (eds), *Choice and Consent* (Routledge-Cavendish, 2007) 41, 42; Sara Ahmad, 'Deconstruction and Law's Other: Towards a Feminist Theory of Embodied Legal Rights' (1995) 4 *Social and Legal Studies* 55, 56; Imogen Tyler, 'Reframing Pregnant Embodiment' in Sara Ahmed et al. (eds), *Transformations: Thinking through Feminism* (Routledge, 2005) 288; Louise Du Toit, *A Philosophical Investigation of Rape: The Making and Unmaking of the Feminine Self* (Routledge, 2009).

cross-interpellation helps us to imagine how individual jurors whose personal ideologies diverge from and even critique rape myth schemas may be drawn into a rape-supportive subject position for the duration of a trial.

Our argument begins with an explanation of rape myth schemas and how narratives have been shown to work at trial. We go on to provide a detailed explanation of interpellation as we use it in our argument. Mapping out the theory of emplacement, enchantment, and enactment, we demonstrate how architectural details and design function as agents of ideology, hailing building users. At this point, we look at the particular susceptibility of jurors to interpellation on the basis of their condition as necessarily unfamiliar with law, as seekers of information and as held in a state of uncertainty throughout their service. We then compare four Australian court constructions to demonstrate the ideological resonance of Greek Revival aesthetics and modernist design. We interrogate the raced and sexed significance of the liberal values of 'reason' and 'neutrality' signified by these aesthetic components and demonstrate how these values are woven through with rape myth schemas. In our conclusion we bring these elements together once again to deliver the argument that court architecture contributes to low conviction rates in rape trials by hailing jurors into subject positions that silence divergent ideologies and prioritise rape myth schemas.

Schemas at trial

Information provided in trials is abundant, inconsistent, and disjointed. It does not unfold as two clear opposing narratives. Rather, it is delivered over a number of days through a question/answer format as numerous witnesses are interrogated and then cross-examined by barristers. At the same time, evidence of 'fact' is entangled with evidence of witness credibility.[4] Each member of the jury is required to gather the available evidence, along with information provided by judges and barristers about the legal structure of the alleged crimes, legal processes, and the specific *legal* definition of otherwise familiar terms. As they gather this information, the jury members must evaluate, remember, and then use it to negotiate with each other on an agreed verdict.

Research from the humanities suggests that individuals rely on 'schemas' to make sense of any information.[5] These are narrative frameworks shared within and across cultural groups. They take the form of 'common knowledge'; 'community values'; and logic, even when not based on reliable evidence. One genre of schema is 'rape myths': Narratively structured misconceptions about sex and sexuality. A particularly powerful one is 'the enduring belief that women say

4 Is the complainant's skirt and knickers *probative* or a ploy to undermine credibility?

5 Richard Sherwin, 'Law Frames: Historical Truth and Narrative Necessity in a Criminal Case' (1994) 47(1) *Stanford Law Review* 39; Rae Kaspiew, 'Rape Lore: Legal Narratives and Sexual Violence' (1995) 20 *Melbourne University Law Review* 350.

"no" when they mean "yes"'.[6] This schema has been identified at work in rape trials, romantic fiction and liberal politico-legal philosophy.[7] In previous work we have argued that numerous factors at trial, including the temporal location of jury directions, encourage jurors to apply rape myths in order to sort the plethora of nebulous and fragmented information delivered.[8] In this chapter we are arguing that the design of court buildings compounds the pressure on jurors to use rape myth schemas during rape trials.

The impetus for the jury to use rape myth schemas comes from frequent prompts scattered throughout rape trials, by the prosecution, the judge, the structure of romance narratives, the structure of consent legislation, and more. Trial transcript analysis and court observation research has demonstrated that carefully formulated question syntax elides complainant accounts of what happened and constructs narratives supporting the accused.[9] Other work has shown that implying specific behaviours in a complainant can foreground rape myth schemas in the minds of jurors.[10] Mock jury research has shown the strength of juror adherence to these schemas throughout deliberation discussions. Ellison and Munro's mock jurors generated extravagant speculative facts never even alluded to in trial, in order to sustain a narrative resisting a complainant's account of rape.[11] Through myriad methods, rape myths are made present in trials as logical schema with which to process evidence.

We have theorised that recognised methods of information-gathering lead each juror to listen for evidence that conforms to their selected schema.[12] Other

6 Nina Philadelphof-Puren, 'Contextualising Consent: The Problem of Rape and Romance' (2010) 20 (46) *Australian Feminist Studies* 31.

7 Du Toit (n 3); Wendy Larcombe, *Compelling Engagements: Feminism, Rape Law and Romance Fiction* (The Federation Press, 2005); Naffine (n 3); Alison Young, 'The Wasteland of the Law, the Wordless Song of the Rape Victim' (1998) 22(2) *Melbourne University Law Review* 442.

8 Kirsty Duncanson and Emma Henderson, 'Narrative, Theatre and the Disruptive Potential of Jury Directions in Rape Trials' (2014) 22(2) *Feminist Legal Studies* 155; Emma Henderson and Kirsty Duncanson, 'A Little Judicial Direction: Can the Use of Jury Directions Challenge Traditional Consent Narratives in Rape Trials?' (2016) 39(2) *University of New South Wales Law Journal* 750.

9 John M Conley and William O'Barr, *Just Words: Law, Language and Power* (Chicago University Press, 1998); Alison Young (n 7).

10 Vanessa Munro and E Finch, 'The Demon Drink and the Demonised Woman: Socio-Sexual Stereotypes and Responsibility Attribution in Rape Trials Involving Intoxicants' (2007) 16(4) *Social and Legal Studies* 591; Louise Ellison and Vanessa Munro, 'A Stranger in the Bushes, or an Elephant in the Room? Critical Reflections upon Received Rape Myth Wisdom in the Context of a Mock Jury Study' (2010) 13(4) *New Criminal Law Review* 781; Louise Ellison and Vanessa Munro, 'Better the Devil You Know? "Real Rape" Stereotypes and the Relevance of a Previous Relationship in (Mock) Juror Deliberations' (2013) 17 *The International Journal of Evidence and Proof* 299.

11 A case in point was the suggestion by a juror that evidential bruises were sustained by the complainant during a rollercoaster ride. The ride had no supportive evidence within the trial: no carnival was mentioned, let alone any reference to the complainant getting into a rollercoaster; see Louise Ellison and Vanessa Munro, 'Reacting to Rape: Exploring Mock Jurors' Assessments of Complainant Credibility' (2009) *British Journal of Criminology* 202, 208.

12 See Duncanson and Henderson (n 8).

non-conforming evidence falls from memory or is simply not 'heard'. Thus, by the end of a trial, each juror has 'sorted' the evidence. Law reform compels judges to caution juries about rape misconceptions, telling them (in Victorian courts, for example) that the presence of typical myth-based facts is not *necessarily* evidence of the presence of consent. However, these warnings come only at the end of the trial, arguably by which time the jury has forgotten divergently aligned evidence. Thus, we argue that these directions come too late: A juror cannot retrieve information they discarded at the time it was delivered. The schematic tool reinforces an already powerful logic working its influence during the trial, and it cannot be easily reversed once the evidence has been delivered.

In this chapter we theorise that part of each juror's use of such schema is shaped by the way in which they are interpellated into their subject position as 'a member of the jury'. This interpellation begins from their receipt of the eligibility letter telling them they have been randomly selected for duty. It continues through their attendance at court, to the judge's direction at the conclusion of the trial. Our interest lies with the interpellative interaction between juror and court building architecture and design.

Interpellation

Establishing a working theory of interpellation will aid us to demonstrate how court building architecture encourages jurors to foreground a particular subjecthood during their duty, silencing other parts of themselves. This subjecthood, we stress, is not an inevitable, automated response. As we elucidate our interpretation of interpellation, we recognise the potential for resistance. However, we ultimately demonstrate the power of interpellation to influence how jury service is undertaken.

The hail

Interpellation is a process through which each individual is situated within an ideologically structured social order. Through this process, each person builds a sense of identity, a personhood woven through with cultural value and meaning, attitudes, beliefs, social roles, and expectations. In this manner, subjecthood is constituted. Althusser explains:

> Ideology 'acts' or 'functions' in such a way that it 'recruits' subjects among the individuals (it recruits them all), or 'transforms' the individuals into subjects (it transforms them all) by that very precise operation which I have called *interpellation* or hailing.[13]

13 Louis Althusser, *Lenin and Philosophy and Other Essays*, tr Ben Brewster (Monthly Review Press, 1971), 118. Emphasis in original.

Each person is conscripted, recruited, or coercively convinced to become part of the dominant ideology and to take on a position within the social order. This is accomplished while still providing the individual with a sense of autonomy.

The process involves what Althusser names 'the hail' – the 'hey you' – of someone/something calling to the individual on the basis of some axis of their multifaceted identity. The police officer hails an individual as a suspect,[14] the teacher hails a student, the catcaller hails an object of masculine pleasure (evaluable primarily on the basis of sexual potential), and so on. And the individual responds: Turning to the police officer or running from them, stopping their disruptive chat in the classroom and paying attention, or 'flipping the bird' at the catcaller. When the individual responds to the hail, they have recognised within themselves the identity articulated by that hail: The suspect of police interest, the disobedient student, or the sexualised body. In the moment of response, the individual simultaneously confirms the existence of: (a) the logic of the ideology (the law, the education curriculum, or the patriarchy); (b) the authority and legitimacy of the someone/something who hailed (the long arm of the law, the agent of indoctrinating education, or the instrument of patriarchy); and (c) their own subject identification (suspect, student, or body). Or, in the case of the finger-raising respondent, the individual might acknowledge the ideological order and their position within it while also demonstrating their resistance and antipathy towards it.

The capital S Subject

In its original iteration, that which articulates the hail is mightier than the individual whom it hails. There are two components to this relationship: A belief that the interpellating agent represents something greater than the interpellated individual, and the collusion between state ideology and violence.

Although the Church exemplifies the presupposed Subject for Althusser, Law as a monolithic, overarchingly powerful edifice is implicitly present in his most famous example: The policeman's hail. It is in the name of Law that the policeman calls into the crowd, 'Hey you!', interpellating all who respond, identifying their subjecthood (who they *really* are) and positioning them accordingly through the ideologically (juridically) structured social order. Bassel describes this as 'binding the law to the one who is hailed'.[15]

Repressive power (violence) and interpellating state ideology

It is important to remember the complementarity of the *ideological* state apparatuses (those that hail) with the *repressive* state apparatuses Althusser describes.

14 Ibid.

15 Leah Bassel, 'Citizenship as Interpellation: Refugee Women and the State' (2008) 43(2) *Government and Opposition* 293, 295.

Repressive apparatuses secure by force the political conditions of a nation in which interpellation might be exercised[16] – that is, by the use of violence or the threat of violence and punitive laws to maintain the ideologically preferred social order. Law functions at a clearly repressive level, using violence to leverage docility and compliance. Court buildings provide a location for one very public set of repressive state rituals: Criminal trials.

However, law also works at an ideological level, where the violence is more coercive than spectacularly performative. For example, Bassel observes legal interpellation working on numerous planes within the relationship between the French Government and Muslim Somali women refugees through the processing of refugee claims as well as in the very definition and circumscription of French public space as politically 'secular'.[17] Specifically, interpellation in this latter form has included consultation and debates directly connected to the creation of law regulating the display of religious symbols in state schools. In Law's name, the women of whom Bassel writes are positioned and granted circumscribed subjecthood (Muslim women compelled to wear the hijab) through the hailing of restricted aspects of their multifaceted identities (they were also mothers, students, employees, political actors, and so forth). Bassel explains that a 'legitimate subject is constituted, and a social identity is provided' for these women by the state.[18] Other parts of their identity are silenced as a consequence. She demonstrates that Muslim women cannot be heard by the French State, unless they speak about specific issues (headscarves) in specific ways (headscarves are an oppressive part of patriarchal Islamic culture). These women are thus interpellated into the subject position of 'Muslim women oppressed by their own patriarchal culture'. Other parts of their identity and alternative experiences of the hijab are ignored, and further dimensions of their lives are diminished, even silenced.

In our argument, we understand Law as functioning as a capital S Subject; as an overarching edifice that is greater and more powerful than any individual subject. Part of its authority derives from its repressive power that takes the form of police, the degradation rituals of trials,[19] and the imposition of punishment. However, we are interested in Law's coercive *ideological* power. The tendrils of its coercion work in myriad ways throughout society. Our lens is narrowed to focus on its interpellative practices that constantly hail people into subject positions across a social order structured according to an ideology of which Law is an integral part.

Thus, although we can observe the jury as repressively controlled by restrictions on movement and speech, not able to go to the toilet without permission from the judge and potentially penalised for falling asleep, the jury is also

16 Althusser (n 13) 101.

17 Bassel (n 15).

18 Ibid 301.

19 Harold Garfinkel, 'Conditions of Successful Degradation Ceremonies' (1956) 61 *American Journal of Sociology* 420.

manipulated at an ideological level. Each member of the jury is interpellated into the temporary subject position of 'juror'. They are told in the pre-trial literature and on empanelment that they must bring forward that part of themselves representing 'community values', rational evaluation, and reason. The other parts of their identity are silenced or suppressed for the duration of the trial.

The hail of micro-gestures and decorative accents

The hail can be articulated by less powerful apparatuses on a smaller scale. Althusser provides far more intimate recognition rituals practised between friends.[20] These friends call to each other on the street or when answering the door in the 'Who's there?', 'It's me' exchange. For Althusser these rituals demonstrate that we are '*always already* subjects'.[21] However, we suggest that these are micro-level interpellative practices in which a person is hailed in an aspect of their identity, and they respond, 'Yes, it's me!'. On this level, we can recognise smaller gestures as a form of ideological hailing, but not just between people: Also between people and objects. This allows us to recognise the hail in the decorative accents of court architecture. Each column, white wall, and wood panel calls out to the individual juror as they pass, finding their way to the jury pool, or as their bored or discomforted gaze roves the courtroom.

We can see interpellation situated endlessly through micro-gestures across court buildings. This means that the ideology expressed through the courtroom may not be internally coherent, and might even be self-contradictory. It also means that there is scope for slippage and inconsistency. This might provoke extra work for a juror in having to suture any rift in the ideological logic. But it might also allow for alternative ideologies and logics to enter the deliberation room, enabling resistance by a non-majority juror or even a conviction.

Recognition of the self in the hail

For the hail to recruit individuals into subjectivity, each individual must recognise an aspect of themselves in the hail ('that is *really* me!'). To be interpellated by the police officer's 'Hey you!', the individual must imagine that they might be the person the police are looking for. Further, they must know themselves to be the student subject to the hailing teacher's authority, and they must know that they are the body assessed by random men in the street on the basis of sexual potential:

> The one who is hailed always recognizes that it is really him who is being hailed … that the hail was 'really' addressed to him, and … not someone else.[22]

20 Althusser (n 13) 117.
21 Ibid. Emphasis in original.
22 Ibid 118.

Recognition is possible because there is some form of identity or subjectivity that pre-exists each unique hail. Althusser is clear in asserting that subject formation begins prior to birth and that interpellation is a constant process that works to reaffirm and continually situate (and resituate) subjects according to the identities established through family, church, and state institutions. Thus, interpellation can be understood as one of the many ways in which subjects are constituted.

Youdell, following Butler, observes interpellation colluding with all of those Foucauldian disciplinary technologies shaping and positioning docile bodies; discourses and knowledges creating that which they name; and those other normalising forces compelling individuals to behave, perform, position, and shape themselves according to the myriad demands, regulations, choices, categorisations, and identifications that work on and through us all.[23] Our subjectivity is created through a range of technologies and mechanisms simultaneous with interpellation.

What Bassel demonstrates happening through the French State's interpellation of Muslim Somali refugee women is a prioritisation of specific components of their multifaceted personhoods.[24] In order to make claims for refugee status, residency, citizenship, or simply participation in public discussion, these women are required to silence those parts of their identity that conflict with a model of compliant Muslim womanhood circumscribed and interpellated by the French state.

In this chapter, we follow Bassel's use of interpellation to theorise that juries are positioned through their interaction with the ideological design of court buildings to prioritise certain aspects of their identity that align with liberal ideology. Silenced in this process are their divergent individual experiences, ideologies, and knowledges. This interactive subject positioning, we argue, determines the schema jurors use for the required period of their subject performance as 'juror'.

Cross-interpellation

In order to understand how an array of people from across society attending court as jurors might be interpellated such that they prioritise rape myth schemas to organise trial information into a comprehensive narrative, the theory of cross-interpellation is vital. The hail calls on individuals to recognise and foreground hegemonic socio-cultural identities nestled within their otherwise divergently intersectional selves.

Cross-interpellation refers to the process whereby a person recognises and foregrounds something within their multifaceted selves that does not correspond

23 Deborah Youdell, 'Subjectivation and Performative Politics: Butler Thinking Althusser and Foucault — Intelligibility, Agency and the Raced-Nationed-Religioned Subjects of Education' (2006) 27(4) *British Journal of Sociology of Education* 511, 516.

24 Bassel (n 15).

with the dominant biologically or culturally situated aspects of their identity. The subject position being hailed (the police suspect, the chatty student, the object of the gaze) may not align with the principal components of a person's socio-cultural identity (as a woman, an Aboriginal person, a queer person, and/or a Muslim). In part this is because the hail calls on them to recognise a subject position within themselves over time. This is a function of institutionalised racism, for example. The #BlackLivesMatter movement has evidenced how visible Aboriginal people feel to the police such that the hail of police triggers a cross-interpellative response that they are a police suspect even as they know that they have not broken the law. Institutionalised educational hierarchies provide so many of us with that easily triggered feeling of being called to the headmaster's office long after graduation. Correspondingly, the #MeToo movement's global social media spread of millions of women revealing that they have been subject to unwanted sexual attention demonstrates how extensively women are aware of their sexual objectification. Thus, even as women might see themselves primarily as competent executives of powerful institutions, the street holler hail can call on that germ of recognition within that they are primarily (in that moment) objects for masculine visual pleasure.

Fiske theorises cross-interpellation in terms of its dislocation from biology.[25] He writes that a 'biological female can have a masculine subjectivity'.[26] This means that a woman 'can make sense of the world and of herself and her place in the world through patriarchal ideology'.[27] Situated within patriarchy, women do not simply have this opportunity to access a masculine perspective. Rather, women are compelled to make sense of the world and of themselves using patriarchal ideology, even as they are simultaneously interpellated into marginalised subject positions by it.

As part of the early cultural studies movement, Fiske's work challenges biological essentialism and allows us to imagine more complex cross-interpellative relations. There is immense pressure to conform to white patriarchal heteronormativity. Divergently identified and marginalised communities are compelled to learn how to make sense of the world through the lenses of these dominating interwoven ideologies. Divergently identifying people might be interpellated to take up subject positions of privilege. This may expand the categorical conditions of privilege (to include black police, formerly excluded people entering the teaching profession, and women catcallers, for example). However, cross-interpellation is regularly realised when divergently identified people conform to the ideological position being hailed, despite their own abhorrence of that ideology.

25 John Fiske, 'British Cultural Studies and Television' in Robert Clyde Allen (ed), *Channels of Discourse Reassembled: Television and Contemporary Criticism* (Routledge, 1987).

26 Ibid 258.

27 Ibid.

In the context of jury service, we are arguing that the hail calls to a germ of liberal ideology within each juror's identity, compelling them to make sense of the world through this lens for the duration of the trial. Thus, although the jury is supposed to imbue the arbitration of justice with a diversity of community values, the liberal ideology of court architecture hails each juror to prioritise a view of the world that fundamentally refuses to acknowledge non-consent to penetrative sex. At the same time, the hail forms part of a suite of mechanisms silencing counter subject positions and schemas.

The illusion of autonomy

By hailing an aspect of subjecthood that corresponds to some component of an individual's identity, interpellation 'obtains from them the *recognition* that they really do occupy the place it designates for them as theirs in the world, a fixed residence'.[28] The hail coerces the individual into identifying themselves in the fixed identity articulated in the hail. In this manner, the creation of subjectivity would seem to come from within the individual, as though they asserted some autonomy in deciding that they *are* that person being hailed (it is *really* me). It is this feeling of autonomous decision-making that renders the process 'recruitment'. Youdell explains that interpellation thus creates the feeling that 'subjecthood is freely taken and subjection is freely accepted by the good subject'.[29] The subject feels that they have agency over their identity and position within the social order. It feels like choice.

Mostly, this autonomy is an illusion. Ian Law emphasises the compelling power of interpellation, writing that we 'are located … precisely because we recognize ourselves, and (this is crucial) *because we have no choice*'.[30] He argues that, despite the sense of agency, we are not actually exercising it. This is because the recognition we feel is so immediate, it is ingrained. Our identity is already embedded. Law explains that we are 'turned into biddable subjects because it becomes instantly obvious to us that we *are* that way and that we *know* that way'.[31]

For Davis, interpellation's efficiency is due to its imperceptible stealth upon the consciousness of the individual; 'the demand and compulsion are so subtle that we apparently do not even recognise their force, [and] in fact seem to welcome them'.[32] Interpellation is able to recruit us not only because we have already been trained to know ourselves in that hailed subjectivity, but also because we

28 Noela Davis, 'Subjected Subjects? On Judith Butler's Paradox of Interpellation' (2012) 27(4) *Hypatia* 881, 891. Emphasis in original.

29 Youdell (n 23) 516.

30 Ian Law, 'On the Subject of the Object: Narrative, Technology and Interpellation' (2000) 8(1) *Configurations* 1, 14. Emphasis in original.

31 Ibid. Emphasis in original.

32 Davis (n 28).

have been trained in the ideological framework and the processes of subject formation. Rather than us feeling coerced or compelled, the experience *can* be (but is not always) one of embracing the identity or feeling it to be natural and unquestionable.

Thus, as an individual juror moves through the court building and recognises themselves in the signage, they may not feel that they are being pressured to silence their critical self. Rather, their embrace of the rational, reasoning, responsible liberal citizen performing a civic duty may feel like a natural, sensible, and decisive response to taking up the offered role of juror.

The potential for resistance

Resistance to the hail is possible and regularly exercised. An Australian example is the moment when Noongar footballer Nicky Winmar responded to the hail of racial vilification from the stands in 1993 – he raised his jumper and 'pointed with pride at the colour of his skin'.[33] This action is celebrated as transformative, instigating an anti-racist movement in Australian Rules Football.[34] Reading Winmar's act through an Althusserian lens, we can see Winmar recognising himself within the identity of 'black' in the abusive hail (yes, I am *really* black), but refuting the denigrating connotations of the vilification by asserting his pride in being black (*this* is what black *really* means). Thus, while Winmar affirmed a subjectivity and the existence of an ideological system, he altered the texture of the subject, asserted significant control over his position within the social order, and challenged the logic of the ideology.

Winmar's act was explicit resistance. However, misrecognition, misinterpretation, and shifting the zeitgeist through the interpellative interaction also reconfigure ideology and subject formation. Interpellation is less monolithic and more like part of the pervasive mechanisms through which discourses struggle, compete, and align. Individuals are hailed from multiple sites, and they respond in various ways, whether affirming or resisting, and thereby constantly changing ideology, subjectivity, and the social order.

While our focus in this chapter is on juror compliance with liberal ideology as supported by interpellative interaction with court buildings, to ignore the scope for resistance would fail to recognise the complexity of subject formation and the capacity for social change. Resistance is possible. Individual jurors may cognitively 'flip the bird' at the symbols of reason, neutrality, and justice embodied across the courtroom. Their interpellative interaction with the figure of Lady Justice may not be one of comfortable recognition, but of alienation (I am *not* the reasonable subject of liberal ideology).

33 Matthew Klugman and Gary Osmond, 'That Picture: Nicky Winmar and the History of an Image' (2009) 2 *Australian Aboriginal Studies* 78, 79.

34 Ibid.

However, our argument is that the conspiracy of interpellating architecture, barrister examination techniques, the interweave of romance and political philosophy, white patriarchal culture, and the many other mechanisms of coercion make resistance difficult. A single resistant juror must also convince eleven other jurors in order to ensure a rape conviction. Further, juror research reveals the significant pressure felt by members of the jury to compromise in order to get back to their busy lives or escape the bullying of other jurors.[35] In some jurisdictions, a majority verdict – where a jury has only one or two dissenting parties – is enough to acquit a charge of rape.

The possibility of resistance is important to recognise in order to avoid asserting a monolithic theory of subject formation in the context of jurors. It is also a component of the theory that may provide an avenue for change. How might resistance to the hail be enabled such that jurors are able to hold on to their divergent selves and their critical awareness?

The mutual and unending reconstitution of Subject (state ideology) and subject (position)

The possiblity of resistance and cross-interpellation exposes the fragility and inconsistency of ideology, which must endlessly reaffirm itself. Ideology is therefore reliant on the subject and the interpellative exchange. Rather, the state and ideology are dependent on each subject's compliant response to the hail. Davis explains that 'as ideology constitutes the social subject, so the subject constitutes the ideology of its society'.[36] That is to say, when the subject responds to the hail by recognising themselves within it, they are also recognising the logic of the system and accepting it as the truth, as logical, and as legitimate. Thus, through the interpellative interaction the Subject and the subject are 'mutually constitutive of each other; they rematerialize in and through each other'.[37] This represents a 'total and productive entanglement of subjects and ideology with each other'.[38] Ideology positions you when it calls to you, but when you respond by recognising yourself in the hail, you are also confirming that the subject position is authentic and that the ideological structure is logical and legitimate.

Interpellation in sum and our argument

Interpellation is a process through which individuals are positioned within an ideologically structured social order. It is an exchange beginning with an agent of ideology's hail ('Hey you!'). The individual hailed recognises themselves in

35 Warren Young, Neil Cameron and Yvette Tinsley, *Juries in Criminal Trials Part Two (Preliminary Paper)* (NZ Law Commission, 1999).

36 Davis (n 28) 888.

37 Ibid.

38 Ibid.

the hail and responds (I am the identity being hailed), thereby colluding with the agent to subjugate themselves via a positioned subjecthood within the ideologically structured social order.

Ideology is discursive and constantly needs to reaffirm itself. At the same time, hailing agents abound and do not only represent dominant ideology: We are hailed by overlapping, competing, and complementary ideologies all the time and from agents both explicit and implicit. In responding to the hail, or choosing to resist, the individual foregrounds certain parts of their identity while silencing others.

The subject position hailed may not align with the dominant identity of the individual. The individual can be cross-interpellated to take on a viewing position or identity based on a different but familiar ideological position (a feminist may be interpellated such that they understand an event through a patriarchal lens). Despite these disjunctures, due to the interactive nature of interpellation, the assumption of the subject position can feel natural, authentic, and autonomous. This is not really the case.

But resistance is possible. The interactive nature of interpellation, the abundance of hailing agents and hails, and the instability produced by the presence of multiple ideologies all create space for slippage and change in ideology, social structures, and the repertoire of subject positions available.

We are arguing that jurors are interpellated throughout their jury service. A significant interpellative exchange is that between juror and court building. The ideological signifiers of court buildings recruit jurors to foreground specific subject positions while silencing others. This subject position may not align with a juror's dominant identity beyond the courtroom. However, trial conditions coerce cross-interpellation and suppress resistance. The interpellation of each juror will not be identical: Slippage happens and resistance is possible. Despite this, the justice system's compellingly consistent failure to convict those accused of sexual assault indicates that a uniform ideology is working its influence in jury deliberations.

Buildings as hailing agents

To understand court buildings as hailing agents we turn to the work of organisational management scholars. In their analysis of a university library construction, Hancock and Spicer argue that architecture creates an 'identityscape', which in this case interpellates students into 'model' worker subjects who will meet the demands of the modern labour market.[39] They build on Foucault's 'analytics of architecture, power and identity' because 'practices of subjectivisation are … spatially located and that particular architectures embed spatial configurations

39 Philip Hancock and André Spicer, 'Academic Architecture and the Constitution of the New Model Worker' (2011) 17(2) *Culture and Organisation* 91, 92.

in ways that contribute to the possibility of such a process'.[40] Perhaps most celebrated for his use of Jeremy Bentham's plans for the Panopticon to theorise disciplinary power, Foucault's work demonstrates the ways in which the management of space shapes bodies and subjecthood. Dale and Burrell sketch out three modes of architecturally facilitated subjectivisation, each of which contributes to the interpellative process Hancock and Spicer observe in their library.[41] These are 'emplacement', 'enchantment', and 'enactment'. Exploring how the three manifest in court buildings allows us to theorise inanimate objects and materials as hailing agents, explore nonverbal signifiers as 'hails', and consider embodied and affective experience in our investigation of juror interpellation.

Emplacement

The management of space exercises 'emplacement', situating particular activities in specific sites through design, while positioning 'bodies, within rigidly conceived geographical and spatial locations'.[42] Emplacement involves 'boundaries and compartments producing effects of fixity', which facilitate 'processes of inclusion within and exclusion from specific spaces'.[43] It is the clear and distinct organisation of space for a purpose.

Emplacement functions powerfully in court buildings. Embodying 'a system of roles and relationships', the courtroom is made up of fixed positions that 'correspond to determinate parties associated with specific meanings and patterns of behaviour'.[44] This is reinforced by fixed seating, barriers, floor levels, steps, and glass partitions. Sharp distinctions are established by the layout between 'the space accorded to those … authorised to invoke the law … And those subject to it'.[45] Despite variation between jurisdictions, there are shared emplacement practices across the common law world. Beyond the courtroom, thoroughfares guide court users through security to registrars, lifts, and waiting areas. There are separate entrances for judges, magistrates, and remanded defendants. Hidden corridors, lifts, chambers, and cells are traversed by segregated parties.

As Foucault argues, spatial management does not simply exert power over bodily movement but also produces bodies and their subjecthood. Carlen demonstrates the way in which court design affects the participation of people in trials.[46] She describes the humiliation of witnesses having to speak intimate details

40 Ibid 93.
41 Karen Dale and Gibson Burrell, *The Spaces of Organisation and the Organisations of Space: Power, Identity and Materiality at Work* (Palgrave MacMillan, 2008).
42 Hancock and Spicer (n 39) 95.
43 Dale and Burrell (n 41) 47–48.
44 Giovan Francesco Lanzara and Gerado Patriotta, 'Technology and the Courtroom: An Inquiry into Knowledge Making in Organisations' (2001) 38(7) *Journal of Management Studies* 947.
45 Emma Rowden and Diane Jones, 'Design, Dignity and Due Process: The Construction of the Coffs Harbour Courthouse' (2015) *Law, Culture and the Humanities* 1, 3.
46 Pat Carlen, *Magistrate's Justice* (Martin Robertson Ltd, 1976).

at volume because of the distance between stand and bench. Held in the dock at the rear of the court, defendants are unable to hear what happens in their cases, while magistrates, raised above the court, are able to see and hear everything, to be heard by everyone, and to wield ultimate control over the space.

Carlen argues that the courtroom is the material manifestation of law's ideology. Similarly, Tait writes that 'legal values are written into the physical layout' of courts.[47] Through the emplacement of individuals in allocated spaces, especially in relationship to each other, the role each individual is expected to play gains significance, is enhanced, and becomes embodied by that individual.

The ubiquity of courtrooms in popular culture means that most people entering the space have some pre-existing knowledge of the key roles patterned across the layout. This has an interpellative impact upon court users as they take up their allocated position within the space. For example, as a defendant is led from the custody suite to the dock, they are compelled to recognise in themselves the subjecthood of 'accused criminal', hailed to them by the already meaningful dock.

Enchantment

The arrangement of space colludes with the materials used to construct it, its form, colour, weight, and texture, as well as overt ideological decoration. Together these elements coerce users into subject positions within a given ideologically structured social order. Enchantment is produced by 'the fusion of the material and the symbolic'; it is the 'linking together of matter and meaning in such a way as to produce various power effects'.[48] Architecture is deliberately used to manifest physical embodiments of an organisation or institution's goals, values, and history.[49] However, the very term 'enchantment' evokes the subtlety with which aesthetics can create meaning in collaboration with the user of the space. Analysing the university library, Hancock and Spicer describe how aesthetics shape not only the image the university projects of itself, but also the way students envisage themselves while they use the library.[50] In this manner, they argue, students are interpellated by the building to understand themselves according to the ideological drives of the vocationally focused university facility.

Court buildings resonate with enchantment. In this volume, his Honour Justice Black describes the consultation process for the design of several Australian court buildings.[51] Noting the corporate aesthetic of the courts being replaced,

47 David Tait, 'Glass Cages in the Dock?: Presenting the Defendant to the Jury' (2011) 86(2) *Chicago-Kent Law Review* 467, 494.

48 Dale and Burrell (n 41) 47–48.

49 Hancock and Spicer (n 39) 94.

50 Ibid 92.

51 Michael Black, 'The Architecture of Law Courts: How Concepts of Justice – Light, Transparency, Access, and Equality – Drove the Design of New and Renovated Courthouses for Federal Courts in Australia', this volume, page 31.

Black emphasises the importance of symbolic architecture to the creation of court space. As well as raising many practical concerns about access and security, his account demonstrates the intention of the State to communicate ideas about law to court users through architecture.

In Chapter 1, Grant and Hook demonstrate the importance of materials, seat shapes, window placement, and the alignment of building with landscape in court architecture to make law accessible and relevant to communities historically alienated and dispossessed by law.[52] By working with local Aboriginal communities and echoing the lines of the landscape of legal significance to those communities, TAG Architects with Iredale Pedersen Hook Architects articulated respect for Aboriginal culture and an intention to recognise Aboriginal law in the legal procedures performed within the Kununurra Courthouse. The Courthouse deliberately counters Western design, which Anthony and Grant note 'symbolises the Australian system's exclusion of Indigenous laws'.[53] The State's values, histories, traditions and intentions are thus manifest and reiterated, but also potentially altered, in the architecture of court buildings.

The signifiers used in court design contribute to the way law is understood by court users, while also influencing the way those users understand themselves in relation to the building and law. This works in concert with court emplacement. The hail of the physically allocated role of the individual is ideologically enriched by the materials and decoration demarcating their position. The historical adornment of the judicial bench illustrates this. Resnik and Curtis explain how art was used in Medieval and Renaissance courts to 'remind' judges to be 'loyal subjects of the state'.[54] Coats of Arms embellish benches across Australia and the United Kingdom, hailing their judicial occupants so they might recognise themselves as loyal subjects to the Crown, and further still, as the embodiment of the body politic in the absence of the actual monarch.[55] This reminder for the judge is embedded in the material and interior design of the building. The hailing agent is thus a conjunction of emplacement (the location of the bench) and enchantment (the Coat of Arms). Together, these initiate the interpellative

52 Elizabeth Grant and Martyn Hook, 'Reimagining Spaces for Indigenous Justice: The Architecture and Design of the Kununurra Courthouse', this volume, page 11.

53 Thalia Anthony and Elizabeth Grant, 'Courthouse Design Principles to Dignify Spaces for Indigenous Users: Preliminary Observations' (2016) 8(1) *International Journal for Court Administration* 43, 44.

54 Judith Resnik and Dennis Curtis, *Representing Justice: Invention, Controversy, and Rights in City States and Democratic Courtrooms* (Yale University Press, 2011) 33–36; Judith Resnik and Dennis Curtis, 'Re-Presenting Justice: Visual Narratives of Judgment and the Invention of Democratic Courts' (2012) 24 *Yale Journal of Law and the Humanities* 19; Judith Resnik and Dennis Curtis, 'The Jayne Lecture: Representing Justice – From Renaissance Iconography to Twenty-First Century Courthouses' (2007) 151(2) *Proceedings of the American Philosophical Society* 139.

55 Ernst Kantorowicz, *The King's Two Bodies: A Study of Mediaeval Political Thought* (Princeton University Press, 1957).

process to which the judge responds by conducting their role in a manner aligned with an ideology of common law.

Enactment

Dale and Burrell use the term 'enactment' to theorise greater dynamism in the relationship between space, power, and the subject.[56] They explain that 'social spaces are lived, are processed through, are experienced through mobility' and that these interactions bring about power effects.[57] For Vålard and Georg, space is not fixed either; it is not 'a static container', but active, enabling, constituting, even generative of practices and experience.[58] Importantly, these practices and experiences are 'imbued with affect and are inherently political'.[59] That is to say, these practices and experiences bear discursive ideology in forms that escape easy articulation or cognitive observation while they are felt in the body. Enactment is central to subject formation because identity is not static but is enacted constantly by bodies through their interactions with the spaces in which they exist and which they move through.[60] The concept of enactment enables us to observe the interpellative relationship between court building and juror as dynamically interactive and embodied.

Court buildings are affective: Their architecture impacts upon the bodies using the space, influencing the sensations experienced by those users and generating significances that inform users' understanding of law and shape their capacity to participate in the legal process. Rowden and Jones observe that 'views of nature [from the courtroom] can have a calming influence during stressful situations … particularly for vulnerable groups such as juveniles, or Aboriginal detainees'.[61] Similarly, natural light has been found to support better, more enduring focus,[62] while Branco speculates that for children delivering testimony, the inhospitable size of courtroom furnishings potentially compounds children's trauma.[63] Brooks notes the hardness of seats and the coldness of courtrooms contributing to the 'profound discomfort' of attending court,[64] while Anthony and

56 Dale and Burrell (n 41).

57 Ibid.

58 Marianne Stang Våland and Susse Georg, 'Spacing Identity: Unfolding Social and Spatial-Material Entanglements of Identity Performance' (2018) 34 *Scandinavian Journal of Management* 193, 194.

59 Ibid.

60 Ibid 109–110.

61 Rowden and Jones (n 45).

62 Linda Mulcahy, *Legal Architecture: Justice, Due Process and the Place of Law* (Taylor and Franci, 2010) 152.

63 Patricia Branco, 'Considering a Different Model for the Family and Children Courthouse Building: Reflections on the Portuguese Experience' (2018) 8(3) *Oñati Socio-Legal Series* 400, 413.

64 Victoria Brooks, 'Interrupting the Courtroom Organism: Screaming Bodies, Material Affects and the Theatre of Cruelty' (2019) 15(2) *Law, Culture and the Humanities* 332, 341.

Grant suggest that 'maintaining sightlines to Country is more likely to improve Indigenous users' sense of safety and wellbeing'.[65] Mulcahy argues that design can be a partner in affecting change in the way that justice is processed and experienced, 'rather than just reflecting it'.[66] Architecture controls access to light, comfort, and vision, each of which affects the bodily experience of stress, safety, trauma, anxiety, helplessness, and agency. These three elements also increase or decrease the physical capacity to focus, remain alert, see, hear, and participate in trials.

These affective, embodied interactions with court architecture have interpellative consequences. If we take the example of the child in the space designed for adults, we can see that part of their distress and discomfort comes from a misalignment of material interpellation. The hail of the chair on which the child witness is required to sit, for example, and the height of the balustrade fencing the stand, call to a witness of a size larger than the child, and a person with greater experience, knowledge, and autonomy. The child cannot recognise themselves in that hail: The subjectivity of 'witness' is *not really* who the child is. Similarly, the European architecture of most court buildings, enchanted with the ornament of liberal philosophy, hails court users who can recognise in themselves a subjectivity familiar with its logics. In its deliberate exclusion of Aboriginal law, Anglo-Australian court architecture alienates Aboriginal court users ('this is *not* who I really am'). As a result, these users might cross-interpellate or recognise within the hail the variously erased and criminalised subjectivities of Aboriginal and Torres Strait Islander peoples within colonising Australian law.

In contrast, architecture generated collaboratively with Aboriginal communities, which echoes the landscape, is woven through with Aboriginal law and grants access to Country, offers Aboriginal court users an interpellative interaction that allows them to recognise at least an aspect of their Aboriginal subjectivity through reflection of their own cultural values and ideology, even subject positions generated within Aboriginal ideologies.

An integral part of these interpellative interactions is the ostensible lack of cognitive processing and the immediate embodied feeling of recognition (that is *really* me). Not only is the inappropriate size of chair and stand for a child physically uncomfortable, but the mis-interpellation it causes is also experienced as further discomfort in the body of the child, as an intensity of affect. Interpellation works at an affective level, engaging the senses in the hail and response.

Althusser's examples of interpellative subject creation are situated in the body, often manifest through physical rituals. A key example is the performance of church rituals through which each individual enacts their role in ceremonies and sacraments. Similarly, interpellation between friends involves rituals of cheek-kissing, hand-shaking, and hugging. Ultimately, in the infamous street scene

65 Anthony and Grant (n 53) 44.
66 Mulcahy (n 62) 139.

the individual *turns* (but does not speak) in the moment of self-recognition in response to the police officer's 'Hey you!'.[67] In each of these examples, there is a bodily action, a physical ritual, bespeaking an affective response that confirms the recognition of the individual as the ideologically situated subject.

Ian Law argues that embodiment precedes the vocal component of interpellation.[68] We are able to recognise ourselves in the hail because we are 'embodiments of relations and gestures' that have been established through rituals of ideology (turning to or running from police, sitting cross-legged in the classroom, or raising the finger at the street heckler).[69] Similarly, Youdell theorises this happening within interpellation as a performance responding to the hail – the ritual of response is an embodied performance of subjecthood.[70] So, when you recognise yourself in the hail, you move your body in ways that align with the subjectivity you recognise interpellated by the hail. Consequently, your subjectivity is confirmed or recreated because, as Butler explains, the performance creates, recreates, confirms, or alters subjecthood. Performance thus *produces* the subjectivity it enacts.[71]

The trial is constituted of many rituals and circumscribed performances. Law students are taught that they cannot 'just go to court and move your body'; they must instead 'act like a barrister'.[72] Thus, as the lawyer situates herself according to the emplacement of courtroom layout, she responds to the hail of her allocated seat, recognises within herself the identity of defence or prosecuting counsel, and performs that role with her demeanour as much as in the language she uses, her cognitive processing of the information she gathers from the questions she asks, and the way that she asks them.

As constructions with a specific purpose, both practical and symbolic, court buildings effect interpellation. This interpellation is a dynamic, embodied, affective interaction (*enactment*) in which the layout (*emplacement*) conspires with the material form and ornamentation (*enchantment*), calling out to court users, prompting them to identify an aspect of themselves in that hail and then to perform that subjectivity within the courtroom. Our argument therefore understands architecture as 'a technology of interpellation'.[73] As such, court architecture encourages jurors to prioritise specific subjectivities. Consequently, other identities and subject positions that jurors may embody across their complex and multifaceted lives are silenced.

67 Althusser (n 13) 118.
68 Law (n 30).
69 Ibid 15.
70 Youdell (n 23) 515.
71 Judith Butler, *Bodies that Matter: On the Discursive Limits of 'Sex'* (Routledge, 1993).
72 Barber Kamler and Rod MacLean, 'You Can't Just Go to Court and Move Your Body: First-Year Students Learn to Write and Speak the Law' (1996) 3 *Law Text Culture* 176.
73 Hancock and Spicer (n 39) 91.

Juror susceptibility

One of the design functions of higher-level courts is the accommodation of juries in their unique and particular role. The specificity of jury needs requires architecture that guides juries through buildings, separates them from other court visitors, and places them advantageously within courtrooms to see and hear trials unfold. Woven through the practical *emplacement* of jurors is an interpellative call asking each juror to find within themselves the subject position of 'juror' in the ideologically structured criminal justice system. An architectural *enchantment* shaped by liberal philosophy textures this subject position, influencing the performance of each juror. The enchantment executes its interpellation through a specifically affective experience of being a juror, and through this we can observe the dynamic *enactment* of design interacting with jurors in the course of the trial. In this section we demonstrate the particular susceptibility of jurors to interpellation due to the conditions of uncertainty, information-seeking, and ambiguity under which they must perform their duty.

Uncertainty is fundamental to jury service. An enduring justification for juries and their symbolic power in legitimising the justice system is that they are laypeople. Jurors are not supposed to know much about law. Indeed, legal education can be a point of exclusion from jury service.[74]

Lack of knowledge means that each juror's information-seeking begins with the task of figuring out where they need to be within the court space. Consequently, architectonic interpellation hits hyperdrive when jurors attend court on their first day. For example, the summoned Victorian juror arrives, as instructed by the Victorian Juries website, from the closest public transport hub, looking for something that resembles a court. They seek those explicit symbols of law and justice that call out to each passer-by, and in doing so they can recognise the relevance of these symbols to their subject position in that moment. While at the Victorian Supreme Court these symbols include columns, the Melbourne County Court (MCC) bears a sculpture of Lady Justice. By contrast, the Kununurra Courthouse echoes the shape of the surrounding geology that holds legal significance for Aboriginal peoples. In Melbourne, the summoned individual recognises their own temporary subject position within a signified ideology: 'I *am* that person being compelled to contribute to *the arbitration of justice*.'

As they enter the court building, passing through the 'airport'-style security, each juror must seek where to 'check in'. At the MCC the entrance to the jury pool is immediately to the left of security, past the artwork *Ngarrn-Gi: Land/Law* by Judy Watson.[75] The sign is discrete, and each juror's gaze is charged

74 Each jurisdiction has different criteria. However, in Victoria the *Juries Act 2000* (Vic) Schedule 2, s 1(e), excludes all Australian lawyers from jury service.

75 Judy Watson is a Waanyi woman, and her family's country is situated in an area now known as north-west Queensland. *Ngarrn-Gi: Land/Law* is a substantial piece, at 50 metres of etched zinc, that was delivered in 2002.

by needing to find it. In this moment, emplacement and enactment work with enchantment. In their uncertainty, the juror makes contact with the sign hailing, 'Hey you, Juror'. The juror recognises that part of themselves that is being called for duty (I am *really* a juror). Thus, as they pass into the jury pool there may be an embodied experience of trepidation mixed with temporary relief that they have got something right. The movement into the jury pool, with its associated intensity of feeling, confirms the ideology of justice embodied by the building and the juror's role within it. Left behind is the possible interruption to European-Australian law that Watson's art might offer as a symbol of the enduring law of Aboriginal and Torres Strait Islander peoples.

Concurrent with individual jurors' lack of familiarity with courts is the uncertainty jury service offers concerning its impact on jurors' lives. The stress of jury duty in the United States (US) is most commonly reported to be the disruption it causes.[76] Although in some jurisdictions jurors are compensated for their time and employers are technically not permitted to penalise staff, the time commitment required impacts upon carer responsibilities, self-employment,, and career benchmarks.[77] Young, Cameron, and Tinsley found that New Zealand jurors felt compelled to complete their regular work at the end of each court day to fulfil their work commitments.[78] Negotiating the disruption is made more difficult by the uncertainty about what offences will be considered in the trial and how long the trial will last.

Increasingly, better and more useful orientation material is delivered to jurors. However, there appears to be little consistency in the form, quality, and timing of such information across jurisdictions, even within nations. For example, Najdovski-Terziovski et al. found that each of the seven Australian state- and territory-based jurisdictions delivers markedly different juror orientation material, using a range of formats including video, handbook, and in-person presentations.[79] In the US, states can have more than 20 judicial districts, each with different juror orientation programmes, most of which Marder found to be inadequate for the task of allaying juror uncertainty.[80] Najdovski-Terziovski et al. noted that juror orientation material generally provides an overview of court procedure and law, the jury environment, and the importance of jury work.[81] At the Old Bailey, England, each juror receives a 'bundle', containing a compendium

76 Sarah A Trescher, Monica K Miller and Brian H Bornstein, 'How Does Jury Service Affect 21st Century Jurors?' in Cynthea Nadjowski and Margaret Stevenson (eds), *Criminal Juries in the 21st Century: Psychological Science and the Law* (Oxford University Press, 2018) 271, 272.

77 Ibid.

78 Young, Cameron and Tinsley (n 35).

79 Elizabeth Najdovski-Terziovski et al., 'What Are We Doing Here? An Analysis of Juror Orientation Programs' (2008) 92(2) *Judicature* 70.

80 Nancy Marder, 'Two Weeks at the Old Bailey: Jury Lessons from England' (2011) 86(2) *Chicago-Kent Law Review* 537, 548.

81 Najdovski-Terziovski et al. (n 79).

of trial evidence to aid juror information-seeking and processing.[82] Other jurisdictions provide notebooks.

Despite this provision of information, jurors struggle. Their struggle goes right to the heart of jury service: The jury must gather the evidence provided at trial and assess it according to verbally delivered legal concepts and principles. Jurors must then negotiate with each other to reach a binary decision of guilty or not guilty. Throughout trial, they are maintained in a condition of information-seeking, not just in terms of evidence, but also in relation to the legal arguments and guidance presented by the opposing counsel and judge. The emphasis is primarily on oral evidence. Trials thus rely heavily on the capacity of jurors to concentrate for long periods of time and to remember what they have heard.[83] Note-taking is a skill that not all jurors possess, but is needed as the delivery of evidence is fragmented, inconsistent, and contradictory. Scientific evidence, legal principle, and instructions delivered can be complex, and jurors often find them difficult to follow.[84] In New Zealand, jurors reported feeling that they had not received sufficient legal or factual knowledge at the beginning of trials to help them evaluate the evidence.[85] Further, jurors receive very little guidance on how to conduct their information-seeking.

McKimmie et al. argue that the weight of each juror's cognitive load is fatiguing.[86] Consequently, jurors are motivated to rely on 'stereotypes and other cues'.[87] These authors suggest that the 'design of the courtroom may provide such cues to help jurors organise their stories'.[88] While McKimmie et al. propose that courtroom features like the dock encourage jurors to read defendants as guilty, we suggest that in the absence of guided note-taking or printed explanations of legal principle, jurors are left to seek evaluative guidance elsewhere. Enchanted with the aesthetics of liberal ideology, courtroom architecture provides this guidance, urging jurors to implement schemas borne by liberal values.

The enchantment of the court works effectively as a hailing agent for jurors in these moments because the court is only one of many hailing agents that interpellate members of the jury from the moment of notification, and throughout the trial. For example, on receiving notification of jury duty, each potential Victorian juror is directed to the Juries Victoria website.[89] As they process their eligibility, every page of the site tells them (bold text in original):

82 Marder (n 80) 548.

83 Young, Cameron and Tinsley (n 35).

84 Tarika Daftary-Kapur, Rafaele Dumas and Steven D Penrod, 'Jury Decision-Making Biases and Methods to Counter Them' (2011) 15(1) *Legal and Criminal Psychology* 133.

85 Yvette Tinsley, 'Juror Decision-Making: A Look Inside the Jury Room' in Roger Tarling (ed), *The British Criminology Conference Selected Proceedings* (Leicester, Vol. 4, October 2001).

86 Blake M McKimmie, Jillian M Hayes and David Tait, 'Just Spaces: Does Courtroom Design Affect How the Defendant is Perceived?' (2016) 23(6) *Psychiatry, Psychology and Law* 885, 887.

87 Ibid.

88 Ibid.

89 See <www.Juries.vic.gov.au>.

> **Juries** bring the values, standards and expectations of **our community** into the courtroom, contributing in a significant way to the administration of **justice** in Victoria.

The prominence and repetition of this statement across the website remind each potential juror of their role within the system. Before arriving at court, the potential juror has thus already been prompted to find in themselves the subject position of 'community representative'.

The evaluation tools offered to jurors to process information are recurrently and explicitly named as 'community values' and 'common sense'. Yet the meaning of 'community' is ambiguous, and Victorian society is not a singular homogenous community. The very idea of 'community' is not monolithic either, as it differs across contexts and cultures. Thus, there is not one but many communities. Those to which a juror might belong are multifaceted, and may be based on ethnicity, sex, class, sexual orientation, marital status, parental status, geography, profession, politics, hobbies, or faith. Each individual performs various roles in the different areas of their lives (such as organiser, lover, worker, mother, tenant, employee, voter, dancer, or consumer). This means that the values held by any individual as a 'community representative' are inevitably multiple and often contradictory.

As the Juries Victoria website hails the juror from '*our* community', it is worth considering Hage's theory of belonging, which reveals a hierarchy of community drawn upon by managerial governance.[90] That is to say, some communities have a greater sense of political will than others, and a greater sense of authority and entitlement to manage the space of the nation. Thus, as the website hails the juror to represent '*our* community', it is asking them to recognise within themselves a community membership that provides them with the authority to engage in national administration.

In the absence of explicit definitions, clear guidance, or useful tools, jurors are vulnerable to the enchanting hail of court buildings. Uncertainty about jury service conspires with the ambiguous demands placed on a 'community representative', so that jurors are left to seek cues elsewhere. The character of jury service is 'information-seeking' on many levels. Within the court building, the juror's searching gaze is constantly met by the ideology of law, hailing them through powerful and longstanding signifiers.

The ideology of court buildings

Two signifiers by which juror gazes are met across the common law world are Grecian decoration and flat, unadorned surfaces. Both are enchanted with white

90 Ghassan Hage, *White National Fantasies of White Supremacy in a Multicultural Australia* (Pluto Press, 1998).

masculinist ideologies of liberal philosophy, manifest in different eras of aesthetic virtue: Eighteenth- and nineteenth-century Greek Revival and twentieth-century modernism. These signifiers hail jurors into subject positions that prioritise neutrality and reason, appearing to set aside culture and diversity. However, these architectural features bear schematic logics that deny sovereignty to non-conforming bodies. Rape myths comprise one such schema. To demonstrate this liberal enchantment, we juxtapose four Australian court spaces that are redolent with ideology: The Victorian Supreme Court (VSC), the MCC, the Kununurra Courthouse, and the Kununurra District Courtroom.

The VSC[91] was constructed in the Renaissance Revival style of the late nineteenth century. Ornament is abundant and the building resonates with enchantment. A double layer of Ionic columns adorns the entrance and is echoed as square Composite column fronts on portico arches. Leaves and scrolls render them 'feminine' according to Vitruvius' 'order' of columns.[92] Inside the courtrooms, plainer columns are made more 'masculine' by the absence of fluting. These are understood to echo the 'beauty of the naked male', always imaginatively juxtaposed against the delicacy and adornment associated with women.[93]

The revival of Greek elements in the construction of courts for an extended period from the mid-eighteenth to early twentieth century represents an explicit use of architecture as 'visual language'.[94] Across the road from the VSC, above the entrance of the MCC, the figure of Lady Justice, an imaginary wind sweeping her draped chiton, also invokes the Greek Revival.[95] Resnik and Curtis map the ubiquity of Lady Justice as a symbol of legal and political justice around the world.[96] As referents, Grecian ornament connotes the values of Ancient Greece celebrated during the Revival and central to Enlightenment thinking, including democracy and reason. While democracy is critical to the legitimacy of law, *reason* has particular significance for juries. Later we examine how reason is specifically consequential for rape trials.

91 Although the Victorian Supreme Court does not have jurisdiction to hear rape cases in the first instance, we are aware of at least one rape trial beginning in the Supreme Court building.

92 Joel Sanders, 'Introduction' in Joel Sanders (ed), *Stud: Architectures of Masculinity* (Princeton Architectural Press, 1996) 10, 12.

93 Ibid 13.

94 John Summerson, *The Classical Language of Architecture* (MIT Press, 1966). This dominance of columns in court architecture across this period is illustrated by their appearance in the re-fronting of the Old Bailey in 1740 and then in its complete reconstruction in 1907; see Clive Emsley, Tim Hitchcock and Robert Shoemaker, 'Historical Background: History of The Old Bailey Courthouse' in *Old Bailey Proceedings Online* (www.oldbaileyonline.org, version 7.0, 1 March 2020).

95 Is it significant that the imaginary wind is blowing her chiton against her female body in an echo of the revival fashion which saw English aristocrats dampening their chitons before social occasions to render them tantalisingly almost transparent? See Daniel James Cole, 'Hierarchy and Seduction in Regency Fashion' (2012) 33(1) *Persuasions On-Line*, no pagination.

96 Resnik and Curtis, *Representing Justice* (n 54).

Although the MCC looks bare against the VSC, constructed in 2002, its design features are no less enchanted. The significance of its modernist minimal decoration is more apparent if compared with the Kununurra Courthouse (discussed in two chapters of this volume).[97] In Kununurra, the Courthouse was designed as an intercultural collaboration purposely foregrounding signifiers of Aboriginal law and values, and incorporating Aboriginal spatial conceptualisation. On the second floor sits the Kununurra District Courtroom (KDC), where jury trials are heard. Against the thoughtful enchantment of the Courthouse, the trial court appears *bereft* of culture with its office-style seating, variegated grey carpet, single window, white walls, and uniform wood panels. In this regard, Grant and Hook note the specific direction from the commissioning authority for the district courtroom to be 'neutral'.[98] This follows a general pattern in which Australian lower courts are granted exceptional licence to digress from rigid courtroom formulas, while trial courtrooms are not.[99] The courtrooms of the MCC are similarly 'neutral,' dominated by uniform panels, unadorned walls, limited windows, and bland carpets. As a manifestation of Lady Justice's blindfold, 'neutrality' is another integral value of common law, imagined to provide equity in the delivery of justice by removing or overcoming markers of difference.

The significance of neutrality

Despite the assertion of 'neutrality', the resonance of meaning never stops. In the moment something enters one's awareness it enters a vortex of abundant cultural discourse and is immediately granted significance. Modernist courtrooms are no less enchanted than the ornamentation of the VSC or the intercultural architecture of Kununurra Court's ground floor. In contemporary court architecture, white walls and uniform blank panels signify 'neutrality' – a 'neutrality' that is entrenched with sexed and raced significance. Although we tend to function as though buildings and their internal spaces are 'neutral containers facilitating … free interaction between sovereign subjects',[100] critical race scholarship has traced 'racial patriarchies'[101] throughout the theory, practice, and structures of modern architecture. For example, while Fields reveals the colonial and slave narratives in Hegel's philosophies of history and aesthetics to demonstrate the deeply rooted intersection of race and architecture ('they were born into the world

97 Grant and Hook (n 52).

98 Ibid page 28.

99 Emma Henderson and Kirsty Duncanson, 'Design and Ideology: Innovation and the Magistrates' Court' (2018) 27(2) *Griffith Law Review* 207.

100 Sanders (n 92) 12.

101 Mabel O Wilson, 'Dancing in the Dark: The Inscription of Blackness in Le Corbusier's Radiant City' in Heidi Nast and Steve Pile (eds), *Places through the Body (*Routledge, 1998) 133, 138.

together'),[102] Fusco[103] and Wilson[104] both reveal whiteness as a raced imperative of modernist design. In fact, the aesthetic manifestation of 'neutrality' as whiteness is theorised in contradistinction from black bodies and culture.

The KDC illustrates this raced ideology, combining recognisably fixed emplacement of elevated hierarchies and positioned legal actors with modernist purposive efficiency. The wood panelling appears particularly uniform in contrast to the striated woodwork in the atrium, which deliberately evokes the Aboriginal law borne by the surrounding lined geological formations.[105] While the height of the single window in the courtroom embodies a goal of English court architecture to remove the distractions of the outside world, it also impedes visual connection with those law-imbued geological formations.[106] This again contrasts with the deliberate use of multiple windows in the magistrate's court below, where visual access to Country was deemed a priority.[107] The regimental seating in the KDC differs from the deliberately fluid seating available in the waiting areas, while the Aboriginal art incorporated into the design of the rest of the Courthouse is notably absent in the courtroom.

White walls are an integral feature of modernist architecture. White, Fusco explains, is praised as the colour 'of civilisation' and a 'marker of purity'.[108] This is because 'white surfaces serve as sensors that allow stains to be seen; anything that is excessive stands out'.[109] Such stains and excess are named by one of the most influential early modernist architects, Le Corbusier, as signs 'of the "Brown World"'.[110] Wilson demonstrates that this 'Brown World' represents the ever-present threat of blackness 'as death, dirt and lawlessness'.[111] It is a world explicitly represented in Le Corbusier as African American bodies and culture.

Through the modernist lens, the KDC appears to achieve neutrality, particularly in contrast with the rest of the Courthouse. The signifiers of Aboriginal culture and law are removed, including visual access to the landscape within which the building is set. While the rest of the Courthouse renders Aboriginal law and culture functional through window positioning, shared spaces, a banister, and seating arrangements, in the KDC all that is Aboriginal is rendered 'ornamentation': Distracting views, art, or excessive patterning. Aboriginal

102 Darell Wayne Fields, *Architecture in Black* (Athlone, 2000) xxvii.

103 Caroline Fusco, 'Cultural Landscapes of Purification: Sport Spaces and Discourses of Whiteness' (2005) 22 *Sociology of Sport* 283.

104 Wilson (n 101) 138.

105 Grant and Hook (n 52).

106 Peter Goodrich, *Languages of the Law from Logics of Memory to Nomadic Masks* (Weidenfeld and Nicolson, 1990) 189; Henderson and Duncanson, 'Design and Ideology' (n 99) 220; Julian Murphy, 'Architecting Aboriginal Access to Justice' (2016) 18 *Flinders Law Journal* 268, 287.

107 Grant and Hook (n 52).

108 Fusco (n 103) 288.

109 Ibid 287.

110 Ibid 288.

111 Wilson (n 101) 147.

signifiers become Other and are 'evicted' by the whitewashing of modernist aesthetics 'in order that respectability can be maintained'.[112] The 'respectability', in this instance, is mainstream law.

The interaction between the KDC and the rest of the Courthouse repeats a motif that pervades the white Australian popular imagination – the depiction of landscapes as ominously empty.[113] In this courtroom, set within a courthouse otherwise incorporating Aboriginal semiotics, the white walls, uniform wood panels, inaccessible window, and bland carpet combine to perform *terra nullius*: The foundational lie that the land was empty (and bore no law) prior to European accession.[114] It is the aesthetic removal of pre-existing sovereignty.[115] The KDC exemplifies the ideological *enchantment* of 'neutrality'.

Modernist architecture involves 'clean lines' and a preferred range of materials. Sanders lists glass, steel, wood panelling, and stone as characterising modernist design. Resnik and Curtis document the use of these materials internationally in contemporary courthouse architecture to embody the semiotics of liberal democracy, transparent legal process, and justice.[116] The MCC features on the cover of Resnik and Curtis' book. Sanders argues that these materials convey the social values associated with masculinity including logic, rationality, hygiene, and truth.[117] They thus embody an aesthetics of neutrality and reason.

The masculinity of modern court spaces is also produced by minimal ornamentation: 'reducing architecture to its bare essentials' for efficiency of purpose.[118] While Crawford[119] argues that 'femininity, women and any hint of queerness' is associated with ornamentation, Sanders observes that, since Vesuvius, women figure in architecture as the artifice of adornment.[120] This is a figuring of the feminine as 'masquerade', which is shared by those rape schemas that understand complainants as always potentially false. In contrast, the naked male is exulted as genuine and unadorned.[121] In juxtaposition, the unadorned is unencumbered, neutral, and able to exercise reason.

In the context of rape trials unfolding in modernist courtrooms, the enchantment of the materials used, and the absence of adornment, echoes the discourse

112 Fusco (n 103) 304.

113 Kirsty Duncanson, '"Native" Landscapes, "Cultivated" Gardens and the Erasure of Indigenous Sovereignty in Two Recent Instances of Australian Cinematic Jurisprudence' (2014) 10(2) *Law, Culture and the Humanities* 237.

114 Kirsty Duncanson, 'The Scene of the Crime: Uneasy Figuring of Anglo-Australian Sovereignty in the Landscape of *Lantana*' (2009) 13 *Law Text Culture* 25.

115 Kirsty Duncanson, 'Being Engaged in Colonial Critique by Mojo Juju's Native Tongue' in K Tranter, K Crawley and K Wienheirt (eds), *Law, Lawyers and Justice through Australian Lenses* (Routledge, 2020).

116 Resnik and Curtis, *Representing Justice* (n 54).

117 Sanders (n 92) 12–14.

118 Ibid 15.

119 Lucas Crawford, 'Refashioning the Architectonics of Gender' (2009) 35(2/3) *English Studies in Canada* 18, 20.

120 Sanders (n 92) 12–13.

121 Ibid.

of gender neutrality in Victorian law. In 1991, the offence of rape was reformed to recognise that objects other than penises could sexually penetrate, and that the sexual penetration of anuses and mouths should be regulated as much as that of vaginas. The law thus recognises that people other than those read by law on the basis of genitalia as 'women' can be raped, and that people other than those categorised as 'men' can be perpetrators. Consequently, both survivor and perpetrator are subsumed under Pateman's 'apparently universal, sexually neuter category of the "individual"' of contemporary liberal philosophy.[122] Such a linguistic manoeuvre is imagined to grant women the legal subjecthood required to consent to or refuse sexual penetration.

Naffine writes that rape law 'may now be gender neutral, but the behaviour is not'[123] – a statement that remains corroborated by the statistics. In 2018, 84 per cent of survivors reporting sexual assault in Victoria identified as female,[124] and data from 2016 shows that 95.2 per cent of perpetrators are male.[125] Changing the linguistically sexed specificity of the crime has not radically altered the sexed identity of survivors and perpetrators, or granted LGBTQIA+ communities access to justice.[126] Neither have the gendered myths about rape been dispelled. Despite the inclusion of differently identifying bodies to the category of 'liberal individual', the presumed characteristics remain masculine (autonomous, singular, *impenetrable*, rational). Boshoff writes that linguistically expanding the category ultimately fails women because it 'does not fit our political, legal, emotional, or intuitive experience' as women.[127] De-gendering the language of law *disguises* rather than overcomes the substantive sexed differences in our culture.

White walls and unadorned surfaces in the KDC and MCC celebrate equitable justice as removing 'ornamentation', while functioning to hide their own raced and sexed ideology. Each blank panel is a referent to a specifically located cultural value that is the denial of its own culture and the hyper-recognition of divergent cultures as Other, artifice, excess, and lacking reason. This is how neutrality is expressed aesthetically and spatially by court architecture.

The sex of legal reason

Reason is understood to be separate from culture. Reasoning is the practice of disconnecting thought from emotion. It is viewed as the capacity to think

122 Carol Pateman, *The Sexual Contract* (Polity Press, 1988).

123 Naffine (n 3) 24.

124 ABS Crime Victimisation Australia 2016–17 (Web Page) <https://www.abs.gov.au/ausstats/abs@.nsf/mf/4510.0>.

125 See <https://www.crimestatistics.vic.gov.au/crime-statistics/historical-crime-data/year-ending-31-december-2016/spotlight-sexual-offences>.

126 Jess Ison, '"It's Not Just Men and Women": LGBTQIA People and #MeToo' in Rachel Loney-Howes and Bianca Fileborn (eds), *#MeToo and the Politics of Social Change* (Palgrave MacMillan, 2020) 151.

127 Boshoff (n 3) 42.

'logically', and to implement a method of knowledge production that disentangles 'truth' from subjective perspective. It is thus deemed to achieve knowledge that is '*perspectiveless*', objective, and neutral, and '*eternally true*, or valid, independent of origins'.[128] Reason is a central value and exercise of law. Jury deliberation is the fantastical manifestation of reason as 'twelve angry men' challenge each other's subjectivity until they reach a reasonable verdict.[129]

Feminist critique has revealed the situatedness of reason. As a logic, it issues from particular bodies that move through the world in specific ways: They are generally economically more powerful, wield greater social capital, and are ostensibly more autonomous because they are not burdened by the abundant minutiae of caring responsibilities. The dimensions of reason have been mapped in contradistinction from the purported logic articulated by women on the basis of their promise of embodied maternal reproduction.[130] Women's bodies defy the singularity of liberal subjecthood with their promise of pregnancy as two beings within one skin (this sex which is not one).[131]

In the context of rape, the very claim to have been sexually penetrated without consent is proof of the absence of this logic: Impenetrability is a central feature of liberal personhood.[132] Women figure as always already potentially penetrated, and thus outside this standard of legal subjecthood. This standard is also a problem for male complainants. While previous laws could not conceive of men being able to consent to sexual penetration at all (no reasonable belief in consent could mitigate a charge of sodomy),[133] the repeal of such laws and the de-gendering of rape place male complainants in the same precarious position of being marked as unreasonable (unbelievable, illogical) as soon as they disclose that they have been penetrated.

In demonstrating the reliance of liberal philosophy on the exclusion of women, Pateman critiques Rousseau.[134] This bastion of social contract theory formulates a critical link between the capacity to reason and the practice of a specific form of heteronormativity. This is the assertion of a husband's will over that of his wife because women are 'creatures of passion' and necessarily chaste, and

128 Elizabeth Grosz, 'Feminism and the Crisis of Reason' in Linda Alcoff and Elizabeth Potter (eds), *Feminist Epistemologies* (Routledge, 2013) 187, 191. Emphaisis in original.

129 Sarat Austen, 'Fathers in Law: Violence and Reason in *12 Angry Men*' (2007) 82 *Chicago-Kent Law Review* 863.

130 Ahmad (n 3) 56; Tyler (n 3) 288; Jennifer Nedelsky, 'Embodied Diversity and the Challenges to Law' (1997) 42 *McGill Law Journal* 91.

131 Luce Irigary, Carolyn Burke (Translator) and Catherine Porter (Translator) *This Sex Which is Not One* (Cornell University Press 1977).

132 Du Toit (n 3).

133 The crime of anal penetration as sodomy has its common law origins not as a crime against a person, but against 'majesty' and nation; see Leslie Moran, *The Homosexual(ity) of Law* (Routledge, 1996) 72.

134 Pateman (n 122) 15.

must lie about their sexual desire.[135] To prove his argument, Rousseau provides an illustrative example of heterosexual intimacy:

> The lips always say 'No,' and rightly so; but the tone is not always the same, and that cannot lie … Must her modesty condemn her to misery? Does she not require a means of indicating her inclinations without open expression? … To win this silent consent is to make use of all the violence permitted in love. To read it in the eyes, to see it in the ways in spite of the mouth's denial … If he then completes his happiness, he is not brutal, he is decent. He does not insult chasteness; he respects it; he serves it. He leaves it the honor of still defending what it would have perhaps abandoned.[136]

Through a feminist lens or contemporary Victorian law this is an account of rape. Although, as Philadelphof-Puren writes, the manner of its delivery, its grammar, 'almost makes it an act of reason'.[137] In the midst of theorising who is able to participate in the social contract, Rousseau uses a metaphor of sexual intimacy as the imposition of heteromasculine desire on a woman's articulated non-consent. This argument is intended to demonstrate that because women oppose men's desire to have sex, they lack reason. Feminine artifice is unequivocal. Rousseau explicitly states that women can never be recognised as refusing consent. Reason is thus, like neutrality, the erasure of divergent narratives and values. It is the embodiment of the hegemonic order, which is heteronormatively masculine.

Rousseau's vignette is not a perverse outlier of political philosophy. Rather, it epitomises the conflation of liberal theory with heteronormativity that lies at the foundation of contemporary democracy and law.[138]

It is also an enduring template for the rape myth schemas that persist throughout popular culture and within courtrooms.[139] It situates duplicity in women as the predetermined condition of democratic structures: That women say 'no' when they mean 'yes' is the justification for contemporary Western governance, necessitating the greater authority of men in politics and law. Here are the myths that women do not know what they want sexually, that they need (sometimes violent) persuasion (for their own pleasure), and that women's chastity is their raison d'être (and thus they lie about having actually consented).

The language of reason and neutrality peppers legal discourse as it is expressed during trials. However, it also enchants court architecture as carefully considered symbols of law's ideology or as implicit echoes of culturally specific aesthetics. This has implications for each juror as they sit within the jury box, grasping for the best tools to process the evidence.

135 Ibid.
136 Ibid 155.
137 Philadelphof-Puren (n 6) 35.
138 Pateman (n 122).
139 Philadelphof-Puren (n 6).

Conclusion: Bringing the pieces together

This chapter has taken a long journey, through an idea that is at once something we all 'know' and something that we are reluctant to take seriously. It is at once obvious that court buildings influence how we feel and act; that they impose upon us law's ideology. However, the idea that architecture influences juror decision-making is only now gaining traction.[140] In this chapter, we have sought to ground this claim by exploring the usefulness of the concept of interpellation to understand the relationship between court architecture and juror; by examining how buildings interact with their users through emplacement, enchantment, and enactment to shape user behaviour and subject position; by exploring the particular vulnerability of jurors to the influence of hailing agents due to their role as information-seekers as well as the ambiguity and uncertainty of this role; and by demonstrating that the ideology borne by court architecture is woven through with rape schemas that have long been used to explain and justify the politico-legal structures of common law states.

Rape conviction rates are extraordinarily low and have decreased in recent history across most common law jurisdictions.[141] Feminist legal research demonstrates that rape myth schemas circulate through rape trials and are used by jurors to deliberate over evidence towards a verdict. We argue that one reason why rape myths remain so powerful is that jurors are hailed by the ideological design elements of court buildings to situate themselves in a rape myth–supporting subject position when processing and deliberating over evidence at trial. This makes it difficult for jurors to find the accounts provided by complainants logical and believable or to convict defendants.

A juror's role is to seek and process information about law, the acts and events in question, and the credibility of witnesses. In the absence of clear guidance or explicit measuring tools, jurors execute their work in a state of uncertainty. *Emplaced* by conventional court architecture, they sit in enforced inactivity to one side of the trial action. Architectural *enactment* restricts their movement and what they see. It also influences their affective experience, intensifying their discomfort and uncertainty.

While they listen to confusing and fragmented oral evidence, we theorise that jurors' eyes rove over the details of their surroundings. Their gaze is met repeatedly by signifiers of legal ideology. In these moments, design elements become agents hailing, 'Hey you, juror!' The cultural significance of columns, sculptures, white walls, and uniform wood panelling transforms the hail into a call for each juror to recognise within themselves the subject position of 'neutral' and 'reasoning' liberal individual.

We have sought to demonstrate that, despite the claim that both of these virtues (neutrality and reason) achieve objectivity through triumphs of thought

140 See here the work of David Tait on the impact of caged and glassed docks, Tait (n 47) 494.
141 Daly and Bouhours (n 1); Larcombe, 'Falling Rape Convictions' (n 1).

over emotion and culture, both are fundamentally situated and defined by rape mythology. Indeed, the very foundation of liberal philosophy implements rape myth schemas to explain and justify the politico-legal structures of most common law states.

Because reason and neutrality are powerful threads of the hegemonic order, they are woven throughout Western culture as normal and recognisable. They are taught in schools, asserted on television, and demanded by state institutions. Thus, even when an individual juror diverges from the logic of liberal philosophy, they easily cross-interpellate to recognise within their multifarious selves subject positions that *do* align with the hegemony. Despite this potential for internal contradiction, cross-interpellation is regularly experienced as natural and logical. However, there is potential for resistance, although this is limited. In the context of a rape trial the limitations are compounded by the pressure on jurors to align their decision-making with the dichotomous verdict and the tight cultural control over signification in the trial space.

Ultimately, we argue that jurors are coerced through the interpellative exchange with court architecture to prioritise specific subject positions within the ideologically structured order. Divergent, critical, or resistant points of subject identification are suppressed for the duration of the trial. The dominant subject position implements a rape myth schema logic that cannot recognise non-consent to sexual penetration and understands masculine sexual penetration as a reasonable act.

Recognition that the material forms of court buildings interact with jurors to position them and coopt them into an ideological position has the potential to aid further thinking and reform in relation to rape law, and beyond to other areas of legal procedure. Court architecture has become an important area for research, examples of which are provided in this collection. Also evidenced here are examples of the way that the cultures of court architecture are changing. Although many constructions continue to follow convention, some court building projects are creating legal spaces that recognise and seek to redress the violence of law. Our hope is that our extended consideration of the influence of court architecture on jurors will contribute constructively to both the burgeoning research field and to the creation of greater access to justice through reconfigured court buildings.

6

THE CHILD SEXUAL ASSAULT TRIAL

Reconceptualising the design of court spaces according to trauma-informed principles

Annie Cossins[1] *and Emma Rowden*[2]

Introduction

It has been well documented that the process of giving evidence for children in a child sexual assault (CSA) trial can be severely traumatising, often characterised as an experience of further abuse.[3] Several factors – including the nature of cross-examination, the potential for seeing the perpetrator, and being required to relive a traumatic episode in a room full of strangers in a public setting – mean that the fundamental nature of testifying is at odds with the requirements for recovering from trauma. These issues are compounded for children who by virtue of their mental development often lack the necessary agency, capacity, and resilience to give evidence when faced with these additional challenges. Thus, children can be prevented from giving their best evidence while trials may collapse due to emotional breakdown and withdrawal of the key witness. In addition to the traumatising nature of the adversarial system, the inability of victims to safely give their evidence has led to a gross failure of our legal system to deliver justice for vulnerable complainants of sexual assault.

In an attempt to address some of these barriers that vulnerable and child witnesses face, several jurisdictions have changed both trial practices and the design of courtroom environments since the 1990s in order to reduce the number of

1 Annie Cossins is responsible for the work in this chapter on trauma-informed theory and trauma-informed courts.which was first published in Anne Cossins, *Closing the Justice Gap for Adult and Child Sexual Assault: Rethinking the Adversarial Trial* (Palgrave MacMillan, 2020)

2 Emma Rowden is responsible for the work in this chapter on courtroom design and the references to her previous research on remote witness facilities.

3 *Royal Commission into Institutional Responses to Child Sexual Abuse* (Criminal Justice Report: Parts VII to X and Appendices, August 2017).

DOI: 10.4324/9780429059858-9

potential trauma triggers for victims. These include the pre-recording of evidence-in-chief and cross-examination or giving live evidence from a remote witness suite that is connected to the courtroom by video link.[4]

There is some evidence to show that these strategies have improved the trial experience for complainants and led to higher levels of complainant satisfaction with the criminal justice system (CJS).[5] Nonetheless, this chapter contends that more needs to be done. We hypothesise that more victims of CSA might be willing and able to participate in adversarial trials if the design of courtrooms, courthouses, and the trial processes within them were more explicitly governed by the principles of "trauma-informed care" (TIC).

TIC is a philosophy of care from the psychological literature for treating patients with a history of psychological trauma. It is also a model that has become integrated into the delivery of public health services as well as other organisations dealing with traumatised people. Its aim is to meet the unique needs of survivors and to avoid re-traumatisation by reorganising the way in which institutions relate to traumatised individuals. In such an approach, service providers are trained about the phenomenon of trauma and its consequences, and why it is important that the physical and social environment of organisations understand the needs of traumatised individuals. Thus, the focus is on creating an experience conducive to healing, and one less likely to be re-traumatising.[6] Since CSA trials are likely to deal with children with histories of psychological trauma, the key question for this chapter is: can we design criminal justice spaces and processes that are trauma-informed?

While the aims of a criminal trial are clearly different from those of a health or counselling service, jurisdictions could improve the experience for complainants of CSA through integrating TIC practices and philosophies into the physical and social environment of the CSA trial. While the American Bar Association has recommended trauma-informed legal practice for lawyers who represent children and families, no one has previously considered whether and how the principles of trauma-informed systems could apply in criminal trials where a child is a complainant of sexual abuse.[7]

In particular, we contend that TIC provides a useful model to understand how and why the particular spatial features of court environments with special measures are succeeding, as well as how they might be improved. The chapter concludes that the concept of TIC has the potential to further inform the

4 Anne Cossins, *Alternative Models for Prosecuting Child Sex Offences in Australia* (National Child Sexual Assault Reform Committee Report, 2010) ('*Alternative Models for Prosecuting Child Sex Offences in Australia*').

5 See for instance, Becky Hamlyn et al., *Are Special Measures Working? Evidence from Surveys of Vulnerable and Intimidated Witnesses* (Home Office Research Study 283, 2004).

6 Susan Wells and Jenifer Urff, *Essential Components of Trauma-Informed Judicial Practice* (Final Draft Report, 2013) 3.

7 American Bar Association, *ABA Policy on Trauma-Informed Advocacy for Children and Youth* (Report, 2014) <www.americanbar.org/content/dam/aba/administrative/child_law/ABA Policy on Trauma-Informed Advocacy.authcheckdam.pdf>.

transformation of the criminal trial into a trauma-informed system which aims to do no further harm, to ameliorate the well-documented effects of adversarialism, and to achieve best evidence.

What are the long-term effects of trauma on victims of CSA?

Experiences of child abuse and neglect can fundamentally alter the way in which a person perceives and responds to the world because of the ways in which trauma impacts the developing brain and a child's identity, with life-long consequences. It is unsurprising then that rates of post-traumatic stress disorder (PTSD) are considerably higher among victims of sexual assault than among the general population.[8]

Overall, the most pervasive consequence of complex trauma for child witnesses, and other sufferers of PTSD and trauma-like symptoms, is the 'dysregulation of emotions and impulses'.[9] Trauma sufferers can experience involuntary and repeated overwhelming feelings of terror and helplessness that are triggered by particular cues, often experienced through nightmares and flashbacks. They may actively seek to avoid such cues, may be hyper-aroused or hyper-vigilant, have problems concentrating, and exhibit exaggerated startle responses.

For traumatised children, the 'most significant consequence of early relational trauma is the loss of the ability to regulate the intensity and duration of effects'[10] especially during high-stress experiences, such as giving evidence in court, since child abuse adversely affects brain development as well a child's nervous and endocrine systems. These effects negatively impact psychosocial development, mastery of social skills, and the ability to regulate emotions.[11] As the frequency of abuse increases, the risk of a child suffering from complex trauma and PTSD also

8 American Psychiatric Association, *Diagnostic and Statistical Manual of Mental Disorders (DSM-5)* (American Psychiatric Publishing, 5th ed, 2013); William E Copeland et al., 'Traumatic Events and Posttraumatic Stress in Childhood' (2007) 64(5) *Archives of General Psychiatry* 577; Vilma Gabbay et al., 'Epidemiological Aspects of PTSD in Children and Adolescents' in Raul R Silva (ed), *Posttraumatic Stress Disorder in Children and Adolescents: Handbook* (Norton, 2004); David J Kolko et al., 'Posttraumatic Stress Symptoms in Children and Adolescents Referred for Child Welfare Investigation: A National Sample of In-Home and Out-Of-Home Care' (2010) 15(1) *Child Maltreatment* 48.

9 Howard Bath, 'The Three Pillars of Trauma-Informed Care' (2008) 17 *Reclaiming Children and Youth* 17, 20.

10 Allan N Schore, *Affect Regulation and the Repair of the Self* (W W Norton, 1st ed, 2003) 141.

11 See 'Helping Traumatized Children: Tips for Judges', *The National Child Traumatic Stress Network* (Fact Sheet, 2009) <https://www.nctsn.org/resources/helping-traumatized-children-tips-judges> ('Helping Traumatized Children: Tips for Judges'); Stephen W Porges, *The Polyvagal Theory: Neurophysiological Foundations of Emotions, Attachment, Communication, Self-Regulation* (Norton, 2011); Bessel A van der Kolk, 'Clinical Implications of Neuroscience Research in PTSD' (2006) 1071(1) *Annals of New York Academy of Sciences* 277 ('Clinical Implications of Neuroscience Research in PTSD'); Bessel A van der Kolk, *The Body Keeps the Score: Brain, Mind, and Body in the Healing of Trauma* (Penguin Books, 2015) ('*The Body Keeps the Score*').

increases,[12] although the symptoms of PTSD vary across different age groups.[13] As Perry explains:

> trauma, neglect, and related experiences of maltreatment [...] interfere with normal patterns of experience-guided neurodevelopment by creating extreme and abnormal patterns of neural and neurohormonal activity. [...] [F]rom speech to motor functioning to social, emotional, or behavioral regulation—developmental trauma and maltreatment increase risk of dysfunction.[14]

When a person is faced with triggers that mimic their original traumatic experiences, the parts of the brain that control emotion are stimulated, while those that control speech and communication exhibit less activity.[15] In fact, 'the stress hormones of traumatised people ... take much longer to return to baseline and spike quickly and disproportionately in response to mildly stressful stimuli'.[16]

In addition to the original trauma, children, particularly adolescents, may have a range of other problems such as drug or alcohol abuse, medical issues, homelessness, unemployment, family problems, and/or legal issues with other government agencies, any of which can exacerbate the impact of the original trauma. As Quas and Goodman observe, CSA victims are already at risk of a number of adverse outcomes including, 'poor mental health, low academic achievement, insecure attachment, and relationship problems', even without involvement in the CJS.[17]

The difficulties facing child complainants when giving evidence in the courtroom

It is obvious that the type of skills necessary to give evidence in court – concentration, comprehension of questions asked, memory recall, accuracy, and clear communication – are likely to be impaired in the traumatised child, especially

12 Bessel A van der Kolk, 'Developmental Trauma Disorder: Towards a Rational Diagnosis for Children with Complex Trauma Histories' (2005) 35(5) *Psychiatric Annals* 401; van der Kolk, *The Body Keeps the Score* (n 11).

13 'Helping Traumatized Children: Tips for Judges' (n 11).

14 Bruce D Perry, 'Examining Child Maltreatment through a Neurodevelopmental Lens: Clinical Applications of the Neurosequential Model of Therapeutics' (2009) 14(4) *Journal of Loss and Trauma* 240, 241.

15 David A Crenshaw and Sarah Caprioli, 'The Culture of Silencing Child Victims of Sexual Abuse: Implications for Child Witnesses in Court' (2017) 57(2) *Journal of Humanistic Psychology* 190; van der Kolk, 'Clinical Implications of Neuroscience Research in PTSD' (n 11); van der Kolk, *The Body Keeps the Score* (n 11).

16 van der Kolk, *The Body Keeps the Score* (n 11) 46.

17 Jodi A Quas and Gail S Goodman, 'Consequences of Criminal Court Involvement for Child Victims' (2012) 18(3) *Psychology, Public Policy, and Law* 392, 395.

during lengthy and age-inappropriate cross-examination. While there is limited empirical evidence to show that testifying in court is *always* negative for a child's mental health, a number of studies have documented the harmful psychological impacts of testifying on children.[18]

As witnesses in court, children face a number of potential triggers that may cause a trauma-related response at various times throughout a lengthy trial process, including the authoritarian nature of courts, lack of control over court processes, court personnel exhibiting a lack of awareness of, and attention to, a child's specific needs (including psychological, cultural, and age-related needs), and the age-inappropriate language used by lawyers.[19]

The physical and social environment of the court setting itself can also be a stressful stimulus for a traumatised child. With its alien and imposing architecture, representations of official power structures, the layout, furnishings, legal language, arcane rituals, and costume can conspire to intimidate and unsettle traumatised witnesses.[20] The child witness might also experience the phenomenon of 'anticipatory stress',[21] meaning they will suffer varying degrees of anxiety while awaiting the trial, leading to a worsening of any existing trauma symptoms, particularly if there are lengthy delays and long waiting periods. On the day of trial, this anxiety may be further exacerbated if the architecture of the courthouse means they will see the defendant outside or in the public waiting areas.[22]

For the CSA complainant, engagement in the adversarial trial process is fraught with danger due to the inherent power imbalance between the individual and court authorities. Testifying may be accompanied by a range of triggers that resurrect the

18 See review in Quas and Goodman (n 17).

19 Samantha J Andrews and Michael E Lamb, 'The Structural Linguistic Complexity of Lawyers' Questions and Children's Responses in Scottish Criminal Courts' (2017) 65 *Child Abuse & Neglect* 182; Samantha J Andrews, Michael E Lamb and Thomas D Lyon, 'Question Types, Responsiveness and Self-Contradictions When Prosecutors and Defense Attorneys Question Alleged Victims of Child Sexual Abuse' (2015) 29(2) *Applied Cognitive Psychology* 253; Ali Behzadnia and Mehdi B Mehrani, 'Young Children's Yes Bias in Response to Tag Questions' (2018) 188(12) *Early Child Development and Care* 1663; Kyndra C Cleveland, Jodi A Quas and Thomas D Lyon, 'Valence, Implicated Actor, and Children's Acquiescence to False Suggestions' (2016) 43 *Journal of Applied Development Psychology* 1; J Zoe Klemfuss, Jodi A Quas and Thomas D Lyon, 'Attorneys' Questions and Children's Productivity in Child Sexual Abuse Criminal Trials' (2014) 28(5) *Applied Cognitive Psychology* 780; Rachel Zajac, Sarah O'Neill and Harlene Hayne, 'Disorder in the Courtroom? Child Witnesses under Cross-Examination' (2012) 32(3) *Developmental Review* 181.

20 Emma Rowden, 'As Instalções à Distância Para Crianças e Testemunhas Vulneráveis: Novas Perspectivas a Propósito De Uma Tipologia Especial Emergente' in Patrícia Brancos (ed) *Sociologia do(s) Espaço(s) da Justiça: Diálogos Interdisciplinares* (CES/Almedina, 2013) [translated title: The Remote Witness Facility for Vulnerable and Child Witnesses: New Perspectives on an Emerging Spatial Typology] ('As Instalções à Distância Para Crianças e Testemunhas Vulneráveis').

21 Sherry D Grogan and Kathleen Pace Murphy, 'Anticipatory Stress Response in PTSD: Extreme Stress in Children (2011) 24(1) *Journal of Child & Adolescent Psychiatric Nursing* 58.

22 Rowden, 'As Instalções à Distância Para Crianças e Testemunhas Vulneráveis' (n 20).

intensity of emotions surrounding the original trauma. These include the alien courtroom environment peopled by strangers – the '*eyes of the courtroom*' upon them – and the impact of the paralysing gaze of the defendant,[23] as well as being questioned, harassed, or intimidated by legal counsel. Delays, adjournments, repeated continuances, and appeals can mean that children remain in a state of high anxiety for sustained periods of time. If this is coupled with the absence of a supportive caregiver, a large number of interviews, or acquittal of the defendant, these factors can be further linked to a 'poorer mental state following legal involvement'.[24]

The adversarial system can also re-trigger the feelings of powerlessness that characterised the original trauma. The criminal trial does not provide for a collaborative relationship with witnesses but a coercive one, whereby witnesses are *required* to attend court to give evidence and are subject to the rules of court with no decision-making capacity other than to participate or withdraw from the process. If a child gives evidence, they must comply with court rules and procedures, no matter how damaging to their psychological health. This creates a culture of power/powerlessness which is antithetical to the basic principles of TIC (discussed below), and is reminiscent of the original dynamic between victim and abuser.

If the child's trauma symptoms remain unaddressed, they are likely to interfere with their ability to fully engage with the requirements of the legal process,[25] as well as exacerbate their symptoms and prolong or prohibit the recovery process. Children who choose to face the ordeal of the trial process will be subject to the gruelling conditions of indefinite cross-examination, as well as the well-documented cross-examination effect, that is, the phenomenon whereby children agree with propositions put to them by the cross-examiner, thereby contradicting their original, truthful evidence.[26] Paradoxically, the involuntary symptoms of trauma are often exploited by defence counsel and misinterpreted by the fact-finder as evidence of lack of veracity. If a child 'cannot control her dissociative symptoms in the face of multiple triggers',[27] such as the types of questions used in cross-examination to exploit children's developmental vulnerability,[28] this may

23 Ibid.

24 Quas and Goodman (n 17) 403.

25 Denise E Elliott et al., 'Trauma-Informed or Trauma-Denied: Principles and Implementation of Trauma-Informed Services for Women' (2005) 33(4) *Journal of Community Psychology* 461.

26 Caroline Bettenay et al., 'Cross-Examination: The Testimony of Children with and without Intellectual Disabilities' (2014) 28(2) *Applied Cognitive Psychology* 204; Saskia Righarts et al., 'Young Children's Responses to Cross-Examination Style Questioning: The Effects of Delay and Subsequent Questioning' (2015) 21(3) *Psychology, Crime & Law* 274; Zajac, O'Neill and Hayne (n 19).

27 Niki A Miller and Lisa M Najavits, 'Creating Trauma-Informed Correctional Care: A Balance of Goals and Environment' (2012) 3(1) *European Journal of Psychotraumatology* 17246/1, 17246/2.

28 Anne Cossins, 'Cross-Examination in Child Sexual Assault Trials: Evidentiary Safeguard or an Opportunity to Confuse?' (2009) 33(1) *Melbourne University Law Review* 68 ('Cross-Examination in Child Sexual Assault Trials').

mean that a child dissociates or freezes, appears 'spaced-out', becomes defiant, jumpy, or fidgety, exhibits dramatic mood changes, refuses to answer questions, agrees with the (perceived) wishes of the examiner, or adopts 'regressive [soothing] behaviours'.[29]

These behaviours can lead to inconsistencies in evidence, confusion, retraction of evidence, misinterpretation of questions, and/or agreement with misunderstood questions, all of which is likely to have a negative impact on credibility assessments of the child by fact-finders.[30] A recent British case study confirms the above experiences, with children reporting that they were under 'extreme pressure to remember events accurately' and that defence questions were 'repetitive, rapid, confusing, and focused on secondary content rather than the central criminal acts'.[31]

Although testifying can be beneficial in certain circumstances, overall, empirical studies reveal that giving evidence in court is harmful to children's mental health.[32] Thus, we need to ask the question: how are fact-finders likely to interpret the type of evidence and emotions that are elicited through a process that re-traumatises the child witness? The fact that it is unlikely that a child will be able to give their best evidence when they cannot regulate the effects of trauma,[33] coupled with the potential acute stress involved in giving evidence, means it is necessary to ask: should children testify in court at all if steps cannot be taken to reduce the potential for re-traumatisation?

Policymakers need to ask whether more might be done to tackle the conditions that prevent children from giving their best evidence, so that fact-finders are not relying on less than best evidence to reach a verdict. The remainder of the chapter explores the role of court-house design, guided by TIC principles, in addressing some of these issues.

29 'Trauma: What Child Welfare Attorneys Should Know', *The National Traumatic Stress Network* (Guide, 2017) 10 <https://www.nctsn.org/resources/trauma-what-child-welfare-attorneys-should-know>; see also van der Kolk, *The Body Keeps the Score* (n 11).

30 Judy Cashmore and Lily Trimboli, *An Evaluation of the NSW Child Sexual Assault Specialist Jurisdiction* (NSW Bureau of Crime Statistics and Research, 2005).

31 Elizabeth Ahern, Marlene Kowalski and Michael E Lamb, 'A Case Study Perspective: The Experiences of Young Persons Testifying to Child Sexual Exploitation in British Criminal Court' (2018) 27(3) *Journal of Child Sexual Abuse* 321, 321.

32 See review in Quas and Goodman (n 17).

33 Sarah Miragoli, Rossella Procaccia and Paola Di Blasio, 'Language Use and PTSD Symptoms: Content Analyses of Allegations of Child Sexual Abuse' (2014) 14(5) *Journal of Forensic Psychology Practice* 355; Sarah Miragoli, Elena Camisasca and Paola Di Blasio, 'The Narrative Fragmentation in Child Sexual Abuse: The Role of Age and Posttraumatic Stress Disorder' (2017) 73 *Child Abuse Neglect* 106 ('The Narrative Fragmentation in Child Sexual Abuse'); Sarah Miragoli, Elena Camisasca and Paola Di Blasio, 'Investigating Linguistic Coherence Relations in Child Sexual Abuse: A Comparison of PTSD and Non-PTSD Children' (2019) 5(2) *Heliyon* e01163 ('Investigating Linguistic Coherence Relations in Child Sexual Abuse').

What is TIC and how is it relevant to the adversarial criminal trial?

This section will outline the principles of TIC to envisage a trauma-informed court environment to facilitate the goals of doing no further harm and the achievement of best evidence. We argue that there is a need for a trauma-informed approach to the CSA trial because of the ways in which the criminal trial currently reinforces the imbalances of power that exist between court personnel and vulnerable witnesses. A systems approach that is influenced by the principles of TIC involves the identification of a client's trauma-induced symptoms along with sensitively conceived spaces and processes that are designed to minimise their re-experiences of these symptoms. This 'do no harm' approach requires training of all organisational staff about the institutional behaviours and processes that mimic the dynamics likely to trigger re-traumatisation. Designers also need to be aware of how institutional environments can trigger trauma symptoms.[34] Such an approach 'perceives trauma not simply as a past event but as a formative one' that continues to contribute to a client's emotional state and coping strategies'.[35]

Harris and Fallot[36] are credited with clarifying 'the conceptualization of trauma-informed care'[37] which is underpinned by three core pillars – safety, healing relationships, and self-management of emotions.[38] These core pillars underpin the ten principles that should guide the delivery of trauma-informed services as set out in Table 6.1.[39]

These ten principles have been developed in the field of mental health services, but are they suitable in a criminal justice context? The first principle recognises that trauma victims may have difficulty regulating their emotions, with their coping strategies developed as adaptations to traumatic events.[40]

A trauma-informed legal system would institute measures that reflect the impact of CSA on children's ability to participate in the legal process. While recovery from trauma (second principle) cannot be a goal of the CJS, employment of an empowerment model (third principle) and maximisation of client choice (fourth principle) would assist in counteracting experiences of

34 Amos Rapoport, *The Meaning of the Built Environment: A Nonverbal Communication Approach* (Sage Publications, 1982).

35 Lisa D Butler, Filomena M Critelli and Elaine S Rinfrette, 'Trauma-Informed Care and Mental Health' (2011) 31 *Directions in Psychiatry* 177, 178.

36 Maxine Harris and Roger D Fallot, 'Envisioning a Trauma-Informed Service System: A Vital Paradigm Shift' (2001) 89 *New Directions for Mental Health Services* 3.

37 Butler, Critelli and Rinfrette (n 35) 180.

38 Bath (n 9) 18.

39 Taken from Elliott et al. (n 25).

40 Anke Ehlers and David M Clark, 'A Cognitive Model of Posttraumatic Stress Disorder' (2000) 38(4) *Behaviour and Research Therapy* 319; Elliott et al. (n 25); van der Kolk, *The Body Keeps the Score* (n 11).

TABLE 6.1 The ten principles of trauma-informed services

1. Recognise the long-term impact of violence and victimisation on development and coping strategies (*)
2. Make recovery from trauma the primary goal
3. Employ an empowerment model (*)
4. Maximise a client's choices and control over recovery from trauma
5. Create a therapeutic relationship that is collaborative, empowering, and safe
6. Create an environment that provides safety, respect, and acceptance (*)
7. Emphasise a client's strengths
8. Minimise re-traumatisation (*)
9. Culturally competent (*)
10. Solicit consumer input in designing and evaluating services

Notes: (*) represents the principles we see as relevant to the implementation of TIC in the context of the criminal adversarial trial, i.e. those that are applicable to 'trauma-informed' services, rather than only 'trauma-specific' services. Trauma-*specific* services are 'those whose primary task is to address the impact of trauma and to facilitate trauma recovery', while trauma-*informed* services include organisations that have 'incorporated an understanding of trauma, including its consequences and the conditions that enhance healing, in all aspects of service delivery' (Roger D Fallot and Maxine Harris, 'Trauma-Informed Approaches to Systems to Care' (2008) 3(1) *Trauma Psychology* Newsletter 6, 6).

powerlessness, fear, and helplessness associated with authority and control, thus 'flatten[ing] the hierarchy' and building on clients' strengths rather than their weaknesses, and creating empowering and safe relationships which are non-shaming and non-blaming.[41] The sixth principle is about creating emotional, social, cultural and physical environments that provide safety, respect and acceptance. Thus, physical settings, like court environments, need to be welcoming and safe spaces for trauma survivors to avoid triggering re-traumatisation (eighth principle) which, in the trial context, would promote best evidence. In particular, a child's trauma symptoms should not be used as evidence of their unreliability as a witness. As well, a child's needs and abilities need to be understood in light of their cultural background (ninth principle) in order to create 'cultural safety'.[42]

Fallot and Harris have distilled the 'five core principles' of a TIC approach as: 'safety, trustworthiness, choice, collaboration, and empowerment',[43] to which, we argue, 'recognition' and 'cultural competence' can be added. The triggers embedded in the physical, social, and cultural environment of the adversarial trial result in a lack of emotional safety for victims, as illustrated by Figure 6.1, although they could be ameliorated by a trauma-informed system approach.

41 Elliott et al. (n 25).

42 Elaine Papps and Irihapetti Ramsden, 'Cultural Safety in Nursing: The New Zealand Experience' (1996) 8(5) *International Journal for Quality in Health Care* 491.

43 Fallot and Harris (n 36) 6.

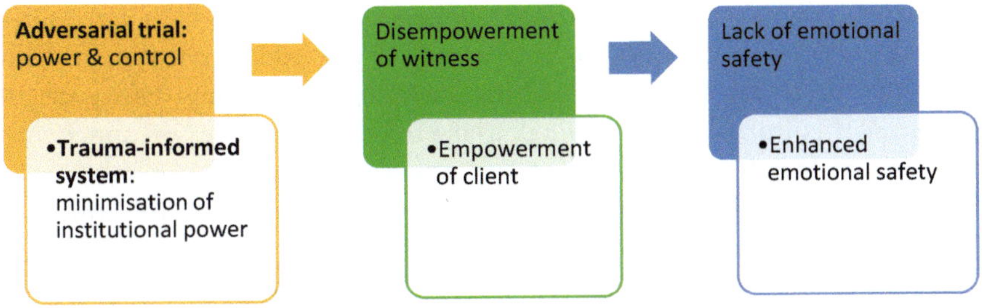

FIGURE 6.1 Comparison of the adversarial trial and a trauma-informed system.

How can TIC principles improve the adversarial system for child victims of sexual assault?

Arguably, there is a need for trauma-informed services within the criminal trial, not for the purposes of dealing with the mental health needs of children, but to allow them to give their best evidence without further re-traumatisation. In other words, the criminal trial provides best evidence to fact-finders when a witness's memory works at its optimum level of recall, something that is impeded when the emotional memories of the original trauma are re-triggered. Since the goals of the criminal trial are entirely different from those of organisations that provide trauma-specific services, it is better to conceive of the criminal trial as engaging in a series of interactions with witnesses and defendants who are subject to the coercive powers of the court. The principles underpinning the evolution of the contemporary criminal trial can be understood within a public order framework which, in turn, is underpinned by the governmental power of the state. However, that power is ameliorated through the fair trial principle (to prevent wrongful convictions) which in recent years has been extended to cover witnesses, notably sexual assault complainants whose unfair treatment has been well-documented.[44]

While recovery from trauma is not a goal of the criminal trial, which only requires the presence of witnesses for short periods of time, it is essential to address the re-traumatising features of the adversarial system in order to ensure a fair trial from victim and community perspectives. A vulnerable child's encounter with the justice system, albeit brief, is likely to have a long-lasting impact on their mental health because of the phenomenon of re-traumatisation. As discussed earlier, compared to the general population, CSA survivors face a greater lifetime risk of developing a range of mental health issues and behavioural disorders, including major depression, anxiety disorder, PTSD, anti-social personality

44 Cossins, 'Cross-Examination in Child Sexual Assault Trials' (n 28); Cossins, *Alternative Models for Prosecuting Child Sex Offences in Australia* (n 4).

disorder, addictions to alcohol and/or drugs, eating disorders, suicidal ideation and suicide attempts.[45] We also acknowledge that there may be certain limits to how far TIC principles can be implemented in an adversarial system which is designed to reveal the inconsistencies in witness testimony. However, the authoritarian culture of the criminal trial produces a number of unnecessary triggers for vulnerable witnesses.

We contend that the ideal forum for the introduction of trauma-informed services is through the use of 'remote witness facilities', such as those used throughout Australia and many other jurisdictions around the world. These spaces find their genesis in the idea of a purpose-built 'child-courtroom' as originally proposed by David Libai in the late 1960s. In this model, the courtroom is divided into a 'judge's room', containing the child, the judge, and the prosecutor, the defence counsel, and the child examiner, which separates them from the accused, the jury, and public, who are located in an adjacent room connected to the proceedings by way of electronics and one-way glass.[46]

However, this alternative method of giving evidence in court is not enough, and its benefits may be readily undermined by other influences. In order to move to a trauma-informed system, training of all personnel (such as judges, lawyers, witness assistance service providers, and other court staff) who have contact or interactions with traumatised victims would be required, with the aim of ensuring the physical and psychological wellbeing of child complainants and avoiding administrative and legal practices that could result in re-traumatisation.

45 Laura P Chen et al., 'Sexual Abuse and Lifetime Diagnosis of Psychiatric Disorders: Systematic Review and Meta-Analysis' (2010) 85(7) *Mayo Clinic Proceedings* 618; David M Fergusson, Joseph M Boden and L John Horwood, 'Exposure to Childhood Sexual and Physical Abuse and Adjustment in Early Adulthood' (2008) 32(6) *Child Abuse & Neglect* 607; David M Fergusson, Geraldine F H McLeod and L John Horwood, 'Childhood Sexual Abuse and Adult Developmental Outcomes: Findings from a 30-Year Longitudinal Study in New Zealand' (2013) 37(9) *Child Abuse & Neglect* 664; Tanja Hillberg, Catherine Hamilton-Giachritsis and Louise Dixon, 'Review of Meta-Analyses on the Association between Child Sexual Abuse and Adult Mental Health Difficulties: A Systematic Approach' (2011) 12(1) *Trauma, Violence & Abuse* 38; Roberto Maniglio, 'The Impact of Child Sexual Abuse on Health: A Systematic Review of Reviews' (2009) 29(7) *Clinical Psychology Review* 647 ('The Impact of Child Sexual Abuse on Health'); Roberto Maniglio, 'Child Sexual Abuse in the Etiology of Anxiety Disorders: A Systematic Review of Reviews' (2013) 14(2) *Trauma, Violence, & Abuse* 96 ('Child Sexual Abuse in the Etiology of Anxiety Disorders'); Debra Rose Wilson, 'Health Consequences of Childhood Sexual Abuse (2010) 46(1) *Perspectives in Psychiatric Care* 56.

46 See further David Libai, 'The Protection of the Child Victim of a Sexual Offense in the Criminal Justice System' (1968–69) 15 *Wayne Law Review* 997, 1016; Natalie Taylor and Jacqueline Joudo, *The Impact of Pre-Recorded Video and Closed Circuit Television Testimony by Adult Sexual Assault Complainants on Jury Decision-Making: An Experimental Study* (Research Report Series No. 68, 2005); Emma Louise Rowden, 'Remote Participation and the Distributed Court: An Approach to Court Architecture in the Age of Video-Mediated Communications' (PhD thesis, The University of Melbourne, 2011)('Remote Participation and the Distributed Court'); Emma Rowden, 'As Instalções à Distância Para Crianças e Testemunhas Vulneráveis' (n 20).

If court personnel do not fully understand the features of the design of remote witness facilities that contribute to protecting complainants from re-traumatisation, these benefits might be lost in the future. While there have been some limited attempts towards this in some jurisdictions,[47] we elaborate on how these spaces, mechanisms, and processes might be improved by a closer alignment with TIC principles.

While not explicitly framed around the principles of TIC, it is clear that the current raft of measures to improve the experience of giving evidence for vulnerable and child witnesses are already compatible with the aims and objectives of trauma-informed service provision. There are several important features of the design of many remote witness facilities (RWFs) that enable vulnerable witnesses to more easily give their evidence.[48] Their success can certainly be explained by reference to TIC principles precisely because they invert some of the power-dynamics intrinsic to the adversarial system and shield a child from the more overt social and behavioural cues[49] of the courthouse environment. By design, therefore, they allow for adequate separation from the intimidating physical and social environment of the courtroom in addition to avoiding exposure to the defendant and their supporters, all of which are potential trauma-triggers.

The following analysis of RWFs is based upon the work of the second author,[50] whose research between 2008 and 2010 with others on the Gateways to Justice project involved conducting site visits at over 40 courthouses and 20 remote witness facility sites in Western Australia and Victoria in order to better understand what the remote experience is like both from the point of view of those in the courtroom and for those in the remote space. The opinions of over 50 stakeholders were sought through semi-structured interviews with judges, magistrates, lawyers, court staff, expert witnesses, and remote court officers who sit in with vulnerable witnesses, child witnesses, or defendants as well as court

47 The concept of TIC is not new to the legal system. Legal professionals who work with children and youth in the United States (US) child welfare and juvenile justice systems are becoming more aware of the negative effects of trauma and trauma-informed practices in order to achieve optimum representation through the lawyer–client relationship. For further examples from the US, see Karen A Reitman, 'Attorneys for Children Guide to Interviewing Clients: Integrating Trauma Informed Care and Solution Focused Strategies', *Publications* (Guide, 2011) <http://www.nycourts. gov/ip/cwcip/Publications/attorneyGuide.pdf>; Laurie A Drabble, Shelby Jones and Vivian Brown, 'Advancing Trauma-Informed Systems Change in a Family Drug Treatment Court Context' (2013) 13(1) *Journal of Social Work Practice in the Addictions* 91; American Bar Association (n 7).

48 See further Rowden, 'Remote Participation and the Distributed Court (n 46); Rowden, 'As Instalções à Distância Para Crianças e Testemunhas Vulneráveis' (n 20); Emma Rowden et al., *Gateways to Justice: Improving Video-Mediated Communications for Justice Participants – Design and Operational Guidelines for Remote Participation in Court Proceedings* (Research Report, 2013) ('*Gateways to Justice*').

49 Rapoport (n 34).

50 Rowden, 'Remote Participation and the Distributed Court' (n 46); Rowden, 'As Instalções à Distância Para Crianças e Testemunhas Vulneráveis' (n 20).

administrators and architects who had some experience in designing and overseeing the construction of RWFs.[51]

Trauma-informed spaces: The provision of safe spaces via remote witness facilities

One of the key features of RWFs is that they provide a safe and separate space away from the defendant and their supporters. RWFs are generally located in either a separate building, in a secure section of the court building with a separate entrance, or as a single room off a main public corridor with no separate access.[52] The fact that the RWF affords a sense of distance, or 'remoteness' to the public court environment was precisely the reason that enabled vulnerable witnesses to give evidence according to several stakeholders who were interviewed. Creating a safe space at the same time as 'flattening the hierarchy' for vulnerable witnesses means that the RWF performs certain shielding and protective functions that are difficult, if not impossible, to achieve in the courtroom. Children see the remote room and restricted areas that surround it as a 'safe place', because of the trained staff and its restricted access.

This point was underlined by the discrepancies in the facilities provided in different courthouses. In some regional areas, RWFs were simply a room off the main hallway in the courthouse which did not provide sufficient separation from the courthouse environment. The need for other 'breakout' spaces (toilets and kitchenettes) within the RWF was a recurring theme in interviews with remote court officers, as it allowed them to have better control over who had contact with the vulnerable witness. It also allowed a child who was struggling to give evidence to have a break without the risk of coming into contact with the defendant and their supporters. Remote court officers preferred this type of supportive environment with buffer zones since if a distressed child flees a less secure remote room, they are less likely to return.[53] In an RWF with sufficient separation from the courtroom and public waiting areas, a child can safely regroup and be assisted with different options for continuing their evidence.

51 Interviews and site visits were conducted primarily with Anne Wallace. The Gateways to Justice project was led by Professor David Tait and funded by an ARC Linkage Grant (LP 0776248). For further information about the project and its methods, see Rowden et al., *Gateways to Justice* (n 48); Rowden, 'Remote Participation and the Distributed Court (n 46); Rowden, 'As Instalções à Distância Para Crianças e Testemunhas Vulneráveis (n 20); Emma Rowden, 'Distributed Courts and Legitimacy: What Do We Lose When We Lose the Courthouse?' (2018) 14(2) *Law, Culture and the Humanities* 263 ('Distributed Courts and Legitimacy').

52 In some remote and regional areas, the only available location is a room within a police station, which is less than ideal. See further Rowden, 'Remote Participation and the Distributed Court' (n 46). In more recent designs, the remote witness room may also be attached to a private and secure area that includes a waiting area and separate amenities such as bathroom and kitchenette facilities, with or without natural light.

53 Rowden, 'Remote Participation and the Distributed Court' (n 46).

As such, remote court officers advocated that successful RWFs required careful planning of the remote room itself and its adjacent spaces which should contain self-contained waiting areas, kitchen facilities, and bathrooms, all of which require secure entry, are not publicly accessible, and can comfortably accommodate child witnesses, their family, and other supporters. These spaces should be stocked with toys and games, as well as teaching aids such as small-scale models of a courtroom, and wigs and gowns for children to try on in order to familiarise themselves with the courtroom.

The more domestically scaled remote witness room can also provide a very different physical setting for the CSA complainant than what is possible in the courtroom which is linked via CCTV or teleconferencing.[54] The significance of the difference in scale, décor, and materiality of the remote witness room, as opposed to the courthouse should not be underestimated. Human behaviour is influenced not only by spatial structure but by room size, shape, as well as architectural materials, features, furnishings, and finishes.[55] In this sense, the environment is a form of nonverbal communication whose messages may or may not be heard, depending on the 'motivations, judgments and culture' of those on the receiving end.[56]

Movement through the sequence of courthouse spaces is designed to prepare court participants for the seriousness of the trial, including appropriate behaviour. According to Rock, these sequences prepare an individual for their forthcoming experience where they must 'quit the everyday world'.[57] Thus, there is a concern that by removing the child witness from the courtroom environment, they are being robbed not only of the mental time to prepare for the trial but also of the environmental behavioural cues that communicate the seriousness of the trial and what the child's appropriate social response should be.[58] However, empirical research into the use of RWFs suggests otherwise.

Despite some concerns being raised by stakeholders in the Gateways to Justice study that there was a mismatch between the design of the courtroom and the design of the RWFs, remote court officers (those closest to child witnesses) were adamant that regardless of these different environments, children were very aware of the '*seriousness*' of their court appearance, whilst benefitting from being shielded from the experience of being 'in court'.[59]

54 The video link equipment in most RWFs is either placed on a movable trolley or built in, and the design brief for the room generally results in a size ranging anywhere from 8 to 15 square metres. Ceiling heights are usually under 3 metres, compared to those of courtrooms, which are generally loftier and taller. See Rowden, 'Remote Participation and the Distributed Court' (n 46); Rowden, 'As Instalções à Distância Para Crianças e Testemunhas Vulneráveis' (n 20).

55 See Rowden, 'Remote Participation and the Distributed Court' (n 46); Rowden, 'Distributed Courts and Legitimacy' (n 51).

56 Charles T Goodsell, *The Social Meaning of Civic Space: Studying Political Authority through Architecture* (University Press of Kansas, 1988) 46.

57 Paul Elliott Rock, *The Social World of an English Crown Court* (Clarendon Press, 1993) 201.

58 Rapoport (n 34).

59 See Rowden, 'Remote Participation and the Distributed Court' (n 46); Rowden, 'As Instalções à Distância Para Crianças e Testemunhas Vulneráveis' (n 20).

A further benefit of an appropriately designed RWF is that it limits the impact of the gaze of the defendant and others in the courtroom on the child: '*they haven't got the fear of walking into a courtroom and a whole pile of eyes looking at them … So basically it can stop them panicking*'.[60] Indeed, it is the very removal of the child from the formality of the courtroom environment that allows a child to focus on the questions being asked of them, thus enhancing their ability to give their best evidence.

Finally, the removal of a child complainant from the public *civic* environment into a more *domestically* scaled space is, arguably, more sympathetic to the types of graphic, sexual information that a child is required to provide as evidence in a CSA trial. In his discussion of what constitutes a civic environment, Goodsell notes that civic space has four key qualities: it is state-owned, publicly accessible, ceremonial, and enclosed. Features that define the characteristics of 'ceremonial' civic spaces are that they are large in scale, impressive in design, and have a material quality that is expressive of their civic value.[61]

The very personal nature of a child complainant's evidence is at odds with the social distances in the courtroom over which evidence is usually imparted.[62] Speaking about sexually abusive experiences potentially exposes a child to re-traumatisation as they describe events which may involve extreme boundary violations, betrayal, powerlessness, fear, terror, and/or humiliation.

The more intimate arrangement enabled by the use of video links and close-up shots may also account for the success of the RWFs for obtaining evidence, particularly in cases of a sexual nature. Here the child sees a face and upper torso of each speaker on two screens (or two persons on one screen if videoconferencing is used), as opposed to being a small person in a large and overwhelming public space talking to others at a distance. According to Hall's theory of proxemics, an Anglo-American sensibility of space dictates that personal information is most comfortably disclosed at distances below 0.9 metres,[63] although the comfort of that distance will vary across different cultures. This stands in stark contrast to the normal spatial distances between participants in a courtroom, where personal information is disclosed over large distances that are more likely to be associated with non-personal information shared across 'public space'.[64] Apart from

60 I004WAR, reported in Rowden, 'Remote Participation and the Distributed Court' (n 46); Rowden, 'As Instalções à Distância Para Crianças e Testemunhas Vulneráveis' (n 20).

61 Goodsell (n 56).

62 Amanda Konradi, 'Pulling Strings Doesn't Work in Court: Moving beyond Puppetry in the Relationship between Prosecutors and Rape Survivors' (2001) 10(1) *Journal of Social Distress and the Homeless* 5; Joyce Plotnikoff and Richard Woolfson, *In Their Own Words: The Experiences of 50 Young Witnesses in Criminal Proceedings* (National Society for the Prevention of Cruelty to Children (NSPCC), 2004); Rowden, 'As Instalções à Distância Para Crianças e Testemunhas Vulneráveis' (n 20).

63 Edward Twitchell Hall, *The Silent Language* (Anchor Books, 1959) 179.

64 Edward Twitchell Hall, *The Hidden Dimension: Man's Use of Space in Public and Private* (The Bodley Head, 1966).

shielding the child from the public areas of the courtroom, the close distance between the child's chair and the TV screens also helps to replicate the personal and intimate distances associated with the sharing of personal information.

The fact that there is now a presumption in favour of the use of RWFs in most Australian jurisdictions for sexual assault complainants gives some indication of its growing acceptance as a preferred way of obtaining evidence from children.[65] Because RWFs are perceived to be 'less hostile' than the courtroom environment,[66] they may be a vehicle for promoting trauma-informed services. While there is a need for further research to ensure that the principles of TIC can be fully realised in the design of RWFs, significant improvements in this type of facility have already taken place and a gradual awareness of the importance of architectural design to the experience for the remote witness is evident.[67]

More recently, the RWFs at Coffs Harbour Courthouse in Australia (designed according to the 'Gateways to Justice' best practice guidelines),[68] have been subsequently remodelled to include more than one secure entrance in order to address the staff feedback that vulnerable victims always need to know that they have several escape options.[69]

The potential of such design improvements also points to the need for researchers and designers to be ever vigilant of the ways in which courtroom environments may be either supportive of, or hinder vulnerable witnesses' ability to access justice.

Trauma-informed processes: Educating the legal profession and court personnel about identifying and mitigating trauma symptoms

Arguably, the design of dedicated RWFs ought to be done in light of TIC principles, since RWFs will work optimally if the personnel within them are trained

65 See, for instance, *Criminal Procedure Act 1986* (NSW) s 294B-C; *Criminal Procedure Act 2009* (Vic) ss 369, 372(1)(d); *Evidence Act 1977* (Qld) s21AB(a).

66 Graham M Davies and Elizabeth Noon, *An Evaluation of the Live Link for Child Witnesses* (Home Office, 1991) 84.

67 This has come from a position of relatively low priority. For instance, it is significant that the first study of the introduction of an RWF in Australia, by Cashmore and Trimboli (n 30), there was a lack of critical analysis of the differences between the environmental conditions of the remote spaces under scrutiny. Furthermore, early concerns about the generally poor design of video link facilities were evident in research from the United Kingdom (UK), which included such criticisms as the confined nature of the space, poor room temperature, poor décor, uncomfortable chairs, poor soundproofing and proximity to toilets, with the most common phrase used by witnesses to describe what they found being 'the TV link room was like a cupboard'; see Plotnikoff and Woolfson (n 62) 38.

68 See Rowden et al., *Gateways to Justice* (n 48).

69 See further Emma Rowden and Diane Jones, 'Design, Dignity and Due Process: The Construction of the Coffs Harbour Courthouse' (2018) 14(2) *Law, Culture and the Humanities* 317.

in these principles. In fact, the introduction of TIC principles into the CJS would require the training of all court personnel about the effects of trauma on abused children, particularly remote court officers who are in direct contact with child complainants.

Generally, those who routinely work within the criminal justice system have a limited understanding of the pervasive 'sensory and environmental trauma triggers'[70] that can pose a threat to a child's mental stability and their ability to give evidence, as well as having few processes to prevent re-traumatisation. Legal personnel will not have the qualifications or resources to diagnose those suffering from PTSD and other mental illnesses so best practice would suggest that all complainants of CSA be treated as trauma survivors,[71] which is consistent with the fact that child complainants of CSA are considered to be vulnerable witnesses in Australian courts.

Common procedures and practices should be introduced that are non-traumatising in order to do no harm, which is also the aim of the design of RWFs.[72] In order to understand the ramifications of trauma on the human brain, court personnel need to be adequately trained about trauma symptoms and their impact on a child's ability to give evidence, how to avoid re-traumatisation, and how to manage the situation when a child is triggered, something that is still possible within a well-designed RWF. This might result in the elimination of some of the more aggressive lawyerly practices that 'most consumers, trauma survivors or not, find frightening and demeaning',[73] particularly cross-examination techniques that exploit the effects of trauma to undermine the reliability of a child's evidence, thus influencing a jury's perceptions of the child's credibility.[74]

The creation of an atmosphere in court that fosters safety, respect, and acceptance is also necessary because the original trauma of CSA occurred in an unsafe environment. As discussed earlier, because the courtroom is configured to represent the authority of the state over defendants and witnesses, a safe court environment would require appropriate trauma-informed behaviour by all legal

70 Miller and Najavits (n 27) 17246/1.

71 Elliott et al. (n 25).

72 For instance, lawyers routinely use leading and suggestive questions, despite the fact that they are the most unreliable method of eliciting information from children – Cossins, 'Cross-Examination in Child Sexual Assault Trials (n 28) 81; see also Michael E Lamb et al., *Tell Me What Happened: Structured Investigative Interviews of Child Victims and Witnesses* (Wiley-Blackwell, 2008); Michael E Lamb and Angèle Fouchier, 'The Effects of Question Type on Self-contradictions by Children in the Course of Forensic Interviews' (2001) 15(5) *Applied Cognitive Psychology* 483; Martine Powell et al., *An Evaluation of How Evidence is Elicited from Complainants of Child Sexual Abuse* (Report for the Royal Commission into Institutional Responses to Child Sexual Abuse, August 2016). While protections against improper questions do exist in some jurisdictions, both empirical and anecdotal evidence shows that these protections are infrequently used by judges (American Bar Association (n 7)); Cashmore and Trimboli (n 30); Cossins, 'Cross-Examination in Child Sexual Assault Trials (n 28).

73 Harris and Fallot (n 36) 10.

74 Cossins, 'Cross-Examination in Child Sexual Assault Trials' (n 28).

personnel along with procedures to protect a complainant from re-traumatisation before and during their evidence in order to equalise relations between complainants and court personnel, and to create emotionally safe interactions with complainants, as RWFs are designed to do. In other words, both court design and the training of court personnel need to be complementary in order remove as many potential triggers as possible for traumatised witnesses.

The issue of safety also arises when considering how the criminal trial emphasises a witness's weaknesses rather than their strengths through the use of humiliating, confusing, and/or hostile forms of cross-examination, something that can still occur despite specially designed RWFs. Thus, the trial process fosters the belief that any degree of confusion, inconsistencies in evidence, and/or gaps in memory can be used as measures of veracity and credibility rather than being understood as the possible symptoms of trauma. Indeed, some CSA complainants will have engaged in risky and self-destructive behaviours after being sexually abused which can also be used by defence counsel to undermine their credibility. However, trauma-informed perspectives view such risky behaviours as coping mechanisms to deal with the effects of trauma.[75]

Both trauma-informed services and systems should seek to be culturally competent, where a person's problems are best understood with respect to their cultural background. However, the criminal trial, traditionally, has no mandated mechanisms for implementing cultural competence. In order to achieve that, as well as oversee cultural change, other court personnel may be required in the shift of a criminal trial towards a trauma-informed system. For example, an innovation in the UK (recently adopted in New South Wales (NSW)) is the use of intermediaries. Vulnerable witnesses, as defined under section 16 of the *Youth Justice and Criminal Evidence Act 1999* (UK), are eligible for assistance from an intermediary who is a trained and registered 'communication specialist whose primary responsibility is to enable complete, coherent and accurate communication' on the part of the vulnerable witness by advising the judicial officer about the witness's communications vulnerabilities and needs, as well as intervening during questioning to 'prevent miscommunication'.[76]

In a trauma-informed system, intermediaries would need to be mandated because it is unlikely that any child or adolescent will have the developmental and language sophistication of judges and lawyers. If intermediaries were compulsory for children giving evidence in CSA trials, they could also assist a court in becoming more culturally competent in relation to children from non-English speaking backgrounds, as well as children from various ethnic and racial backgrounds. Within a trauma-informed system, a wider role for intermediaries

75 Lisa M Najavits, Roger D Weiss and Sarah R Shaw, 'The Link between Substance Abuse and Posttraumatic Stress Disorder in Women' (1997) 6(4) *The American Journal on Addictions* 273.

76 Judicial College, *Equal Treatment Bench Book* (2013–2015) 5–11 <www.judiciary.gov.uk/wp-content/uploads/2013/11/equal-treatment-bench-book-2013-with-2015-amendment.pdf>.

could be envisaged in order to remove the power differential between examiner and complainant. This might mean the intermediary being an advocate for protecting the complainant from abusive questioning strategies or the intermediary becoming the examiner, as is the case in Norway.[77]

While this chapter has focused on the ways in which the trial has traditionally imposed power imbalances between court personnel and witnesses through the lack of appropriately trained personnel and authoritarian court architecture, it should be noted that any adjustments to the design of courtrooms, courthouses and their associated spaces should be mindful of the need to respect the rights of the defendant, and how the court environment can impinge upon those rights.[78]

Conclusions

Despite recent reforms designed to improve the court experience for sexual assault complainants, such as the use of CCTV for giving evidence or pre-recorded evidence,[79] the criminal trial has limited means or imagination for dealing with a child suffering from trauma symptoms who is required to give evidence about being sexually abused. Although support persons are available in most Australian jurisdictions when children testify, courts do not, generally, employ therapists who can provide psychological support to the complainant before, during, or after giving evidence. While children may be able to give their evidence via CCTV from an RWF, thus providing an emotionally safer place, the possibility of re-traumatisation is likely due to the conduct of legal personnel.

Because of the possible triggers that presently exist within the CSA trial, RWFs ought to be carefully designed in conjunction with those who understand trauma-informed principles. Our discussion of the Gateways to Justice project findings here suggest that RWFs should be designed to provide an important buffer zone which can prevent a child's exposure to the defendant, and in which remote court officers can calm a distraught child within a safe place, thus allowing them to finish giving evidence. An RWF also provides a safe haven away from the public spaces of the court, both for children and their families, and should be designed with multiple safe points of exit. Furthermore, the dimensions of the RWF should replicate a domestic-scaled space that is conducive to giving evidence of a private, intimate, and personal nature, something that is often hindered by the scale and distances between speakers within the public space of the courtroom. Overall, the RWF should protect a child from the over-stimulation

77 See Trond Myklebust, 'The Position in Norway' in John R Spencer and Michael E Lamb (eds), *Children and Cross-Examination: Time to Change the Rules?* (Hart Publishing, 2012).

78 See further Linda Mulcahy and Emma Rowden, *The Democratic Courthouse: A Modern History of Design, Due Process and Dignity* (Routledge, 2020) and McKay's contribution in this edited collection.

79 Cossins, *Alternative Models for Prosecuting Child Sex Offences in Australia* (n 4).

of the courtroom since a number of triggers could result in re-experiencing the emotions associated with the original trauma.

But what about the relationship between child complainants and legal personnel within the courtroom? Compared to the criminal trial, '[t]he core of the service relationship in a trauma-informed system is open and genuine collaboration between provider and consumer at all phases of the service delivery'.[80] The question is whether this is desirable and attainable within the criminal trial context. Nonetheless, collaborative relationships between complainants and key personnel in the justice system are possible in relation to pre-trial issues. Police and prosecutors can explain the reasons for their decisions and can prepare the complainant for court which is already undertaken in some jurisdictions (see for instance the Witness Assistance Service in the Office of the Director of Public Prosecutions in NSW, the Child Witness Unit in Victoria, or the Citizens Advice Witness Service in the UK). But it is the actual trial itself where the relationships of power – between judge and witness, and examiner and witness – easily replicate 'the most damaging dynamics of childhood trauma'.[81]

Is it ever possible for these relationships to do no harm? A re-interpretation of the importance of witness evidence in the context of the CSA trial would recognise that the child, as the prosecution's chief witness, must have the mental and physical stamina to participate in the trial process. The interests of justice require a traumatised witness to be able to give their *best* evidence rather than evidence that is the product of re-traumatisation as the result of hostile, power relationships created through the adversarial process.

Moving to a trauma-informed system requires a 'paradigm shift' because it is necessary for the issue of trauma to 'move to the center' of an organisation's interactions with the public.[82] With the recognition that trauma-informed systems are 'content specific, time limited and outcome focused', trauma-informed interactions require a commitment to change by 'integrating knowledge about violence and abuse' into the organisation's practices and procedures.[83] In a criminal trial context, this paradigm shift is not about delivering trauma-specific services (that is, psychological counselling) – rather, the integration of knowledge would involve the adoption of a trauma-systems approach aimed at achieving cultural and environmental change.

In order to create a trauma-informed adversarial trial, it would be necessary to introduce legal procedures and architectural designs to prevent the unavoidable triggers of the CSA trial. These changes would require a review of all aspects of how complainants are interviewed, before trial, how they are examined in court,

80 Harris and Fallot (n 36) 19.
81 Ibid.
82 Ibid 21.
83 Ibid 16.

and how they are debriefed after their experience in order to envisage a trauma-informed physical and social environment for the CSA trial.

First, training about the long-term impact of trauma for all those who interact with complainants would be needed: police, prosecutorial staff, and all court personnel, including security guards, clerks, tipstaff, defence lawyers, judges, sheriffs, and remote court officers. There are already excellent resources for training staff on the impact of trauma.[84] These do, however, require adequate funding. The design and conduct of trauma-informed training programmes without such funds would be a major barrier to their successful implementation.

Second, a review of the policies and procedures[85] of the criminal trial would include the identification of practices that 'replicate trauma dynamics', in particular 'dynamics that characterize abusive relationships', such as boundary violations, practices that deny or invalidate a child's experiences, or practices that reconstruct reality in a way that 'represent[s] the values and beliefs of the abuser'.[86] While witness assistance services provided before trial are designed to limit re-traumatisation by familiarising complainants with the court process and preparing them for examination and cross-examination, preparing someone for the triggers that may re-traumatise them may not be sufficient to do no harm. As discussed above, a paradigm shift could involve the introduction of non-legal personnel into the legal system who can initiate and oversee cultural change which has been achieved in some jurisdictions while best practice would treat all complainants as trauma survivors by introducing non-traumatizing procedures and practices as standard.

Further, strategies designed to eliminate or reduce unavoidable triggers ought to involve the core principles of empowerment and choice. This would facilitate a more collaborative relationship between complainant and prosecutor, rather than a relationship characterised by authority and control, be more conducive to feelings of safety, and counteract the fear and helplessness of victimization[87] which would empower the complainant to give their best evidence. Well-funded specialist prosecutorial units which commit to the creation of collaborative relationships with complainants are one solution[88] while legal representation is another. Nonetheless, the latter suggestion faces considerable barriers, such as

84 See D E Elliott, *Difficult Conversations: A Training Curriculum on Becoming Trauma-Informed* (Franklin County Women's Research Project, 2003) for non-clinicians; Lisa Pilnik and Jessica R Kendall, 'Identifying Polyvictimization and Trauma among Court-Involved Children and Youth: A Checklist and Resource Guide for Attorneys and Other Court-Appointed Advocates', *Office Juvenile Justice and Delinquency Prevention* (Web Page, January 2012) <https://ojjdp.ojp.gov/sites/g/files/xyckuh176/files/programs/safestart/IdentifyingPolyvictimization.pdf> for lawyers.

85 Harris and Fallot (n 36) 9.

86 Ibid.

87 Elliott et al. (n 25).

88 American Bar Association (n 7).

government funding, and a prevalent belief that legal representation for witnesses is inconsistent with the adversarial trial process.[89]

While RWFs constitute a vehicle for introducing trauma-informed processes into CSA trials, providing clear benefits for child complainants while giving evidence, these benefits are in danger of being lost without the knowledge of just *how* and *why* they work. As we have demonstrated here, TIC provides us with an appropriate frame of analysis for reaching this understanding. Furthermore, we argue that without an accompanying package of reforms that are trauma-informed, re-traumatisation is still the likely outcome for a child complainant in a CSA trial, whether or not there is a conviction. The utility of a trial process that impedes the ability of children from giving their best evidence, and the jury from hearing the best evidence of the prosecution's chief witness, must be questioned, the more so if such trials result in jury decisions that amount to wrongful acquittals. Neither complainants nor the community benefit from a non-trauma informed system of justice.

Bibliography

Articles/books/reports

Ahern, Elizabeth, Marlene Kowalski and Michael E Lamb, 'A Case Study Perspective: The Experiences of Young Persons Testifying to Child Sexual Exploitation in British Criminal Court' (2018) 27(3) *Journal of Child Sexual Abuse* 321

American Bar Association, *ABA Policy on Trauma-Informed Advocacy for Children and Youth* (Report, 2014) <www.americanbar.org/content/dam/aba/administrative/child_law/ABA Policy on Trauma-Informed Advocacy.authcheckdam.pdf>

American Psychiatric Association, *Diagnostic and Statistical Manual of Mental Disorders (DSM-5)* (American Psychiatric Publishing, 5th ed, 2013)

Andrews, Samantha J and Michael E Lamb, 'The Structural Linguistic Complexity of Lawyers' Questions and Children's Responses in Scottish Criminal Courts' (2017) 65 *Child Abuse & Neglect* 182

Andrews, Samantha J, Michael E Lamb and Thomas D Lyon, 'Question Types, Responsiveness and Self-Contradictions When Prosecutors and Defense Attorneys Question Alleged Victims of Child Sexual Abuse' (2015) 29(2) *Applied Cognitive Psychology* 253

Bath, Howard, 'The Three Pillars of Trauma-Informed Care' (2008) 17 *Reclaiming Children and Youth* 17

Behzadnia, Ali and Mehdi B Mehrani, 'Young Children's Yes Bias in Response to Tag Questions' (2018) 188(12) *Early Child Development and Care* 1663

Bettenay, Caroline, Anne M Ridley, Lucy A Henry and Laura Crane, 'Cross-Examination: The Testimony of Children with and without Intellectual Disabilities' (2014) 28(2) *Applied Cognitive Psychology* 204

Butler, Lisa D, Filomena M Critelli and Elaine S Rinfrette, 'Trauma-Informed Care and Mental Health' (2011) 31 *Directions in Psychiatry* 177

89 Anne Cossins, 'Is There a Case for the Legal Representation of Children in Sexual Assault Trials?' (2004) 16(2) *Current Issues in Criminal Justice* 160.

Cashmore, Judy and Lily Trimboli, *An Evaluation of the NSW Child Sexual Assault Specialist Jurisdiction* (NSW Bureau of Crime Statistics and Research, 2005)

Chen, Laura P, Hassan M Murad, Molly L Paras, Kristina M Colbenson, Amelia L Sattler, Erin N Goranson, Mohamed B Elamin, Richard J Seime, Gen Shinozaki, Larry J Prokop and Ali Zirakzadeh, 'Sexual Abuse and Lifetime Diagnosis of Psychiatric Disorders: Systematic Review and Meta-Analysis' (2010) 85(7) *Mayo Clinic Proceedings* 618

Cleveland, Kyndra C, Jodi A Quas and Thomas D Lyon, 'Valence, Implicated Actor, and Children's Acquiescence to False Suggestions' (2016) 43 *Journal of Applied Development Psychology* 1

Copeland, William E, Gordon P Keeler, Adrian Angold and Jane E Costello, 'Traumatic Events and Posttraumatic Stress in Childhood' (2007) 64(5) *Archives of General Psychiatry* 577

Cossins, Anne, 'Is There a Case for the Legal Representation of Children in Sexual Assault Trials?' (2004) 16(2) *Current Issues in Criminal Justice* 160

Cossins, Anne, 'Cross-Examination in Child Sexual Assault Trials: Evidentiary Safeguard or an Opportunity to Confuse?' (2009) 33(1) *Melbourne University Law Review* 68

Cossins, Anne, *Alternative Models for Prosecuting Child Sex Offences in Australia* (National Child Sexual Assault Reform Committee Report, 2010)

Crenshaw, David A and Sarah Caprioli, 'The Culture of Silencing Child Victims of Sexual Abuse: Implications for Child Witnesses in Court' (2017) 57(2) *Journal of Humanistic Psychology* 190

Davies, Graham M and Elizabeth Noon, *An Evaluation of the Live Link for Child Witnesses* (Home Office, 1991)

Drabble, Laurie A, Shelby Jones and Vivian Brown, 'Advancing Trauma-Informed Systems Change in a Family Drug Treatment Court Context' (2013) 13(1) *Journal of Social Work Practice in the Addictions* 91

Ehlers, Anke and David M Clark, 'A Cognitive Model of Posttraumatic Stress Disorder' (2000) 38(4) *Behaviour and Research Therapy* 319

Elliott, D E, *Difficult Conversations: A Training Curriculum on Becoming Trauma-Informed* (Franklin County Women's Research Project, 2003)

Elliott, Denise E, Paula Bjelajac, Roger D Fallot, Laurie S Markoff and Beth Glover Reed, 'Trauma-Informed or Trauma-Denied: Principles and Implementation of Trauma-Informed Services for Women' (2005) 33(4) *Journal of Community Psychology* 461

Fallot, Roger D and Maxine Harris, 'Trauma-Informed Approaches to Systems to Care' (2008) 3(1) *Trauma Psychology* Newsletter 6

Fergusson, David M, Joseph M Boden and L John Horwood, 'Exposure to Childhood Sexual and Physical Abuse and Adjustment in Early Adulthood' (2008) 32(6) *Child Abuse & Neglect* 607

Fergusson, David M, Geraldine F H McLeod and L John Horwood, 'Childhood Sexual Abuse and Adult Developmental Outcomes: Findings from a 30-Year Longitudinal Study in New Zealand' (2013) 37(9) *Child Abuse & Neglect* 664

Gabbay, Vilma, Melvin D Oatis, Raul R Silva and Glenn S Hirsch, 'Epidemiological Aspects of PTSD in Children and Adolescents' in Raul R Silva (ed), *Posttraumatic Stress Disorder in Children and Adolescents: Handbook* (Norton, 2004)

Goodsell, Charles T, *The Social Meaning of Civic Space: Studying Political Authority through Architecture* (University Press of Kansas, 1988)

Grogan, Sherry D. and Kathleen Pace Murphy, 'Anticipatory Stress Response in PTSD: Extreme Stress in Children (2011) 24(1) *Journal of Child & Adolescent Psychiatric Nursing* 58

Hall, Edward Twitchell, *The Hidden Dimension: Man's Use of Space in Public and Private* (The Bodley Head, 1966)

Hall, Edward Twitchell, *The Silent Language* (Anchor Books, 1959)
Harris, Maxine and Roger D Fallot, 'Envisioning a Trauma-Informed Service System: A Vital Paradigm Shift' (2001) 89 *New Directions for Mental Health Services* 3
Hillberg, Tanja, Catherine Hamilton-Giachritsis and Louise Dixon, 'Review of Meta-Analyses on the Association between Child Sexual Abuse and Adult Mental Health Difficulties: A Systematic Approach' (2011) 12(1) *Trauma, Violence & Abuse* 38
Klemfuss, J Zoe, Jodi A Quas and Thomas D Lyon, 'Attorneys' Questions and Children's Productivity in Child Sexual Abuse Criminal Trials' (2014) 28(5) *Applied Cognitive Psychology* 780
Kolko, David J, Michael S Hurlburt, Jinjin Zhang, Richard P Barth, Laurel K Leslie and Barbara J Burns, 'Posttraumatic Stress Symptoms in Children and Adolescents Referred for Child Welfare Investigation: A National Sample of In-Home and Out-Of-Home Care' (2010) 15(1) *Child Maltreatment* 48
Konradi, Amanda, 'Pulling Strings Doesn't Work in Court: Moving beyond Puppetry in the Relationship between Prosecutors and Rape Survivors' (2001) 10(1) *Journal of Social Distress and the Homeless* 5
Lamb, Michael E and Angèle Fouchier, 'The Effects of Question Type on Self-contradictions by Children in the Course of Forensic Interviews' (2001) 15(5) *Applied Cognitive Psychology* 483
Lamb, Michael E, Irit Hershkowitz, Yael Orbach and Phillip W Esplin, *Tell Me What Happened: Structured Investigative Interviews of Child Victims and Witnesses* (Wiley-Blackwell, 2008)
Libai, David, 'The Protection of the Child Victim of a Sexual Offense in the Criminal Justice System' (1968–69) 15 *Wayne Law Review* 997
Maniglio, Roberto, 'The Impact of Child Sexual Abuse on Health: A Systematic Review of Reviews' (2009) 29(7) *Clinical Psychology Review* 647
Maniglio, Roberto, 'Child Sexual Abuse in the Etiology of Anxiety Disorders: A Systematic Review of Reviews' (2013) 14(2) *Trauma, Violence & Abuse* 96
Miller, Niki A and Lisa M Najavits, 'Creating Trauma-Informed Correctional Care: A Balance of Goals and Environment' (2012) 3(1) *European Journal of Psychotraumatology* 17246/1
Miragoli, Sarah, Rossella Procaccia and Paola Di Blasio, 'Language Use and PTSD Symptoms: Content Analyses of Allegations of Child Sexual Abuse' (2014) 14(5) *Journal of Forensic Psychology Practice* 355
Miragoli, Sarah, Elena Camisasca and Paola Di Blasio, 'Investigating Linguistic Coherence Relations in Child Sexual Abuse: A Comparison of PTSD and Non-PTSD Children' (2019) 5(2) *Heliyon* e01163
Miragoli, Sarah, Elena Camisasca and Paola Di Blasio, 'The Narrative Fragmentation in Child Sexual Abuse: The Role of Age and Posttraumatic Stress Disorder' (2017) 73 *Child Abuse Neglect* 106
Mulcahy, Linda and Emma Rowden, *The Democratic Courthouse: A Modern History of Design, Due Process and Dignity* (Routledge, 2020)
Myklebust, Trond, 'The Position in Norway' in John R Spencer and Michael E Lamb (eds), *Children and Cross-Examination: Time to Change the Rules?* (Hart Publishing, 2012)
Najavits, Lisa M, Roger D Weiss and Sarah R Shaw, 'The Link Between Substance Abuse and Posttraumatic Stress Disorder in Women' (1997) 6(4) *The American Journal on Addictions* 273
Papps, Elaine and Irihapetti Ramsden, 'Cultural Safety in Nursing: The New Zealand Experience' (1996) 8(5) *International Journal for Quality in Health Care* 491

Perry, Bruce D, 'Examining Child Maltreatment Through a Neurodevelopmental Lens: Clinical Applications of the Neurosequential Model of Therapeutics' (2009) 14(4) *Journal of Loss and Trauma* 240

Plotnikoff, Joyce and Richard Woolfson, *In Their Own Words: The Experiences of 50 Young Witnesses in Criminal Proceedings* (National Society for the Prevention of Cruelty to Children (NSPCC), 2004)

Porges, Stephen W, *The Polyvagal Theory: Neurophysiological Foundations of Emotions, Attachment, Communication, Self-Regulation* (Norton, 2011)

Powell, Martine, Nina Westera, Jane Goodman-Delahunty and Anne Sophie Pichler, *An Evaluation of How Evidence is Elicited from Complainants of Child Sexual Abuse* (Report for the Royal Commission into Institutional Responses to Child Sexual Abuse, August 2016)

Quas, Jodi A and Gail S Goodman, 'Consequences of Criminal Court Involvement for Child Victims' (2012) 18(3) *Psychology, Public Policy, and Law* 392

Rapoport, Amos, *The Meaning of the Built Environment: A Nonverbal Communication Approach* (Sage Publications, 1982)

Righarts, Saskia, Fiona Jack, Rachel Zajac and Harlene Hayne, 'Young Children's Responses to Cross-Examination Style Questioning: The Effects of Delay and Subsequent Questioning' (2015) 21(3) *Psychology, Crime & Law* 274

Rock, Paul Elliott, *The Social World of an English Crown Court* (Clarendon Press, 1993)

Rowden, Emma, 'As Instalções à Distância Para Crianças e Testemunhas Vulneráveis: Novas Perspectivas a Propósito De Uma Tipologia Especial Emergente' in Patrícia Brancos (ed), *Sociologia do(s) Espaço(s) da Justiça: Diálogos Interdisciplinares* (CES/Almedina, 2013) [translated title: The Remote Witness Facility for Vulnerable and Child Witnesses: New Perspectives on an Emerging Spatial Typology]

Rowden, Emma, 'Distributed Courts and Legitimacy: What Do We Lose When We Lose the Courthouse?' (2018) 14(2) *Law, Culture and the Humanities* 263

Rowden, Emma and Diane Jones, 'Design, Dignity and Due Process: The Construction of the Coffs Harbour Courthouse' (2018) 14(2) *Law, Culture and the Humanities* 317

Rowden, Emma, Anne Wallace, David Tait, Mark Hanson and Diane Jones, *Gateways to Justice: Improving Video-Mediated Communications for Justice Participants – Design and Operational Guidelines for Remote Participation in Court Proceedings* (Research Report, 2013)

Royal Commission into Institutional Responses to Child Sexual Abuse (Criminal Justice Report: Parts VII to X and Appendices, August 2017)

Schore, Allan N, *Affect Regulation and the Repair of the Self* (W W Norton, 1st ed, 2003)

Taylor, Natalie and Jacqueline Joudo, *The Impact of Pre-Recorded Video and Closed Circuit Television Testimony by Adult Sexual Assault Complainants on Jury Decision-Making: An Experimental Study* (Research Report Series No. 68, 2005)

van der Kolk, Bessel A, 'Developmental Trauma Disorder: Towards a Rational Diagnosis for Children with Complex Trauma Histories' (2005) 35(5) *Psychiatric Annals* 401

van der Kolk, Bessel A, 'Clinical Implications of Neuroscience Research in PTSD' (2006) 1071(1) *Annals of New York Academy of Sciences* 277

van der Kolk, Bessel A, *The Body Keeps the Score: Brain, Mind, and Body in the Healing of Trauma* (Penguin Books, 2015)

Wells, Susan and Jenifer Urff, *Essential Components of Trauma-Informed Judicial Practice* (Final Draft Report, 2013)

Wilson, Debra Rose, 'Health Consequences of Childhood Sexual Abuse (2010) 46(1) *Perspectives in Psychiatric Care* 56

Zajac, Rachel, Sarah O'Neill and Harlene Hayne, 'Disorder in the Courtroom? Child Witnesses Under Cross-Examination' (2012) 32(3) *Developmental Review* 181

Legislation

Criminal Procedure Act 1986 (NSW)
Criminal Procedure Act 2009 (Vic)
Evidence Act 1977 (QLD)
Youth Justice and Criminal Evidence Act 1999 (UK)

Other

Hamlyn, Becky, Andrew Phelps, Jenny Turtle and Ghazala Sattar, *Are Special Measures Working? Evidence from Surveys of Vulnerable and Intimidated Witnesses* (Home Office Research Study 283, 2004)

'Helping Traumatized Children: Tips for Judges', *The National Child Traumatic Stress Network* (Fact Sheet, 2009) <https://www.nctsn.org/resources/helping-traumatized-children-tips-judges>

Judicial College, *Equal Treatment Bench Book* (2013–2015) <www.judiciary.gov.uk/wp-content/uploads/2013/11/equal-treatment-bench-book-2013-with-2015-amendment.pdf>

Pilnik, Lisa and Jessica R Kendall, 'Identifying Polyvictimization and Trauma among Court-Involved Children and Youth: A Checklist and Resource Guide for Attorneys and Other Court-Appointed Advocates', *Office Juvenile Justice and Delinquency Prevention* (Web Page, January 2012) <https://ojjdp.ojp.gov/sites/g/files/xyckuh176/files/programs/safestart/IdentifyingPolyvictimization.pdf>

Reitman, Karen A, 'Attorneys for Children Guide to Interviewing Clients: Integrating Trauma Informed Care and Solution Focused Strategies', *Publications* (Guide, 2011) <http://www.nycourts.gov/ip/cwcip/Publications/attorneyGuide.pdf>

Rowden, Emma Louise, 'Remote Participation and the Distributed Court: An Approach to Court Architecture in the Age of Video-Mediated Communications' (PhD thesis, The University of Melbourne, 2011)

'Trauma: What Child Welfare Attorneys Should Know', *The National Traumatic Stress Network* (Guide, 2017) <https://www.nctsn.org/resources/trauma-what-child-welfare-attorneys-should-know>

PART III

Justice outwith buildings

7

'AND THAT'S WHY STREET-WISE COMPLAINANTS NOW ALWAYS GIVE EVIDENCE BEHIND SCREENS, LIVE'

Exploring the intensive affects of the courtroom

Anna Carline, Clare Gunby, and Jamie Murray

Introduction

The use of 'special measures' aimed at supporting the complainant through the criminal justice process and enabling the delivery of 'best evidence' is now commonplace in sexual offence cases. Such measures include the use of the police video-recorded interview as evidence-in-chief, the use of screens in the courtroom to shield the complainant from the defendant, and cross-examination by a live link. Drawing upon semi-structured interviews with 39 barristers across England and Wales, this chapter explores practitioners' perspectives regarding the use of these measures and situates our analysis within a consideration of the intensive affects of bodies in the space of the courtroom. More specifically, in order to explore the space of justice, the chapter draws upon theories of affect and the intensive ontological register to make sense of barristers' widely held and enduring belief that testimony that is delivered 'remotely' has significantly less impact upon a jury and, in turn, renders a conviction less likely. As will be shown, these perspectives frequently influenced the advice given to complainants in the cases explored in this chapter.

To commence, the chapter outlines the legal and policy context surrounding the introduction of special measures and the methods we used to gather our data. Thereafter, the theory of affects and the concept of the intensive ontological regime are introduced, before a critical analysis of barristers' perspectives is undertaken. This analysis examines the following themes that emerged during our research: 'Courtroom affects and the impact of special measures', 'Affectual relationality: the jury dynamic', 'Harnessing intensive affects and ideal victim discourses', and 'Affect and practice: advising the complainant'. In conclusion, it will be argued that an appreciation of the role of affects in the space of the courtroom may enhance our understanding of, and responses to, the challenges

DOI: 10.4324/9780429059858-11

of developing and implementing provisions that aim to improve the criminal justice response to rape.

Background to the introduction of special measures

Introduced by the *Youth Justice and Criminal Evidence Act 1999* (England and Wales) (hereafter, YJCEA), special measures are intended to support vulnerable or intimidated witnesses (hereafter, VIWs, see later for a definition) to participate effectively within the criminal justice system.[1] Given that many VIWs may be reluctant to come forward and report allegations and/or provide testimony, special measures aim to offer reassurance and protection, ameliorate the stress and anxiety of giving evidence during a trial and, ultimately, improve the quality of testimony.[2] These measures can be seen to be part of two wider and interlinked political agendas which focus upon placing the victim at the centre of the criminal justice system and, more specifically, improving the criminal justice response to rape.[3] In relation to the latter, successive governments have introduced various policy and law reforms designed to improve the rates of conviction and attrition in rape cases and enhance the experiences of sexual violence complainants in the criminal justice process.[4] At the same time, there is a well-known 'implementation gap', whereby many of the well-meaning policies and reforms are either not implemented at all or not utilised as expected.[5] There is also a wealth of

1 Home Office, *Speaking Up for Justice: Report of the Interdepartmental Working Group on the Treatment of Vulnerable or Intimidated Witnesses in the Criminal Justice System* (Home Office, 1998).

2 Ibid.

3 See, for example, HM Crown Prosecution Service Inspectorate (HMCPSI) and HM Inspectorate of Constabulary (HMIC), *A Report on the Joint Inspection into the Investigation and Prosecution of Cases Involving Allegations of Rape* (Investigation Report, April 2002); HM Crown Prosecution Service Inspectorate (HMCPSI) and HM Inspectorate of Constabulary (HMIC), *Without Consent: A Report on the Joint Review of the Investigation and Prosecution of Rape Offences* (Inspection Report, January 2007); HM Inspectorate of Constabulary (HMIC), *Making the Victim Count* (Crime Recording Report, November 2014); HM Government, *Ending Violence against Women and Girls: Strategy 2016–2020* (Strategy Report, March 2016); Ministry of Justice, *Code of Practice for Victims of Crime* (Her Majesty's Stationery Office, 2015).

4 See, for example, Crown Prosecution Service (CPS) and Police, *Joint CPS and Police Action Plan on Rape* (Rape Action Plan Report, 2002); Crown Prosecution Service (CPS) and Police, *Joint CPS and Police Action Plan on Rape* (Rape Action Plan Report, April 2015); Home Office, *Setting the Boundaries: Reforming the Law on Sex Offences* (Consultation Paper Vol. 1, July 2000); Home Office, *Protecting the Public: Strengthening Protection against Sex Offenders and Reforming the Law on Sexual Offences* (Cm 5668, 2002); Home Office, *Convicting Rapists and Protecting Victims: Justice for Victims of Rape* (Consultation Paper, Spring 2006); Home Office, *Sexual Offences Act 2003: A Stocktake of the Effectiveness of the Act since Its Implementation* (Home Office, 2006); Vivien Stern, *A Report by Baroness Vivien Stern CBE of an Independent Review into How Rape Complaints Are Handled by Public Authorities in England and Wales: The Stern Review* (Home Office Report, 2010).

5 See Anna Carline and Patricia Easteal, *Shades of Grey: Domestic and Sexual Violence against Women – Law Reform and Society* (Routledge, 1st ed, 2014); Anna Carline and Clare Gunby, 'Rape Politics, Policies and Practice: Exploring the Tensions and Unanticipated Consequences of Well-Intended Victim-Focused Measures' (2017) 56(1) *The Howard Journal of Crime and Justice* 34. See,

literature that explores the difficulties in achieving successful prosecutions, the ongoing influence of various rape 'myths' and misconceptions, concerns relating to the treatment of sexual violence victims within the criminal justice system, and the extent, and impact, of secondary victimisation.[6] Further, and as is well-known, in sexual violence cases the complainant's testimony tends to be pivotal to the case, due to the perceived lack of independent evidence. Accordingly, their involvement within the process is highly significant and it is vital that the quality of their testimony is in no way compromised.

The YJCEA introduced two provisions that pertain explicitly to sexual offences: section 34 prohibits a defendant from personally cross-examining a complainant during a trial and section 41 reforms the law relating to the introduction of sexual history evidence. The broader special measures that may be used in cases involving VIWs include screens to shield the witness from the accused (section 23), giving evidence via a live link (section 24), giving evidence in private (section 25), removal of wigs and gowns by judges and barristers (section 26), video-recorded evidence-in-chief (commonly referred to as the ABE, or Achieving Best Evidence interview) (section 27), video-recorded cross-examination and re-examination (section 28), and examination through an intermediary (section 29). Under section 17, a sexual violence complainant is considered to be an intimidated witness on the basis that they are likely to suffer fear and apprehension when giving evidence. Indeed, the Home Office emphasised that 'giving evidence of an intimate nature in a public courtroom was likely to be an intimidating experience for the majority of rape and sexual offence complainants'.[7] A complainant may also be 'vulnerable', which relates to those witnesses who require assistance due to age and/or incapacity (section 16).

Significantly, a sexual violence complainant is deemed to be automatically eligible to apply for special measures. This, as Ellison notes,

> has the welcome effect of precluding challenges to eligibility in cases of acquaintance or 'date rape' on the unwarranted ground that the complainant knows the defendant and is therefore less likely to be intimidated by him than a victim of rape by a stranger'.[8]

---

for example, Kate Cook, 'Rape Investigation and Prosecution: Stuck in the Mud?' (2011) 17(3) *Journal of Sexual Aggression* 250; Liz Kelly, Jo Lovett and Linda Regan, *A Gap or a Chasm? Attrition in Reported Rape Cases* (Home Office Research Study 293, 2005); Sue Lees, *Carnal Knowledge: Rape on Trial* (Women's Press, 2nd ed, 2002); Stern (n 4).

6 See, for example, Carline and Easteal (n 5); Kelly, Lovett and Regan (n 5); Alison Saunders, 'Speech on the Prosecution of Rape and Serious Sexual Offences by Alison Saunders' (Speech, Crown Prosecution Service, 2012); Stern (n 4); Jennifer Temkin, 'Prosecuting and Defending Rape: Perspectives from the Bar' (2000) 27(2) *Journal of Law and Society* 219; Jennifer Temkin and Barbara Krahé, *Sexual Assault and the Justice Gap: A Question of Attitude* (Hart Publishing, 2008).

7 Home Office (n 1) [para 9.1].

8 Louise Ellison, *The Adversarial Process and the Vulnerable Victim* (Oxford University Press, 1st ed, 2001) 38.

A special measures application may be made by any party to the proceedings, or by the court on its own motion (s19(1)). In deciding whether to grant the application, a court must determine whether the measure(s) will be likely to maximise the quality of the evidence. It must also take into account any views expressed by the witness and whether the measures might inhibit such evidence being effectively tested by a third party (s19(2)). However, by virtue of the *Coroners and Justice Act 2009* (England and Wales), if a special measure is applied for, a court *must* give a special measure direction with regard to section 27 (video-recorded evidence-in-chief) *unless* it considers that the measure 'would not be likely to maximize the quality of the complainant's evidence' (section 101). At the time of the introduction of this legislation, the then government justified this approach 'on the basis that it would enable complainants to have early certainty about the way their evidence would be given'.[9]

Evaluating the implementation and impact of special measures

A 2005 monitoring exercise indicated that applications for special measures had a very high success rate (at 98%),[10] with the TV link most frequently applied for (90%), followed by video-recorded evidence-in-chief (41%) and screens (10%).[11] It needs to be noted, however, that section 28 (pre-recorded cross-examination) has only recently been piloted and is still in the process of being incrementally implemented nationally.[12] Hamlyn et al.'s survey of VIWs demonstrated that many of these witnesses were assisted and supported by the special measures, with 33 per cent indicating that they would not have been willing to testify otherwise.[13] VIWs who accessed special measures reported reduced levels of distress and were also less likely to have 'been upset a lot' during cross-examination, compared with those who had not accessed special measures.[14] The survey also highlighted that the provisions had increased satisfaction in, and improved opinions of, the criminal justice system, with VIWs reporting that 'they were more likely to believe that the CJS [criminal justice system] was effective in bringing

9 Laura C H Hoyano, 'Coroners and Justice Act 2009: Special Measures Directions Take Two: Entrenching Unequal Access to Justice?' (2010) 5 *Criminal Law Review* 345, 365. See also Office for Criminal Justice Reform, *Convicting Rapists and Protecting Victims: Justice for Victims of Rape* (Consultation Paper, Spring 2006); Office for Criminal Justice Reform, *Convicting Rapists and Protecting Victims: Justice for Victims of Rape, Responses to Consultation* (Office for Criminal Justice Reform, 2007).

10 Debbie Cooper and Paul Roberts, *Special Measures for Vulnerable and Intimidated Witnesses: An Analysis of Crown Prosecution Service Monitoring Data* (Crown Prosecution Service, 2005) 111.

11 Ibid 78.

12 Joyce Plotnikoff and Richard Woolfson, 'Worth Waiting for: The Benefits of Section 28 Pre-trial Cross Examination' (2016) 8 *Archbold Review* 6.

13 Becky Hamlyn et al., *Are Special Measures Working? Evidence from Surveys of Vulnerable and Intimidated Witnesses* (Home Office Research Study 283, June 2004) 78.

14 Ibid xiv.

criminals to justice, meets the needs of the victim and treats witnesses fairly and with respect'.[15]

Nevertheless, Hamlyn et al.'s study demonstrated that levels of anxiety remained higher among VIWs, and that they were generally less satisfied than other witnesses.[16] Furthermore, 10 per cent stated that they did not find the live link helpful,[17] and other research also indicates that VIWs often feel that they have little choice regarding the format of the delivery of their testimony,[18] which may only be compounded by the presumption in favour of using the ABE as the evidence-in-chief. In addition, previous research has identified numerous problems and issues regarding the implementation of and processes related to the use of special measures. Applications for special measures are frequently made late in the process, and sometimes not until the first day of trial;[19] the identification of, and communication with VIWs, is often found wanting; and the needs of the witness are often given insufficient regard.[20] Concerns have also been expressed in relation to the quality of the videos that may be shown as evidence-in-chief,[21] which has been said to be limited by the adoption of an overly rigid and counterproductive interview structure and inappropriate interviewing techniques, excessively long interviews, and amateurish recording.[22] In addition, prosecutors have expressed disquiet that the format of the ABE conflicts with what they consider to be a credible and persuasive testimony – that which provides a linear, coherent, and consistent account of the assault.[23]

It is also recognised that the use of the live link is 'not a panacea for all problems that prosecution witnesses encounter',[24] particularly where the victim remains in a relationship with the defendant. Moreover, the use of technology may do little to ameliorate the ordeal of being cross-examined. Accordingly,

15 Ibid.
16 Ibid xii.
17 Ibid 70.
18 Matthew Hall, 'The Use and Abuse of Special Measures: Giving Victims the Choice?' (2007) 58(8) *Journal of Scandinavian Studies in Criminology and Crime Prevention* 33.
19 Corrine Charles, *Special Measures for Vulnerable and Intimidated Witnesses: Research Exploring the Decisions and Actions Taken by Prosecutors in a Sample of CPS Case Files* (Crown Prosecution Service Research Report, April 2012); Mandy Burton, Roger Evans and Andrew Sanders, *Are Special Measures for Vulnerable and Intimidated Witnesses Working? Evidence from the Criminal Justice Agencies* (Home Office Online Report 01/06, 2006).
20 Burton, Evans and Sanders (n 19); Mandy Burton, Roger Evans and Andrew Sanders, 'Implementing Special Measures and Vulnerable and Intimidated Witnesses: The Problem of Identification' (2006) *Criminal Law Review* 229.
21 Stern (n 4).
22 Ibid 69.
23 Nina J Westera et al., 'Does the Narrative Style of Video Evidence Influence Judgements about Rape Complainant Testimony?' (2015) 29 *Applied Cognitive Psychology* 637; Nina J Westera, Martine B Powell and Becky Milne, 'Lost in the Detail: Prosecutors' Perceptions of the Utility of Video Recorded Police Interviews as Rape Complainant Evidence' (2017) 50(2) *Australian and New Zealand Journal of Criminology* 252.
24 Burton, Evans and Sanders (n 19) 56.

in Hamlyn et al.'s study, VIWs still considered being cross-examined to be the most upsetting experience of the trial process, with being called a liar by defence counsel causing significant distress.[25] It remains to be seen, however, whether the implementation of pre-recorded cross-examination may ameliorate some of the distress caused by cross-examination. A common concern is that the use of 'remote testimony' (that is, the ABE and live link) reduces the emotional impact of the evidence on the jury, which could negatively impact upon conviction rates,[26] despite experimental research, including that with mock jurors, suggesting otherwise.[27] As will be discussed later, this perception was prominent among the barristers we interviewed and frequently influenced their practice and the advice they provided to a complainant.

Methodology

In 2010, Carline and Gunby conducted a small-scale study with 14 barristers in the North West of England to explore the implementation and impact of the reforms contained in the *Sexual Offences Act 2003* (England and Wales). In addition to discussing the substantive law reforms,[28] counsel also spoke at length about the rates of attrition and conviction in rape cases, along with the impact and implementation of other reform and policy measures aimed at improving the victim's experience of the criminal justice system.[29] Recognising the small-scale nature of this initial study, and wishing to explore these factors further, another 39 interviews were conducted between 2014 and 2016, supported by funding from the British Academy (BA). In an effort to attain a purposive sample, participants were recruited from the four largest cities in the four Crown Prosecution Service (CPS) regions that had prosecuted the most rape cases during 2011–2012 (the time at which the BA application was being developed). This resulted in the interviewing of six barristers from two chambers in Birmingham, six barristers from two chambers in Leeds, nine barristers from three chambers in Manchester, and eighteen barristers from nine chambers in London.

25 Hamlyn et al. (n 13) 53.

26 Council of HM Circuit Judges, *Convicting Rapists and Protecting Victims: A Consultation Response of the Council of Her Majesty's Circuit Judges* (Consultation Response Report, 2006); Hamlyn et al. (n 13); Sara Payne, *Rape: The Victim Experience Review* (Home Office Review Report, 2009).

27 See, for example, Graham Davies, 'The Impact of Television on the Presentation and Reception of Children's Testimony' (1999) 22(3–4) *International Journal of Law and Psychiatry* 241; Louise Ellison and Vanessa Munro, 'A "Special" Delivery? Exploring the Impact of Screens, Live-Links and Video Recorded Evidence on Mock Juror Deliberation in Rape Trials' (2014) 23(1) *Social & Legal Studies* 3.

28 Anna Carline, Clare Gunby and Caryl Beynon, 'Alcohol-Related Rape Cases: Barristers' Perspectives on the Sexual Offences Act 2003 and Its Impact on Practice' (2010) 74(6) *Journal of Criminal Law* 579; Anna Carline and Clare Gunby, '"How an Ordinary Jury Makes Sense of It Is a Mystery": Barristers' Perspectives on Rape, Consent and the Sexual Offences Act 2003' (2011) 32(3) *Liverpool Law Review* 237.

29 See Carline and Gunby (n 5).

Barristers were recruited via a mix of approaching existing contacts, emailing individuals who were identified from their chamber's websites as having experience in prosecuting and defending rape, and contacting the clerks of chambers that dealt heavily with sexual offence cases to request that they disseminate an email about the research. This email invitation outlined the nature of the study and what participation would include. At the end of the interviews, barristers were asked to recommend colleagues who may be interested in participating, and individuals were also recruited via this means. The final sample comprised 18 male and 21 female barristers. The majority of participants were highly experienced, with the number of years spent working on rape cases ranging from four to forty years. Thirty-four participants had a mixed practice of defending and prosecuting rape, while four only defended and one only prosecuted. The interviews were conducted at chambers, at Crown Court, or over the telephone (n=14), and lasted an average of 57 minutes.

The semi-structured interview schedule was devised following a review of the previous study data and relevant policy and academic literature. In addition to questions relating to the rates of attrition and conviction and the challenges involved in prosecuting and defending rape cases, the participants were asked about their opinions regarding the substance and impact of various law and policy reforms – including special measures – upon the criminal justice response to rape and the victim's experience of the criminal justice system. Reading and analysing the transcripts revealed the significant extent to which barristers continually referred to emotions and the body. Our participants frequently reflected upon how emotions and bodies operated within the space of the courtroom and how their presence or absence could fundamentally impact upon the trial, particularly the jury. From a theoretical perspective, it can be argued that the barristers in our research were talking about affects and intensities.

Exploring the affective turn

Many disciplines, particularly across the social sciences and humanities, have seen the advent of what is often referred to as the 'affective turn',[30] although this has been less evident in law and criminology.[31] While there exists a level of contestation regarding the concept of affects, the classic formulation of affect is that developed by Spinoza: 'the affections of the body by which the body's power of acting is increased or diminished, helping or hindering, and at the same time the idea of the affections'.[32] It is possible to identify numerous key features of affects – although it is important to emphasise that no hierarchy is

30 Patricia Clough, *The Affective Turn: Theorising the Social* (Duke University Press, 1st ed, 2007); Melissa Gregg and Gregory Seigworth, *The Affects Theory Reader* (Duke University Press, 2010).

31 For an example, see Andreas Philipopoulos-Mihalopoulos, *Spatial Justice: Body, Lawscape, Atmosphere* (Routledge, 1st ed, 2015).

32 Baruch Spinoza, *Ethics* (Oxford University Press, 2000) 164.

to be assumed. First, one way to describe affect is as a feeling or sensation. This can include 'basic emotions' such as anger, joy, and fear, but also other sensations such as 'apprehension, pity, disappointment, shame, excitement or hope' which infuse our lives and bodies.[33] However, affect also includes those feelings that are ineffable: those bodily sensations that we cannot quite describe or represent with language. These feelings and sensations may be fleeting or sustained, negative or positive; but, importantly, they are central to how we experience life.

Second, affect theory places significant emphasis on the body – the lived embodied experience. Feelings and sensations reside within the body.[34] Hence, by focusing on affects, we are concerned with exploring how feelings and sensations emerge within bodies, how bodies transmit affects and sensations, and how bodies respond to affects. Nevertheless, it is important to note that the concept of body used in this context is to be understood in the widest sense, and hence is by no means limited to human – or fleshy – bodies. Furthermore, there is a significant body of literature that explores the affective nature of atmospheres:[35] atmospheres are productive of feelings, sensations, and change within bodies, and are themselves affected by bodies. It is possible to intuitively understand how atmospheres affect us, and how atmospheres within a setting can shift as bodies move around, in and out of spaces. We can also intuitively understand how a courtroom is designed to produce certain affects – feelings and sensations in bodies – and behavioural change. As Gherardi notes: 'Affective atmospheres are physically inscribed in an architectural project and … realized through the participation of people who embody a feeling and express it through situational practices.'[36]

Acknowledging that affect is embodied leads us to identify the following further features: affect is relational, and is a force of and for change. In relation to the former, affect theory is concerned with the relationship between bodies: affects arise out of the interactions between different bodies.[37] Hence, as Wetherell notes, affect 'is not an object inside the self … but is in relation to others, a response to a situation, to the world … Affect is never wholly owned, always intersecting and interacting'.[38] Consequently, these interactions produce change; and, as such, it is recognised that an affect 'takes us or moves us in ways that we cannot help or prevent'.[39] Affects can either enhance or diminish the

33 Eeva Sointu, 'Discourse, Affect and Affliction' (2016) 64(2) *The Sociological Review* 312, 312.
34 Sointu (n 33).
35 Ben Anderson, 'Affective Atmospheres' (2009) 2(1) *Emotion, Space and Society* 77; Teresa Brennan, *The Transmission of Affect* (Cornell University Press, 2004); Silvia Gherardi, 'One Turn … and Now Another One: Do the Turn to Practice and the Turn to Affect Have Something in Common?' (2017) 48(3) *Management Learning* 345.
36 Gherardi (n 35) 7.
37 Sara Ahmed, 'Killing Joy: Feminism and the History of Happiness' (2010) 35(3) *Signs* 571.
38 Margaret Wetherell, *Affect and Emotion: A New Social Science Understanding* (Sage Publications, 2012) 22.
39 Ian Burkitt, *Emotions and Social Relations* (Sage Publications, 2014) 10.

capacities of a body, and hence they can be negative as well as positive. While residing within and among bodies, affect is – or can be – preconscious: it can arise and impact upon the body without us being consciously aware of it, and thus may produce autonomic responses.[40] While affectual cognisance frequently emerges, some argue that there is always an excess to an affect that remains unknowable.[41] However, while some affects, or aspects of affects, may escape conscious perception, this is not to assert that there is no relationship between discourse and affects. Numerous scholars illustrate how discourse (the social and cultural scripts that produce identities and meanings) and affects intertwine to produce meaning – we frequently draw upon discourses to make sense of the affects we encounter.[42] As Sointu notes, '[a]ffect unfolds in relation to discursive meaning'.[43] Moreover, in addition to making sense of affects, discourse and language also produce affects in bodies; in this regard, cross-examination is a very good example of a discourse that can negatively affect a complainant.

Accordingly, affects are a non-representational, sensed intensity – they are sensed and thought by bodies, with bodies emitting affects according to their speeds and slownesses and differential relations with other bodies, affecting other bodies in their zones of affect and being affected when they fall into a neighbouring zone of affect. A body's capacities and potential for relational interactions may be increased or decreased through these emergent relations of affecting and being affected.[44] As such, an affect is an emergent event that is in excess of the sum of the relational forces that produce the emission of an event.

Affects and the intensive ontological register

Drawing upon the work of Deleuze and Guattari, an affect can be described as both productive of and the outcome of a transformative event that occurs in the intensive ontological field.[45] Hence, in order to better understand affects, it is important to grasp the distinction between two ontological registers – the actual and the intensive. As conceptualised by Deleuze and Guattari,[46] the actual register is that which is both real and actual, and exists extensively; it can be explained as

40 Brian Massumi, 'The Autonomy of Affect' (1995) 31 *Cultural Critique Part II* 83; Elspeth Probyn, *Blush: Faces of Shame* (University of Minnesota Press, 2005); Wetherell (n 38).

41 Massumi (n 40).

42 See Wetherell (n 38).

43 Sointu (n 33) 314.

44 Clough (n 30); Gregg and Seigworth (n 30); see generally Brian Massumi, *A User's Guide to Capitalism and Schizophrenia* (MIT Press, 1992); Brian Massumi, *Parables for the Virtual: Movement, Affect, Sensation* (Duke University Press, 2002); Brian Massumi, *Politics of Affect* (Polity, 1st ed, 2015).

45 Gilles Deleuze and Félix Guattari, *What Is Philosophy?* (Verso, 2015); Gilles Deleuze and Félix Guattari, *A Thousand Plateaus* (Bloomsbury, 2017).

46 Deleuze and Guattari, *What Is Philosophy?* (n 45); Deleuze and Guattari, *A Thousand Plateaus* (n 45).

that which we understand and comprehend as existing in the world and as being real. It is corporeal and material. In contrast, the intensive register is real, but not actual – it exists intensively, and is incorporeal and immaterial. Bonta and Protevi explain that the notion of the intensive field has been used to describe 'the characteristic properties of thermodynamic systems (for example, temperature, pressure) which when driven past a critical threshold trigger a change in the quality of the system'.[47] These can be contrasted with the 'extensive [or actual] properties of a system, such as length or volume, which are measured by an external 'metric' or standard (a cubic centimetre stays the same whether it is used to measure water or oil)'.[48] Delanda further explains this in the following manner:

> While extensive quantities (such as volume, area, length, amount of energy or entropy) are additive, intensive quantities are not. For example, if one adds two equal volumes of water one gets twice the amount of water. But if one adds two quantities of water at forty five degrees of temperature one does not get a body of water at ninety degrees but one at the original temperature.[49]

Rather, for a change to occur in the intensive regime, there must be a '*difference* ... in [the] degree of intensity'.[50] This difference needs to be more than 'a simple addition, but the emergence of a spontaneous flow or movement', such as an affect, event, or a force, which in turn fundamentally changes the properties of the system. As such, '*intensive differences are productive*'.[51]

There is, however, a complex mutual relay of productive creation between the two ontological registers. Operations and developments in the intensive incorporeal register create and shape material and expressive matters that will become actualised in the register of corporeal things and words. In turn, the actual register is sampled by the intensive register, readjusting the operations of the latter. Deleuze and Guattari's point is that understanding change and creation in the actual register is unthinkable without the pre-operation of real (but not actual) intensive and incorporeal ontological processes and operations.[52] The widest point of the register of the intensive is that it is always adjacent to every actual state and circumstance and can be sensed by corporeal bodies in both critical and everyday states and circumstances.

47 Mark Bonta and John Protevi, *Deleuze and Geophilosophy: A Guide and Glossary* (Edinburgh University Press, 1st ed, 2004) 101.

48 Ibid.

49 Manuel Delanda, 'Space: Extensive and Intensive, Actual and Virtual' in Buchanan Ian and Lambert Gregg (eds), *Deleuze and Space* (Edinburgh University Press, 2005) 80, 80.

50 Ibid 81. Emphasis in original.

51 Ibid. Emphasis in original.

52 Deleuze and Guattari, *What Is Philosophy?* (n 45); Deleuze and Guattari, *A Thousand Plateaus* (n 45).

In applying this theory to the discussion of special measures, the starting point is to conceptualise the courtroom, in its broadest possible sense, as both an intensive and an actual field. This incorporates, inter alia, the physical, architectural courtroom and courtroom furniture; the wider court building and the streets abutting the court building; all the bodies that enter these spaces, including those of judges, barristers, court officials, defendants, complainants, witnesses, police officers, family members, solicitors, and reporters; and all the expressive materials that pass between these bodies and across these spaces – the words, noises, looks, gazes, smells, and clothing. As such, it incorporates intensive incorporeal affects that are real, but not actualised. These affects include, for example, the atmosphere of the courtroom, the affectual capacities of the bodies of the numerous trial participants, and all the embodied transformative forces and events that flow from their interrelationships and interconnections.

The courtroom can thus be understood as involving a battle of incorporeal and intensive forces – forces that are not actual or extensive, in the sense that it is not possible to physically grasp them, but which are not unreal; they are affects that can be sensed. These forces and affects emanate from the various bodies at different degrees of speed and slowness – different affective capabilities – with some forces eventually overpowering others. Significantly, it is this battle of forces that will establish what will eventually be actualised – or brought into being. When one affective intensive force prevails over another, the emerging state of the world is significantly shifted. As such, in the intensive field of the courtroom we have superpositions of multiple states of bodies – in the intensive regime, incorporeal bodies and states are indeterminate. Defendants are simultaneously guilty and not guilty, witnesses are simultaneously telling the truth and not telling the truth. During the trial, a battle of intensive forces is played out, and the conquering force will determine what will ultimately be actualised: that is, a guilty or not guilty verdict. One of the central arguments of this chapter, based on our findings, is that affects and the intensive field are intuitively well understood by barristers and already worked within court practices. Through their practice, barristers marshal affects, sensations, and beliefs across the intensive field of the courtroom, which generally unravel into an actualisation, an establishment of a verdict, which is in fact an ex post facto representation of what is really a battle of affects.

Courtroom affects and the impact of special measures

The barristers in our research noted that special measures were commonplace in cases involving sexual violence. Reflecting the official rationale and extant research, our participants contemplated that the use of such measures had increased reporting: 'I think they must have had an impact for the good in terms of encouraging victims to come forward' (B11). When contemplating the necessity and positive effects of special measures for rape complainants, the barristers highlighted the pivotal role that such provisions play in decreasing the negative affects that providing evidence produces for the witness. For example, it was commented that the provisions made the 'experience far less distressing', which was appropriate because 'it shouldn't be trial by ordeal' (B28). In expressing this sentiment, the barristers frequently referred to the body of the complainant: 'nobody should take a kicking for being brave enough to make an allegation' (B22). This participant emphasised that it was 'the state's duty to protect them [complainants] in cotton wool, insofar as possible'. Through these discussions, we can see how the barristers conceptualised giving evidence as involving embodied intensive affects, as the process and experience of appearing in court could move and transform the complainant, frequently in a negative manner.

However, despite voicing approval for the adoption of special measures in principle, the counsel we interviewed overwhelmingly expressed significant concerns regarding the use of 'remote evidence' – ABEs and cross-examination via a live link – on the basis that these involved the complainant not being physically present in the courtroom. The barristers felt that such measures were 'a mistake for the evidential value of the Crown's case' (B17), and attached greater weight to having the complainant physically present in court: 'having a witness in court, even behind the screen, watching their video, in front of the jury, can sometimes be the most powerful piece of evidence' (B18). Indeed, all of the barristers believed that the use of remote evidence had impacted negatively upon conviction rates. For example, one participant commented that having the complainant in the courtroom 'rather than the face on the screen, honestly, I swear, makes a difference between sometimes getting a conviction or not' (B8). In exploring these perspectives, we are able to see the importance that the barristers attach to producing intensive affects in the courtroom – or, to be more precise, the importance of affecting the jury.

Reflecting previous research,[53] some of the barristers' concerns related to the production of poor-quality ABEs:

> The video camera is normally about six feet above their head and about twenty feet away. So, the jury don't see the intimate sort of reaction to questions of the pain of them giving you their account.
>
> *(B29)*

Here we can again see how the barristers placed significant emphasis upon the body of the complainant, and the ability of that body – particularly the face – to emit affects and thereby transform others. Hence, our participants stressed how important it is that the ABE and live link enable the jury to see the complainant's face '[b]ecause, obviously, you can tell so much from people's faces … And if they can't see the person's eyes then it seems more remote and detached' (B28). However, their concerns regarding the affectual ability of the evidence were not limited to poorly conducted and constructed ABEs. Rather, all of the

53 Stern (n 4).

participants emphasised that, if prosecuting, they would prefer the complainant to be physically present in the courtroom for at least some of her testimony. Confirming anecdotal evidence in England and Wales, and resonating with the views of practitioners in other jurisdictions, the barristers in this research maintained that, by placing the complainant outside the courtroom, ABEs and live links have a negative impact upon a trial, as they reduce the emotional impact of her evidence upon the jury. It was argued that such measures 'dehumanise' (B10) the complainant, and that you lose 'that bit of human intimacy' (B7) and 'the emotion [and] the tension' (B19). Furthermore, our participants claimed that jurors expect to see the complainant, as 'they like to watch them' (B7). In the absence of the complainant being physically present in the courtroom, it was considered impossible for the jury to 'pick up on the nuances of body language'; and one barrister noted that, 'because so often you pick up on those things … you really understand the meaning of something as opposed to just the words that are spoken' (B14). In this regard, meaning was recognised as being both actual and intensive.

Based on these discussions, we can see how our barrister participants recognised and were concerned about the ability of the complainant to emit intensive affects that would move the jury. Hence, it was deemed important for the victim to be physically present in the courtroom so that the jury can 'see the whites of their eyes' (B20) and 'get a sense of them' (B7). Further, the sensory and transformative capacities of the various bodies in the courtroom are not limited to the visual, but include other senses: 'you can almost smell the person three or four feet away' (B38). Such considerations developed into a wider understanding and appreciation of the importance of affective atmospheres, with it being noted that 'having someone actually in court giving their evidence and, you know, you can feel the emotion, you can feel the atmosphere changing in court, it makes a big difference to the trial' (B14). Therefore, in drawing upon the theoretical framework we can see how the barristers placed significant emphasis on both the actual (spoken) and intensive (unspoken) properties and capacities of the body. Proximity to the complainant's fleshy body was seen as vital to producing, and overcoming, intensive and affective forces that would ultimately move the jury, shifting these forces from an intensive superposition (simultaneously guilty/not guilty and victim/not victim) to an actualised – that is, delivered – verdict.

Affectual relationality: The jury dynamic

In relation to the introduction of special measures, one concern that has frequently been voiced is that their use may lead the jury to assume that the defendant is guilty. However, our data clearly indicates that this is not the case. Indeed, a common theme to emerge from our interviews was that the use of remote testimony works to the advantage of the defence. It was noted that a defendant would frequently give evidence within the courtroom and without the use of the screen, and therefore the jury are 'gonna see him in the flesh' (B3). Where remote witness testimony is used, the defendant's fleshy performance was considered to stand in stark contrast with that of the 'sterilised' complainant, whom the jury have 'never met' and therefore are not 'able to evaluate' (B11). Concerns were expressed by our participants that the jury would often 'switch off' (B13) during the presentation of video evidence, but that the presence of the defendant in the courtroom would then change the atmosphere and dynamic: 'defence come on and everyone starts to wake up, oh, what's going on here' (B13). It was also highlighted that, in this situation, the cross-examination of the defendant was the 'first sort of reality the jury have got' (B12).

In exploring the impact of the defendant's physical presence in the courtroom, the barristers placed particular emphasis on the relational nature of affect. More specifically, they commented on how being physically present enables the defendant to establish a connection with, and respond to, the jury – an opportunity that would not be available to the complainant if her evidence was delivered remotely. A few barristers discussed this issue at length. B5, for example, highlighted that, in contrast to the complainant, 'the defendant is eyeballing the jury', and that, if he made the jury laugh, this would be a 'disastrous sign for the prosecution'. While recognising that a complainant would be unlikely to invoke a similar response, she may nevertheless 'get some reaction out of them'. However, given her absence, she would be unaware of any such reaction and therefore unable to alter her performance accordingly. Thus, not being in physical proximity to the jury was considered to hamper the complainant's ability to establish an intensively reciprocal relationship with them, through which the affects emitted by the array of bodies within the courtroom can be sensed and bring about transformations.

Accordingly, this inability to register and subsequently respond to the jury's reactions was perceived to negatively impact upon the performance of the complainant. It was felt that, in these circumstances, witnesses seek to be reassured that the jury are engaged and receptive to their testimony. However, the jury could be 'raising eyebrows and all sorts' or 'looking down at their notes' and not really listening (B5). In contrast, B9 reflected upon a case in which the complainant, while delivering her testimony within the courtroom, engaged in an action that was seen to have a lasting and transformative affect and effect upon the jury:

> that moment where … the witness looks past you when you're asking them questions and they just go, I just want him to know I've never forgotten. And it's dynamite. You can't pay for stuff like that. As a prosecutor it's absolutely amazing.

By emphasising the importance and performative nature of the nonverbal interaction between the jury and those giving evidence, it is clear that the barristers recognise the embodied, relational and unconscious nature of affects. What is said, and how it is said, impacts upon and transforms others on both an intensive and actual level. Verbal and nonverbal communications have the ability to provoke a range of sensations and reactions. These may be both physical and emotional, and can also be unconscious and autonomic (such as a sudden and automatic flinch) as well as conscious.

Harnessing intensive affects and ideal victim discourses

In exploring and recognising the relational and transformative nature of affects, our barrister participants also appreciated the importance of and our ability to produce, harness, and manage intensive forces. The quote above by B9 describes an unexpected intensively forceful event that arose during the trial process and was identified by the prosecution as a pivotal moment in the trial. It also provides an interesting example of an agential performance that sits in contrast with gendered stereotypes around passive victimhood. However, the participants' conceptualisations of performances that can have the desired transformative impact upon the jury were frequently influenced by stereotypes regarding the actions and reactions of 'real rape' victims. Herein we can see not only barristers' desire to produce and harness certain affects, but also the interplay between discourses and affects.

Previous research has amply illustrated the existence of ideal or 'real' rape victim discourses, which include the notions that only stranger rape is 'real rape'; that a 'real victim' would resist, suffer physical injuries, and report the crime immediately; that false allegations are common; and that victims who drink or engage in what is deemed to be risky or irresponsible behaviour are to blame for their victimisation.[54] These discourses can be seen to influence key decision-making processes at all points of the criminal justice system.[55] Such decisions include a victim's initial decision to report the offence; police and prosecutorial decisions to arrest, charge, and prosecute an offender; and the jury's ultimate verdict. What arose during many of the interviews was the expectation that a victim would be traumatised in a particular way and, more specifically, that this trauma

54 See, for example, Kimberly A Lonsway and Louise F Fitzgerald, 'Rape Myths: In Review' (1994) 18(2) *Psychology of Women Quarterly* 133; Saunders (n 6).

55 Carline and Easteal (n 5); Louise Ellison and Vanessa Munro, 'Reacting to Rape: Exploring Mock Jurors' Assessments of Complainant Credibility' (2009) 49 *British Journal of Criminology* 202; Louise Ellison and Vanessa Munro, 'Getting to (Not) Guilty: Examining Jurors' Deliberative Processes in and beyond the Context of a Mock Rape Trial' (2010) 30 *Legal Studies* 74; Louise Ellison and Vanessa Munro, 'A Stranger in the Bushes, or an Elephant in the Room? Critical Reflection upon Received Rape Myth Wisdom in the Context of a Mock Jury Study' (2010) 13 *New Criminal Law Review* 781; Emily Finch and Vanessa Munro, 'The Demon Drink and the Demonised Woman: Socio-Sexual Stereotypes and Responsibility Attribution in Rape Trials Involving Intoxicants' (2007) 16 *Social and Legal Studies* 591; Katrin Hohl and Elisabeth Stanko, 'Complaints of Rape and the Criminal Justice System: Fresh Evidence on the Attrition Problem in England and Wales' (2015) 13 *European Journal of Criminology* 324; Kelly, Lovett and Regan (n 5); Temkin and Krahé (n 6).

would be emotionally displayed during the trial. In this regard, most barristers maintained that, if prosecuting, they would want to have 'the complainant in court, crying her eyes out, a real person' (B6). Similar views were expressed by those who defended, and it was suggested that the witness breaking down would confirm the truth of the allegation: 'if you're defending, you don't want the jury to see anybody breaking down and crying, looking at your client, because it just reinforces the truth of the account' (B14). Such perspectives, however, draw upon 'ideal rape' victim discourses, which assume that a real rape victim will react in a certain manner, that the jury will expect to see such a performance and that this performance will in turn produce certain intensive affects, which will shape the outcome of the case. And these discourses persist despite the introduction – albeit relatively recently – of judicial directions that warn the jury not to rely upon mistaken assumptions, including the expectation that all complainants will display certain emotions during the trial process.[56] Hence, in their desire to produce and harness transformative affects, the barristers in our research problematically drew upon and reinforced certain stereotypical discourses. That this was problematic and unethical, was not, however, lost on the participants: 'I'm not sure how professional it is for me to say it but … I wanted in front of the jury, that breakdown' (B24).

These views regarding the 'real rape' victim performance can also be linked to wider assumptions concerning the ability of the jury to read the truth from the live and embodied testimony of the complainant:

> if you sit in the courtroom and if you watch somebody who is finding the process very difficult, and you can tell very quickly listening to somebody if they're telling the truth or not.
>
> *(B14)*

In a similar vein, B31 noted: '[the jury] can see the victim, they can see how he or she relates to what's happened to them'. These perspectives, however, contrast with psychological research that shows that people tend to (mistakenly) assume that they are better able to tell if a person is lying or telling the truth when that person is in the flesh, and overestimate their ability to do so.[57] Nevertheless, the barristers' concern to produce certain intensive affects within the courtroom could be seen to drive their desire to have the complainant physically present,

56 Judicial College, *The Crown Court Compendium: Part 1 – Jury and Trial Management and Summing Up* (The Judicial College, 2018).

57 Sara Landström, Pär Anders Granhag and Maria Hartwig, 'Witnesses Appearing Live versus on Video: Effects on Observers' Perception, Veracity Assessments and Memory' (2005) 19 *Applied Cognitive Psychology* 913; Maureen O'Sullivan, Paul Ekman and Wallace V Friesen, 'The Effect of Comparisons on Detecting Deceit' (1988) 12 *Journal of Nonverbal Behavior* 203; Aldert Vrij, *Detecting Lies and Deceit: The Psychology of Lying and Implications for Professional Practice* (John Wiley & Sons, 2000).

and to deliver testimony in a particular way, even though this raises significant ethical and professional issues.

Affects and practice: Advising the complainant

The barristers' perspectives regarding the negative impact of special measures upon conviction rates and the importance of having the complainant physically present in the courtroom fundamentally influenced their practice and their advice to complainants.

Early on, following the introduction of special measures, prosecutors would always request a live link. However, 'it took them a few years to realise that that was not very clever' (B6). Subsequently, an inverse situation arose, whereby prosecutors would generally try to 'disapply special measures' (B9), while defence barristers would raise no objections to their use. B13, for example, commented:

> I was getting a bit too clever in the early days getting all these ABEs excluded and then the person would come live. And I just started losing these cases ... and I thought ... because the victim was all of a sudden there, it's like so much more impact. So, actually I don't ever argue [against] admissibility of ABEs any more ... it was just tactically a disaster.

However, prosecutors' disinclination towards the use of special measures did not apply across the board. For example, most of our participants expressed support for the use of screens, as these would ensure the complainant's presence in the courtroom. As B17 noted: 'most regular [sexual offences] prosecutors always try and get the complainant into court with a screen, because it's so much more effective'. Significantly, this preference for a screen had a profound influence on their practice: 'I always, if I get the opportunity, try and encourage complainants to give evidence in court from behind a screen' (B19). While one barrister stated that 'to say that I'll persuade them to come into court is probably putting it too highly' (B11), another noted: 'I always twist witnesses' arms to come into the courtroom by hook or by crook' (B5). Overall, it was observed that 'street-wise complainants now always give evidence behind screens, live' (B13).

Conclusion

This chapter has provided new insights into the space of the courtroom by drawing upon theories of affects, the intensive ontological regime, and empirical research with barristers. To this end, we have explored practitioners' views of special measures by engaging with the 'affective turn', which hitherto has been under-utilised within the fields of law, criminal justice, and criminology. In applying this theoretical framework, it has been possible to establish that counsel placed significant emphasis upon the affective capacity of the body during the trial and its ability to move or influence the jury, and that this understanding of the body informed their opinions of, and use of, 'remote testimony'. While the use of special measures was commonplace, the barristers frequently considered that the pre-recorded ABE and use of live link reduced the emotional – or affectual – impact of the complainant's testimony, which in turn negatively affected the evidential value of the case and ultimately conviction rates. Consequently, our barrister participants argued that, when prosecuting, they wanted the complainant to deliver their testimony live in the courtroom, and their justification for this was linked to the affective capabilities of the body: the ability of the body to bring about a transformation in the jury. In turn, this fundamentally influenced their practice, as they would endeavour to persuade the complainant to eschew the remote special measures. Through their observations, we can see how the barristers were intuitively aware of affects and the intensive regime; they demonstrated a good understanding of the affectual force of the body and its ability to bring about transformations in others. However, in so doing, the barristers frequently drew upon various problematic 'ideal rape victim' discourses on the assumption that the more emotional courtroom performance would be more affective.

None of this should be taken to suggest that we support abolishing special measures that place the complainant outside the courtroom. Undoubtedly, such provisions do help complainants, and it is important to shield witnesses from the negative effects and affects of the trial process – and the barristers we interviewed recognised this. However, the importance of applying a theoretical framework to a field of practice that is already intuitively understood is that barristers can become far more self-reflective and self-reflexive in responding to the challenges of new court practice innovations and technological developments. While perhaps different in nature to their in-person counterparts, intensive affects will nevertheless flow from remote testimony. Hence, the question to explore with practitioners is how the forces of affects can be most productively harnessed to bring about the shifts and transformations desired.

To this end, we argue that policymakers need to appreciate the importance of the incorporeal intensive affects that inform barristers' practice and shape the dynamics of the courtroom. As such, the theoretical framework adopted herein offers a novel approach to examining and understanding the pervasive 'implementation gap' that exists within this field. While financial resources (or the lack thereof) and myths and misconceptions regarding sexual violence are undoubtedly instrumental,[58] this chapter highlights the importance of developing a bottom-up analysis that appreciates the intensive affects that emerge within the courtroom and how these influence practice and the outcomes of cases. Indeed, a few barristers expressed frustration at the continuous production of provisions and reforms by those who had little, if any, experience and knowledge of the everyday reality of courtroom dynamics. For example, it was

58 See, for example, Anna Carline and Clare Gunby, 'Justice for Rape Complainants: Limitations and Possibilities' in Pat Carlen (ed), *Justice Alternatives* (Routledge, 2019).

noted that policy is often 'made by people who have no real experience of what goes on in a courtroom … When you're actually in a courtroom, it's completely different' (B19). This indicates that it is important to produce measures that are influenced by the working reality of the courtroom and take into account both the intensive (incorporeal) and actual (corporeal) ontological registers. In contrast, a top-down approach that fails to acknowledge the importance of affects and the embodied battle of forces that plays out within the courtroom is unlikely to be utilised as expected, if at all.

Acknowledgements

We would like to thank the editors for their feedback and comments on an earlier draft of this chapter. Dr Carline would also like to thank the editors for inviting her to present a paper on this topic at the Space of Justice Symposium held at La Trobe University in July 2017.

Bibliography

Articles/books/reports

Ahmed, Sara, 'Killing Joy: Feminism and the History of Happiness' (2010) 35(3) *Signs* 571

Anderson, Ben, 'Affective Atmospheres' (2009) 2(1) *Emotion, Space and Society* 77

Bonta, Mark and John Protevi, *Deleuze and Geophilosophy: A Guide and Glossary* (Edinburgh University Press, 1st ed, 2004)

Brennan, Teresa, *The Transmission of Affect* (Cornell University Press, 2004)

Burkitt, Ian, *Emotions and Social Relations* (Sage Publications, 2014)

Burton, Mandy, Roger Evans and Andrew Sanders, *Are Special Measures for Vulnerable and Intimidated Witnesses Working? Evidence from the Criminal Justice Agencies* (Home Office Online Report 01/06, 2006)

Burton, Mandy, Roger Evans and Andrew Sanders, 'Implementing Special Measures and Vulnerable and Intimidated Witnesses: The Problem of Identification' (2006) *Criminal Law Review* 229

Burton, Mandy, Roger Evans and Andrew Sanders, 'Vulnerable and Intimidated Witnesses and the Adversarial Process in England and Wales' (2007) 11(1) *International Journal of Evidence and Proof* 1

Carline, Anna and Clare Gunby, '"How an Ordinary Jury Makes Sense of It Is a Mystery": Barristers' Perspectives on Rape, Consent and the Sexual Offences Act 2003' (2011) 32(3) *Liverpool Law Review* 237

Carline, Anna and Clare Gunby, 'Rape Politics, Policies and Practice: Exploring the Tensions and Unanticipated Consequences of Well-Intended Victim-Focused Measures' (2017) 56(1) *The Howard Journal of Crime and Justice* 34

Carline, Anna and Clare Gunby, 'Justice for Rape Complainants: Limitations and Possibilities' in Pat Carlen (ed), *Justice Alternatives* (Routledge, 2019)

Carline, Anna, Clare Gunby and Caryl Beynon, 'Alcohol-Related Rape Cases: Barristers' Perspectives on the Sexual Offences Act 2003 and Its Impact on Practice' (2010) 74(6) *Journal of Criminal Law* 579

Carline, Anna and Patricia Easteal, *Shades of Grey – Domestic and Sexual Violence against Women: Law Reform and Society* (Routledge, 1st ed, 2014)

Charles, Corrine, *Special Measures for Vulnerable and Intimidated Witnesses: Research Exploring the Decisions and Actions Taken by Prosecutors in a Sample of CPS Case Files* (Crown Prosecution Service Research Report, April 2012)

Clough, Patricia, *The Affective Turn: Theorising the Social* (Duke University Press, 1st ed, 2007)

Cook, Kate, 'Rape Investigation and Prosecution: Stuck in the Mud?' (2011) 17(3) *Journal of Sexual Aggression* 250

Cooper, Debbie and Paul Roberts, *Special Measures for Vulnerable and Intimidated Witnesses: An Analysis of Crown Prosecution Service Monitoring Data* (Crown Prosecution Service, 2005)

Council of HM Circuit Judges, *Convicting Rapists and Protecting Victims: A Consultation Response of the Council of Her Majesty's Circuit Judges* (Consultation Response Report, 2006)

Crown Prosecution Service (CPS) and Police, *Joint CPS and Police Action Plan on Rape* (Rape Action Plan Report, 2002)

Crown Prosecution Service (CPS) and Police, *Joint CPS and Police Action Plan on Rape* (Rape Action Plan Report, April 2015)

Davies, Graham, 'The Impact of Television on the Presentation and Reception of Children's Testimony' (1999) 22(3–4) *International Journal of Law and Psychiatry* 241

Delanda, Manuel, 'Space: Extensive and Intensive, Actual and Virtual' in Buchanan Ian and Lambert Gregg (eds), *Deleuze and Space* (Edinburgh University Press, 2005)

Deleuze, Gilles and Félix Guattari, *What Is Philosophy?* (Verso, 2015)

Deleuze, Gilles and Félix Guattari, *A Thousand Plateaus* (Bloomsbury, 2017)

Ellison, Louise, *The Adversarial Process and the Vulnerable Victim* (Oxford University Press, 1st ed, 2001)

Ellison, Louise and Vanessa Munro, 'Reacting to Rape: Exploring Mock Jurors' Assessments of Complainant Credibility' (2009) 49 *British Journal of Criminology* 202

Ellison, Louise and Vanessa Munro, 'A Stranger in the Bushes, or an Elephant in the Room? Critical Reflection upon Received Rape Myth Wisdom in the Context of a Mock Jury Study' (2010) 13 *New Criminal Law Review* 781

Ellison, Louise and Vanessa Munro, 'Getting to (Not) Guilty: Examining Jurors' Deliberative Processes in and beyond the Context of a Mock Rape Trial' (2010) 30 *Legal Studies* 74

Ellison, Louise and Vanessa Munro, 'A "Special" Delivery? Exploring the Impact of Screens, Live-Links and Video Recorded Evidence on Mock Juror Deliberation in Rape Trials' (2014) 23(1) *Social & Legal Studies* 3

Finch, Emily and Vanessa Munro, 'The Demon Drink and the Demonised Woman: Socio-Sexual Stereotypes and Responsibility Attribution in Rape Trials Involving Intoxicants' (2007) 16 *Social and Legal Studies* 591

Gherardi, Silvia, 'One Turn … and Now Another One: Do the Turn to Practice and the Turn to Affect Have Something in Common?' (2017) 48(3) *Management Learning* 345

Gregg, Melissa and Gregory Seigworth, *The Affects Theory Reader* (Duke University Press, 2010)

Gregory, Jeanne and Sue Lees, 'Attrition in Rape and Sexual Assault Cases' (1996) 36(1) *The British Journal of Criminology* 1.

Hall, Matthew, 'The Use and Abuse of Special Measures: Giving Victims the Choice?' (2007) 58(8) *Journal of Scandinavian Studies in Criminology and Crime Prevention* 33

Hamlyn, Becky, Andrew Phelps, Jenny Turtle and Ghazala Sattar, *Are Special Measures Working? Evidence from Surveys of Vulnerable and Intimidated Witnesses* (Home Office Research Study 283, 2004)

HM Crown Prosecution Service Inspectorate (HMCPSI) and HM Inspectorate of Constabulary (HMIC), *A Report on the Joint Inspection into the Investigation and Prosecution of Cases Involving Allegations of Rape* (Investigation Report, April 2002)

HM Crown Prosecution Service Inspectorate (HMCPSI) and HM Inspectorate of Constabulary (HMIC), *Without Consent: A Report on the Joint Review of the Investigation and Prosecution of Rape Offences* (Inspection Report, January 2007)

HM Government, *Ending Violence against Women and Girls: Strategy 2016–2020* (Strategy Report, March 2016)

HM Inspectorate of Constabulary (HMIC), *Making the Victim Count* (Crime Recording Report, November 2014)

Hohl, Katrin and Elisabeth Stanko, 'Complaints of Rape and the Criminal Justice System: Fresh Evidence on the Attrition Problem in England and Wales' (2015) 13 *European Journal of Criminology* 324

Home Office, *Speaking Up for Justice: Report of the Interdepartmental Working Group on the Treatment of Vulnerable or Intimidated Witnesses in the Criminal Justice System* (Home Office, 1998)

Home Office, *Setting the Boundaries: Reforming the Law on Sex Offences* (Consultation Paper Vol. 1, July 2000)

Home Office, *Protecting the Public: Strengthening Protection against Sex Offenders and Reforming the Law on Sexual Offences* (Cm 5668, 2002)

Home Office, *Convicting Rapists and Protecting Victims: Justice for Victims of Rape* (Consultation Paper, Spring 2006)

Home Office, *Sexual Offences Act 2003: A Stocktake of the Effectiveness of the Act since Its Implementation* (Home Office, 2006)

Hoyano, Laura CH, 'Coroners and Justice Act 2009: Special Measures Directions Take Two – Entrenching Unequal Access to Justice?' (2010) 5 *Criminal Law Review* 345

Judicial College, *The Crown Court Compendium: Part 1 – Jury and Trial Management and Summing Up* (The Judicial College, 2018)

Kelly, Liz, Jo Lovett and Linda Regan, *A Gap or a Chasm? Attrition in Reported Rape Cases* (Home Office Research Study 293, 2005)

Landström, Sara, Pär Anders Granhag and Maria Hartwig, 'Witnesses Appearing Live versus on Video: Effects on Observers' Perception, Veracity Assessments and Memory' (2005) 19 *Applied Cognitive Psychology* 913

Lees, Sue, *Carnal Knowledge: Rape on Trial* (Women's Press, 2nd ed, 2002)

Lonsway, Kimberly A and Louise F Fitzgerald, 'Rape Myths: In Review' (1994) 18(2) *Psychology of Women Quarterly* 133

Massumi, Brian, *A User's Guide to Capitalism and Schizophrenia* (MIT Press, 1992)

Massumi, Brian, 'The Autonomy of Affect' (1995) 31 *Cultural Critique Part II* 83

Massumi, Brian, *Parables for the Virtual: Movement, Affect, Sensation* (Duke University Press, 2002)

Massumi, Brian, *Politics of Affect* (Polity, 1st ed, 2015)

Ministry of Justice, *Code of Practice for Victims of Crime* (Her Majesty's Stationery Office, 2015)

Office for Criminal Justice Reform, *Convicting Rapists and Protecting Victims: Justice for Victims of Rape* (Consultation Paper, Spring 2006)

Office for Criminal Justice Reform, *Convicting Rapists and Protecting Victims: Justice for Victims of Rape, Responses to Consultation* (Office for Criminal Justice Reforms, 2007)

O'Sullivan, Maureen, Paul Ekman and Wallace V Friesen, 'The Effect of Comparisons on Detecting Deceit' (1988) 12 *Journal of Nonverbal Behavior* 203

Payne, Sara, *Rape: The Victim Experience Review* (Home Office Review Report, 2009)

Philipopoulos-Mihalopoulos, Andreas, *Spatial Justice: Body, Lawscape, Atmosphere* (Routledge, 1st ed, 2015)
Plotnikoff, Joyce and Richard Woolfson, 'Worth Waiting for: The Benefits of Section 28 Pre-trial Cross Examination' (2016) 8 *Archbold Review* 6
Probyn, Elspeth, *Blush: Faces of Shame* (University of Minnesota Press, 2005)
Saunders, Alison, 'Speech on the Prosecution of Rape and Serious Sexual Offences by Alison Saunders' (Speech, Crown Prosecution Service, 2012)
Sointu, Eeva, 'Discourse, Affect and Affliction' (2016) 64(2) *The Sociological Review* 312
Spinoza, Baruch, *Ethics* (Oxford University Press, 2000)
Stern, Vivien, *A Report by Baroness Vivien Stern CBE of an Independent Review into How Rape Complaints Are Handled by Public Authorities in England and Wales: The Stern Review* (Home Office Report, 2010)
Temkin, Jennifer, 'Prosecuting and Defending Rape: Perspectives from the Bar' (2000) 27(2) *Journal of Law and Society* 219
Temkin, Jennifer and Barbara Krahé, *Sexual Assault and the Justice Gap: A Question of Attitude* (Hart Publishing, 2008)
Vrij, Aldert, *Detecting Lies and Deceit: The Psychology of Lying and Implications for Professional Practice* (John Wiley & Sons, 2000)
Westera, Nina J, Blake M McKimmie, Mark R Kebbell, Rebecca Milne and Barbara Masser, 'Does the Narrative Style of Video Evidence Influence Judgements about Rape Complainant Testimony?' (2015) 29 *Applied Cognitive Psychology* 637
Westera, Nina J, Martine B Powell and Becky Milne, 'Lost in the Detail: Prosecutors' Perceptions of the Utility of Video Recorded Police Interviews as Rape Complainant Evidence' (2017) 50(2) *Australian and New Zealand Journal of Criminology* 252
Wetherell, Margaret, *Affect and Emotion: A New Social Science Understanding* (Sage Publications, 2012)

Legislation

Coroners and Justice Act 2009 (UK)
Sexual Offences Act 2003 (UK)
Youth Justice and Criminal Evidence Act 1999 (UK)

8

DIGITAL JUSTICE AND VIDEO LINKS

Connecting and conflating courtroom and carceral space

Carolyn McKay

Introduction

With a focus on the criminal justice system, this chapter scrutinises the uptake of digital technologies in criminal procedure and the resulting shift in the spatial relationships involved in legal adjudication. Concentrating specifically on the increasing use of audiovisual link technologies (also known as video links, live links, or videoconferencing) that connect public courtrooms with non-public sites of custody or detention, this chapter examines how courtroom space is in the process of being delocalised, dispersed, distributed, or dematerialised to prison video link studios and other remote sites.[1] What are the implications for the administration of justice when the courtroom becomes virtual or fully digitised and the physical presence of certain key actors is no longer required? This chapter seeks to enhance understandings of the profound transformation that is occurring in court space and the implications for the delivery of justice as

1 L Mulcahy, *Legal Architecture: Justice, Due Process and the Place of Law* (Routledge, 2011); E Rowden, 'Distributed Courts and Legitimacy: What Do We Lose When We Lose the Courthouse?' (2018) 14(2) *Law, Culture and the Humanities* 263–281; E Rowden, 'Remote Participation and the Distributed Court: An Approach to Court Architecture in the Age of Video-Mediated Communication' (PhD Thesis, University of Melbourne, 2011); C Licoppe and L Dumoulin, 'The "Curious Case" of an Unspoken Opening Speech Act: A Video-Ethnography of the Use of Video Communication in Courtroom Activities' (2010) 43(3) *Research on Language and Social Interaction* 211–231; R Mohr, 'In between Power and Procedure: Where the Court Meets the Public Sphere' in *A Thousand Eyes: Media Technology, Law and Aesthetics* (Sternberg Press, 2011); D Tait et al., 'Towards a Distributed Courtroom' (2017) <http://courtofthefuture.org/wp-content/uploads/2017/07/170710_TowardsADistributedCourtroom_Compressed.pdf>; A Wallace, SR Anleu and K Mack, 'Judicial Work and AV Use: Perceptions from Australian Courts' (2017) 7(4) *Oñati Socio-Legal Series* [online] 691–716 <http://ssrn.com/abstract=3034200>.

DOI: 10.4324/9780429059858-12

the system shifts from the terrestrial realm to the digital. The coronavirus pandemic has distilled the significance of closely examining the emergence of digital justice.

The chapter commences with an overview of twenty-first century digital society and the pervasiveness of the screen to provide context to the digitisation of criminal procedure and the justice system. The drivers of and rationales for technological change are outlined, as well as concerns regarding technologies operating in criminal justice – a high-stakes context where accused people face prosecution and potential punishment. In the next section, 'Physical courtrooms with physical people', I start to unpack how buildings such as courts and prisons represent a 'combination of function and expression'.[2] First, I examine how 'traditional' physical courtrooms and the physical co-presence of all parties have been central to legal rituals and procedural justice principles; that is, spatiality and corporeality have long underpinned issues of fairness in procedure. Shifting to a consideration of 'Virtual courts with virtual people', I then discuss the introduction of video links into criminal procedure and how this technology has effected a radical change in the method of producing incarcerated defendants to court. In many jurisdictions and for a range of criminal processes, digital or electronic production by video link has become the default situation, meaning that defendants increasingly 'appear' in court from a custodial setting, instead of being transported physically to court. This, in turn, has led to the conceptual expansion of courtroom space into prisons and police cells, and the converse situation of prisons and police cells conceptually intruding into courts. At the same time, the need for a physical courthouse is diminishing as criminal procedure evolves into a digitised and despatialised paradigm.

Drawing on the findings of my previous empirical research,[3] in 'The prison endpoint of video links' I examine the video link spaces within prisons that are used for custodial court appearance. When these spaces are used, the courtroom custody dock is effectively relocated to the prison video link studio so that prisoners' legal experiences are framed by the surrounding carceral environment, instead of by the ambience of a dignified court space. In contrasting the qualitative attributes of prison video link 'court' facilities and those of actual courtrooms, I discuss the significant spatial – and sonic – disjuncture that arises. I also examine contemporary courtroom technological developments in 'The courtroom endpoint of video links' to unpack the tensions between pragmatism, efficiency drivers, ensuring access to justice, and emerging modes of electronic justice. This section scrutinises the uptake of screens and digital technologies in

2 L Fairweather and S McConville, *Prison Architecture: Policy, Design and Experience* (Architectural Press, 2003) 10.

3 C McKay, *The Pixelated Prisoner: Prison Video Links, Court 'Appearance' and the Justice Matrix* (Routledge, 2018).

courtrooms, the gradual depopulation of defendants and other actors in physical courtrooms, and the diminishing 'bricks and mortar' of the court estate.

In 'Conflating court spaces with prisons' I examine how the prison video link studio is treated, pursuant to legislative provisions, as a conceptual extension of the courtroom, resulting in a conflation of the space of the administration of justice with the non-neutral and closed environment of state prosecution and punishment. Does this spatial conflation blur the lines between the functions of the judiciary and the executive and undermine the principles of open and impartial justice? There appears to be a gradual merging of criminal procedure with offender management. In view of these technological and spatial changes, I articulate some provocations presented to procedural justice values and the legitimacy of criminal procedure. In particular, I examine the implications for the principles of open justice, equality of arms, confrontation, and the presumption of innocence and highlight the need for further research into how the new digitised paradigm can spatially reflect justice. The chapter concludes with observations concerning the unstoppable march of technologies and the fact that criminal procedure has always been an ever-evolving, 'plastic' creature. Nevertheless, I conclude that technologies are transformative of the fundamentals of criminal procedure and the space in which criminal justice is administered.

Digitising criminal justice

The massive transformations brought about by digital technologies are well recognised and, in developed nations, few sectors of society have not been radically affected. Health, education, research, business, finance, media, and science, to name a few, have all undergone significant change, altering the way citizens interact with institutions and each other. In the twenty-first-century digital society, technologies are integral and embedded in key functions[4] and society is increasingly networked such that internet access is considered as important as basic electricity supply.[5] Aligned with the pervasive use of technologies in day-to-day existence, technological innovations are transforming legal practice and procedure[6] and, as a consequence, the spaces in which these occur. The digitisation of the law is fuelled not only by the mere existence of information and communication technologies (ICT), but also by efficiency and expediency

4 G Stratton, A Powell and R Cameron, 'Crime and Justice in Digital Society: Towards a "Digital Criminology"?' (2016) 6(2) *International Journal for Crime, Justice and Social Democracy* 17–33; D Lupton, *Digital Sociology* (Routledge, 2014).

5 R Smith, *Digital Delivery of Legal Services to People on Low Incomes* (Legal Education Foundation, 2014).

6 J Donoghue, 'The Rise of Digital Justice: Courtroom Technology, Public Participation and Access to Justice' (2017) 80(6) *The Modern Law Review* 995–1025; LW McDonald et al., 'Digital Evidence in the Jury Room: The Impact of Mobile Technology on the Jury' (2015) 27 *Current Issues in Criminal Justice* 179; R Susskind and D Susskind, *The Future of the Professions: How Technology Will Transform the Work of Human Experts* (Oxford University Press, 2015).

concerns.[7] Certainly, these concerns are important drivers for the introduction of technologies into legal practice and procedure in many countries, including England and Wales, the United States (US), Canada, New Zealand (NZ), and Australia, where digitisation facilitates case management and court registers, the handling of documentation, the presentation of evidence, and the appearance of expert witnesses, vulnerable witnesses, victims, and accused persons. For instance, in England and Wales, the government has embarked on a £1.2-billion court modernisation project that aims to streamline process, provide more connectivity between institutions, and make greater use of online portals such as an online plea service for low-level offences.[8] Central to this digital reform are video link technologies that may eventually enable 'fully video hearings' where all parties participate through a web browser and no one is required to appear in a courtroom,[9] thereby diminishing the need for a physical court estate[10] and co-present physical parties.

While there may be clear benefits for the just, quick, and cheap delivery of *civil* justice,[11] there are particular concerns in relation to the technologisation of *criminal* justice. Criminal justice presents the ultimate high-stakes proceedings in which people face criminalisation, state punishment, and the loss of liberty – 'the highest of high stakes'.[12] Additionally, because the technologies are operated by the state within spaces of prosecution and punishment and they displace the physical presence of accused persons in courtrooms, technological change in this context is not at all benign.[13] The use of technologies in criminal justice

7 The Rt Hon Sir B Leveson, *Review of Efficiency in Criminal Proceedings* (2015) <https://www.judiciary.uk/wp-content/uploads/2015/01/review-of-efficiency-in-criminal-proceedings-20151.pdf>; J Ward, 'Transforming "Summary Justice" through Police-Led Prosecution and "Virtual Courts" is "Procedural Due Process" Being Undermined?' (2015) 55(2) *British Journal of Criminology* 341–358; Donoghue, 'The Rise of Digital Justice' (n 6).

8 Her Majesty's Courts & Tribunals Service (HMCTS) *Reform Update*, May 2018, <https://assets.publishing.service.gov.uk/government/uploads/system/uploads/attachment_data/file/711535/HMCTS_Reform_Update_May_2018.pdf> 7.

9 HMCTS, *Reform Update* (n8) 9, 18; Courts and Tribunals Judiciary, *Judicial Ways of Working – 2022: Crime*, April 2018 <http://www.transformjustice.org.uk/wp-content/uploads/2018/05/jwow-2022-crime.pdf>; M Rossner and M McCurdy, *Implementing video hearings (Party-to-State): A process evaluation* (The London School of Economics and Political Science, 2018) <https://www.gov.uk/government/publications/implementing-video-hearings-party-to-state-a-process-evaluation>.

10 HMCTS, *Fit for the Future: Transforming the Court and Tribunal Estate* (2018) <https://consult.justice.gov.uk/digital-communications/transforming-court-tribunal-estate/supporting_documents/hmctsstrategyapproachconsultation.pdf>.

11 See, for example, *Civil Procedure Act 2005* (NSW) s 56; A Zuckerman et al., *Zuckerman on Australian Civil Procedure* (LexisNexis, 2018); M Kumar, M Legg and I Vickovich, *Civil Procedures in New South Wales* (Thomson Reuters, 2016).

12 K Leader, 'The Trial's the Thing: Performance and Legitimacy in International Criminal Trials' (2018) *Theoretical Criminology* 1–17, 4. doi: 10.1177/1362480618806923.

13 AB Poulin, 'Criminal Justice and Videoconferencing Technology: The Remote Defendant' (2003) 78 *Tulane Law Review* 1089; Rowden, 'Remote Participation' (n 1); Mulcahy, *Legal Architecture* (n 1); McKay, *The Pixelated Prisoner* (n 3); L Dumoulin and C Licoppe, 'Trial at a

is transformative of legal experience and is therefore providing challenges and provocations to contemporary designers and architects interested in creating spaces that continue to represent and enable procedural justice values.[14]

Physical courtrooms with physical people

Spatiality is an important concept in the law, relevant to expressions of jurisdiction, territory, hierarchy, and power.[15] Criminal justice has traditionally operated within civic courthouses that contain open and public courtrooms, and with all relevant parties, particularly the defendant, present in that shared space.[16] As Leader observes, the criminal trial, at least, can be analysed as a 'communal ritual' that is effective only if participants are removed from normal or daily life to appear in a special, if not, 'sacred' space.[17] Thus, both the physical presence of the people involved as well as the physical space of legal adjudication have been critical in underpinning the legitimacy of the law.

In terms of the physical space, the courtroom has been seen as emblematic of the gravitas of criminal procedure and of the power of the state to prosecute and punish transgressors, while its design has been understood as reflecting fairness and impartiality.[18] In court space, there are 'aesthetic and architectural representations of the law', legal iconography, and symbols[19] that function to reinforce solemnity. These tangible spaces have been seen as 'formal and ritualistic' social settings[20] with a 'multiplicity of symbolic cues'[21] that represent society's conceptions of justice[22] in their dignified yet hierarchical design and zones of

Distance: Videoconference Technology as a Policy Tool?' (2015) 1(5) *International Conference in Public Policy*.

14 R Lulham et al., *Audio Visual Links Suites in Custodial Contexts: Basic Ergonomic and Technical Recommendations* (University of Technology Sydney, 2017) <https://www.designforsocialjustice.xyz/>.

15 L Farmer, *Criminal Law, Tradition and Legal Order* (Cambridge University Press, 1997).

16 Mulcahy, *Legal Architecture* (n 1); C Graham, 'A History of Law Court Architecture in England and Wales: SAVE Britain's Heritage' in *Silence in Court: The Future of the UK's Historic Law Courts* (Save Britain's Heritage, 2004) 36–47; J Hodgson, 'Conceptions of the Trial in Inquisitorial and Adversarial Procedure' in A Duff et al. (eds), *Judgment and Calling to Account* (Hart Publishing, 2006) 223–242; Rowden, 'Distributed Courts and Legitimacy' (n 1); K Leader, 'Trials, Truth-Telling and the Performing Body' (Thesis, University of Sydney, 2008).

17 Leader, 'The Trial's the Thing' (n 12) 4, 6.

18 D Tait, 'Glass Cages in the Dock: Presenting the Defendant to the Jury' (2011) 86 *Chicago-Kent Law Review*. 467.

19 D DesBaillets, 'Representing Canadian Justice: Legal Iconography and Symbolism at the Supreme Court of Canada' (2018) March 14(1) *International Journal of Law in Context* 132–156, 132.

20 P Carlen, 'The Staging of Magistrates' Justice' (1976) 16(1) *The British Journal of Criminology* 48–55, 50.

21 JB Thompson, 'The New Visibility' (2005) 22(6) *Theory, Culture & Society* 31–51, 32.

22 NW Spaulding, 'Enclosure of Justice: Courthouse Architecture, Due Process, and the Dead Metaphor of Trial' (2012) 24 *Yale Journal of Law & the Humanities* 311; ET Bellone, 'Private

segregation.[23] Court space has thus been considered to be an architectural manifestation of the symbolic weight and majesty of the law,[24] which should offer 'generosity and dignity' in its expression of 'our fundamental commitment as a civil society to the rule of law'.[25]

Courtrooms are buildings of civic importance that are generally open to public scrutiny. From the public gallery, citizens can bear witness to the impartial dispensing of justice and the power of the state to prosecute. As Johnston argues, the principle of open justice has been premised on courts being accessible and subject to external public oversight.[26] Referencing Jeremy Bentham, Johnston states: 'decision-making should be public … the physical structures in which [decision-making takes] place should architecturally enable transparency, scrutiny and public accountability'.[27] Of course, the reality is that considerable legal negotiation and pre-trial plea resolution occur privately behind closed doors and away from public oversight.[28]

Closely connected with the significance of the material courtroom space has been the privileging of the co-presence of the parties and the importance of 'liveness', that is, face-to-face interaction and confrontation facilitated by in-person physical appearance.[29] The presence of the accused has been of particular value – indeed, the 'crux'[30] and 'master symbol'[31] of criminal procedure given that it is the accused who is central to prosecution, trial, and possible punishment. Further, the physical presence of defendants has ensured that they can effectively exercise their rights of defence,[32] hear and answer a case brought against them, confront their accusers, and participate in the process. Corporeal presence in the shared space of an open courtroom has also underpinned the presentation of viva voce evidence. The spontaneity of live oral testimony and the ability to

---

Attorney-Client Communications and the Effect of Videoconferencing in the Courtroom' (2013) 8 *Journal of International Commercial Law and Technology* 24.

23 J Hanson, 'The Architecture of Justice: Iconography and Space Configuration in the English Law Court Building' (1996) 1(4) *Architectural Research Quarterly* 50–59; J Resnik and DE Curtis, *Representing Justice: Invention, Controversy, and Rights in City-States and Democratic Courtrooms* (Yale University Press, 2011); J Resnik, 'The Contingency of Courts: Changing the Experiences and Logics of Publics' Role in Court-Based ADR' (2015) 15 *Nevada Law Journal* 951.

24 R McDougall, 'Designing the Courtroom of the Future' (paper presented at the International Conference on Court Excellence – Singapore, January 2016) 1–25.

25 Graham (n 16) 19.

26 J Johnston, 'Three Phases of Courts' Publicity: Reconfiguring Bentham's Open Justice in the Twenty-First Century' (2018) 14(4) *International Journal of Law in Context* 525–538. doi:10.1017/S1744552318000228.

27 Ibid 527.

28 Resnik and Curtis (n 23).

29 Leader, 'Trials, Truth-Telling' (n 16); P Auslander, *Liveness: Performance in a Mediatized Culture* (Routledge, 2008).

30 Leader, 'Trials, Truth-Telling' (n 16) 88, 90.

31 A Hyde, *Bodies of Law* (Princeton University Press, 1997) 8.

32 F Cassim, 'The Accused's Right to be Present: A Key to Meaningful Participation in the Criminal Process' (2005) 38(2) *The Comparative and International Law Journal of South Africa* 285–303.

confront, examine, and cross-examine physically present witnesses are linked to the concepts of open justice and the production of authentic evidence.[33] All in all, criminal procedure has been premised on dialogical, face-to-face interaction, where all parties share a 'common spatial-temporal framework' and co-present context.[34]

Spatial and physical attributes are intimately entwined with procedural justice principles – values that have developed through the common law in countries such as Australia, may be enshrined in constitutional rights in certain jurisdictions such as the US, and are referenced in human rights measures in countries including the United Kingdom (UK), certain European countries, NZ, and Canada. Combined with the rule of law, procedural justice values legitimate the operation of criminal law and procedure.[35] While the term defies precise definition,[36] procedural justice relates to the concepts of fairness, due process, open and impartial justice, equality of arms, the 'right' to confrontation, the presumption of innocence, and the right to hear and answer the case.[37] In evaluating whether procedural justice is being upheld, it is clear that the courts must balance the rights of all parties against each other as well as against the interests of the community.[38] As this chapter will reveal, these procedural justice principles are being challenged by the technologisation of criminal procedure and by a criminal justice system that is rapidly becoming a space that is 'digital by default'.[39]

Virtual courts with virtual people

The uptake of video link technologies, in particular, has altered the criminal justice landscape, shifting from a reliance on a physical environment to reliance on a digital one. In general terms, audiovisual link technologies enable the real-time or 'live' audio and/or visual connection between two or more people in different locations – a 'virtual face-to-face interaction'.[40] For instance, in the

33 L Re, 'Oral v Written Evidence: The Myth of the Impressive Witness' (1983) 57 *Australian Law Journal* 679–689; I Dennis, *The Law of Evidence* (Sweet & Maxwell, 2007) vol 604; ES Magner, 'The Best Evidence: Oral Testimony or Documentary Proof?' (1995) 18 *University of New South Wales Law Journal* 67; Leader, 'Trials, Truth-Telling' (n 16).

34 Thompson (n 21) 32.

35 S Bronitt and B McSherry, *Principles of Criminal Law* (Lawbook Company, 2017).

36 Dennis, *The Law of Evidence* (n 33).

37 L Mulcahy, 'Putting the Defendant in Their Place: Why Do We Still Use the Dock in Criminal Proceedings?' (2013) 53(6) *British Journal of Criminology* 1139–1156.

38 I Dennis, 'The Right to Confront Witnesses: Meanings, Myths and Human Rights' (2010) 4 *The Criminal Law Review* 255–274.

39 Ministry of Justice, *Transforming our Justice System: Joint Statement by the Lord Chancellor, the Lord Chief Justice and the Senior President of Tribunals*, September 2016, 8–9.

40 E Schellhammer, 'A Technology Opportunity for Court Modernization: Remote Appearances – A White Paper Prepared for Association of Canadian Court Administrators and Canadian Centre for Court Technology' (2013) <http://docplayer.net/6302452-A-technology-opportunity-for-court-modernization-remote-appearances.html> 11.

author's jurisdiction of the Australian state of New South Wales (NSW), video links are used to enable vulnerable witnesses to safely give evidence and to connect remote expert witnesses[41] and remote interpreters to courtrooms.[42] Video links are promoted as enhancing the security of victims of crime and vulnerable witnesses, including by protecting them from physical confrontation with the alleged offender.[43] In addition, video links connect incarcerated defendants with distant courts and remote legal representatives,[44] minimising the security concerns associated with bringing prisoners into courtrooms.[45] A rationale for using video links, especially in large countries such as Australia and Canada, is the cost-saving derived from minimising the transportation of prisoners to and from courts.[46] In this way, video links provide a means to connect and interact with others who may not share the same spatial context[47] and, simultaneously, to segregate those with whom we do not wish to have co-presence.[48]

Video links are also seen as enabling a more streamlined and efficient criminal justice system at a time of dwindling government resources[49] as there are costs to be saved by minimising the use of court real estate and staff. For instance, in England and Wales, the 'hugely ambitious' digital court reform programme has its sights set on embracing ICT, online adjudication and virtual procedures, especially

41 *Evidence (Audio and Audio Visual Links) Act 1998* (NSW); A Wallace, 'Justice and the "Virtual" Expert: Using Remote Witness Technology to Take Scientific Evidence' (PhD Thesis, University of Sydney, 2011); Rowden, 'Remote Participation' (n 1); E Rowden et al., *Gateways to Justice: Design and Operational Guidelines for Remote Participation in Court Proceedings* (2013) <http://researchdirect.westernsydney.edu.au/islandora/object/uws%3A15505/datastream/PDF/view>.

42 J Napier, 'Here or There? An Assessment of Video Remote Signed Language Interpreter-Mediated Interaction in Court' in S Braun and JL Taylor (eds), *Videoconference and Remote Interpreting in Criminal Proceedings* (University of Surrey, 2011) 145–85, <http://www.videoconference-interpreting.net/wp-content/uploads/2014/04/09_Napier.pdf>.

43 J Cashmore, 'The Use of Video Technology for Child Witnesses' (1990) 16 *Monash University Law Review*, 228; L Ellison and VE Munro, 'A "Special" Delivery? Exploring the Impact of Screens, Live-Links and Video-Recorded Evidence on Mock Juror Deliberation in Rape Trials' (2014) 23(1) *Social and Legal Studies* 3–29; Rowden, 'Remote Participation' (n 1); Rowden, 'Distributed Courts and Legitimacy' (n 1).

44 McKay, *The Pixelated Prisoner* (n 3).

45 Polycom, *White Paper: Enhancing Courts and Justice with Technology – A Polycom Perspective* (2016) <http://www.polycom.com/content/dam/polycom/common/documents/whitepapers/courtroom-video-applications-whitepaper-enus.pdf>.

46 N Donnelly, *The Impact of Audio Visual Links (AVL) in Courtrooms on Prison Transport Costs* (Issue Paper No 137, Bureau of Crime Statistics and Research, September 2018) <https://www.bocsar.nsw.gov.au/Documents/BB/2018-Report-The-impact-of-audio-visual-links-(AVL)-BB137.pdf>; J Bailey, J Burkell and G Reynolds, 'Access to Justice for All: Towards an "Expansive Vision" of Justice and Technology' (2013) 31 *Windsor Year Book of Access to Justice* 181–207.

47 Thompson (n 21).

48 Rowden, 'Remote Participation' (n 1).

49 J Donoghue, 'The Rise of Digital Justice: Courtroom Technology, Public Participation and Access to Justice' (2017) 80(6) *The Modern Law Review* 995–1025; Courts and Tribunals Judiciary (n 9).

for summary matters.[50] Part of this process has involved 'rationalising the court estate' – that is, closing courthouses[51] and employing fewer people.[52] *The Guardian* reported that, since 2010, 162 of 323 magistrates' courts have been closed, and 6 more are scheduled for closure,[53] while the Courts and Tribunals Judiciary state that 'the 460 buildings that made up the court estate has been reduced to 350 so far, with more reductions due to come'.[54] As Resnik and Curtis posit, courthouses face 'technological obsolescence' and 'are at risk of being anachronistic'.[55] Therefore, progressively, the question will be: where is the court?[56]

The rise of video links is rupturing the significance of co-present shared space and physical courtrooms. As the bricks and mortar of courthouses give way to a justice system premised on ICT and the internet, criminal law is entering the 'videosphere'[57] of screens, networks, and digital environments in which adjudication occurs in dematerialised or virtual spaces or multi-sited distributed spaces.[58] The 'traditional' spatial-temporal paradigm of criminal procedure is thus shifting to a model of 'de-spatialized simultaneity' in which we can see and/or hear other parties who are spatially remote in real time.[59] The focus is on centralised and integrated networks, repositories, and 'common platforms',[60] or what I have previously referred to as the 'justice matrix' connecting the disparate sites of police stations, prisons, courts, and an array of other justice institutions.[61] Moreover, the procedural and/or evidential statutes of many jurisdictions have established presumptions in favour of custodial court appearance by audiovisual link for certain criminal matters, replacing traditional presumptions in favour of physical appearance in physical courtrooms. Such jurisdictions are increasingly adopting a default situation of digital appearance from custodial video studios, so that video links are 'the new normal' in criminal procedure.[62] The courthouse

50 J Rozenberg, *The Online Court: Will IT Work?* (2019) The Legal Education Foundation <https://long-reads.thelegaleducationfoundation.org/> no page; Ward (n 7).
51 Rozenberg (n 50) no page.
52 Courts and Tribunals Judiciary (n 9).
53 O Bowcott and P Duncan, 'Half of Magistrates Courts in England and Wales Closed since 2010' *The Guardian* (online, 28 January 2019) <https://www.theguardian.com/law/2019/jan/27/half-of-magistrates-courts-in-england-and-wales-closed-since-tories-elected>.
54 Courts and Tribunals Judiciary (n 9) 17.
55 Resnik and Curtis (n 23) 336.
56 Rowden, 'Distributed Courts and Legitimacy' (n 1).
57 P Goodrich, 'Screening Law' in *A Thousand Eyes: Media Technology, Law and Aesthetics* (Sternberg Press, 2011) 163; C Vismann, 'Tele-Tribunals: Anatomy of a Medium' in *A Thousand Eyes: Media Technology, Law and Aesthetics* (Sternberg Press, 2011).
58 Mulcahy, *Legal Architecture* (n 1); Rowden, 'Distributed Courts and Legitimacy' (n 1); Rowden, 'Remote Participation' (n 1); Licoppe and Dumoulin (n 1); Mohr (n 1).
59 Thompson (n 21) 37.
60 Courts and Tribunals Judiciary (n 9) 5.
61 McKay, *The Pixelated Prisoner* (n 3) 175.
62 P Gibbs, *Defendants on Video: Conveyor Belt Justice or a Revolution in Access?* (2017) Transform Justice <www.transformjustice.org.uk/wp-content/uploads/2017/10/Disconnected-Thumbnail-2.pdf> 2.

is thus transitioning from the analogue terrestrial world to a more nebulous but digital environment connecting with, and operating within, police cells and prisons.

The prison endpoint of video links

In this section, much is drawn from my empirical research that examined the prison endpoint of video links and prisoners' technologised legal experiences.[63] There are many possible endpoints in the use of audiovisual links. For instance, in the UK's emergent 'video-enabled justice' system, there are around 300 endpoints connecting police, lawyers, prisons, and judicial officers.[64] In my study, I chose to focus on the prison endpoint given that it is difficult to access, is rarely seen, and the people appearing from that location have a great need for access to justice in terms of court appearances, legal information, advice, and representation. Moreover, my literature review indicated that the prison endpoint was under-examined. In that study, my overarching research question was: how does appearance by video link from correctional facilities affect prisoners and their experiences of legal proceedings? To answer this question, I sought and received human ethics clearance to interview prisoners in two correctional facilities in NSW and ultimately interviewed 31 prisoners, both men and women. The majority of the people I interviewed were on remand – that is, pre-trial – and were using video links primarily to appear in remote courts, as well as to seek legal advice and give instructions to distant lawyers.

I found in this study that audiovisual link technologies are becoming integrated into the infrastructure of carceral sites so that technologised legal hearings are, in effect, being conducted within these custodial spaces. In this regard, I have argued that video link technologies cannot be treated merely as *courtroom* technologies; they are also significant emergent *prison* technologies affiliated with offender management and penal policy.

In the incremental shift away from the requirement for the physical presence of incarcerated defendants in physical courtrooms towards their appearance from custodial spaces via audiovisual link, the courtroom custody dock is conceptually relocated from the courtroom to the prison video link studio or the police station.[65] The video link technology and enabling legislation spatially construct

63 McKay, *The Pixelated Prisoner* (n 3); C McKay, 'Video Links from Prison: Permeability and the Carceral World' (2016) 5(1) *International Journal for Crime, Justice & Social Democracy* 21–37; C McKay, 'Face-to-Interface Communication: Accessing Justice by Video Link from Prison' in Asher Flynn and Jackie Hodgson (eds), *Access to Justice: Comparative Perspectives on Unmet Legal Need* (Hart Publishing, 2017) 103–121; C McKay, 'Video Links from Prison: Court "Appearance" within Carceral Space' (2018) 14(2) *Law, Culture and the Humanities* 242–262.

64 Sussex Police and Crime Commissioner, 'Sussex PCC Secures £11m for Regional Video-Enabled Justice Programme' (online, 5 September 2017) <https://www.sussex-pcc.gov.uk/about/news/sussex-pcc-secures-11m-for-regional-video-enabled-justice-programme/>.

65 Mulcahy, *Legal Architecture* (n 1).

the custodial space as a metaphysical extension of the remote courtroom. But, as Mulcahy argues, the court no longer sets the aesthetic tone of that custodial endpoint and the significance of courtroom 'architecture and design is marginalised, if not completely denied'.[66] On that basis, it is important to understand the unique qualitative attributes of prison video link studios within the general carceral prison space as it is these elements that set the tone for prisoners' legal experiences.

Prisons are built environments that function as and express state punishment and prosecution. They are 'total institutions'[67] that seek to regulate all aspects of inmates' lives, isolate them from society and render them 'docile'.[68] The attributes of the prison have been well documented by numerous prison scholars and criminologists,[69] convict criminologists,[70] carceral geographers[71] and in literature.[72] Moran contends that the discipline of carceral geography, in particular, foregrounds the significance of spatiality in prison. The built environment of prison enables constant supervision, surveillance, discipline, and secure containment of the inmate population.[73] Penal expression is found in the prison's architectural components and the correlation between 'regime and building and technology'.[74] Prison design is underpinned by geometry and mathematics and, while some correctional facilities may have a humane built environment that encourages penitence, reformation, and rehabilitation, many other prisons are seemingly designed for the building itself to exact punishment and retribution.[75] Prisons are typically cellular, with solid and unforgiving surfaces, many gates,

66 Ibid 172.

67 E Goffman, *Essays on the Social Situation of Mental Patients and Other Inmates* (Doubleday, 1961).

68 M Foucault, *Discipline and Punish: The Birth of the Prison* (Vintage, 1977).

69 B Crewe, 'The Prisoner Society' in *Power, Adaption and Social Life in an English Prison* (Oxford University Press, 2009); B Crewe, 'Inside the Belly of the Penal Beast: Understanding the Experience of Imprisonment' (2015) 4(1) *International Journal for Crime, Justice & Social Democracy* 50–65; M Halsey, 'On Confinement: Resident and Inmate Perspectives of Secure Care and Imprisonment' (2007) 54(4) *Probation Journal* 338–367; P Hancock and Y Jewkes, 'Architectures of Incarceration: The Spatial Pains of Imprisonment' (2011) 13(5) *Punishment & Society* 611–629; B Naylor, 'Human Rights and Respect in Prisons: The Prisoners' Perspective' in B Naylor, J Debeljak and A Mackay (eds), *Human Rights in Closed Environments* (Federation Press, 2014) 84; P Scraton, 'Bearing Witness to the "Pain of Others": Researching Power, Violence and Resistance in a Women's Prison' (2016) 5(1) *International Journal for Crime, Justice & Social Democracy* 5–20; L Wacquant, 'The Curious Eclipse of Prison Ethnography in the Age of Mass Incarceration' (2002) 3(4) *Ethnography* 371–397.

70 R Earle, 'Insider and Out Making Sense of a Prison Experience and a Research Experience' (2014) 20(4) *Qualitative Inquiry* 429–438.

71 D Moran, *Carceral Geography: Spaces and Practices of Incarceration* (Ashgate, 2015).

72 JH Abbott, *In the Belly of the Beast: Letters from Prison* (Vintage, 1991); O Wilde, *De Profundis: The Ballad of Reading Gaol and Other Writings* (Wordsworth Editions, 1999).

73 Moran (n 71); Foucault (n 68).

74 Fairweather and McConville (n 2) 12.

75 NB Johnston, *Forms of Constraint: A History of Prison Architecture* (University of Illinois Press, 2000); see also B Naylor, J Debeljak and A Mackay (eds), *Human Rights in Closed Environments* (Federation Press, 2014).

grates, and grilles and looping lengths of razor wire, all potent signifiers of hard authority and subjugation.

So, what are the prison video studio spaces like? The prisoners I interviewed explained that, while awaiting appearance in the video link 'court', they were kept in nearby holding cells, sometimes for extended periods of time. The male prisoners in particular complained about the state of these holding cells. They described how these cells, integral to the designated space of technologised court appearance, were unhygienic, cramped, and generally undignified. It is from these degrading holding cells that prisoners would emerge to step into the video link studio for their court matter or legal conference. As for the audio-visual link studios in which prisoners are contained during their court hearings, even the video link technology vendors, such as Polycom,[76] have recognised that the prison endpoint of the technology is a taxing environment compared with a civic and open courtroom. Like the surrounding detention-grade fixtures and fittings that are standard in custodial situations, the video link facilities are designed to be durable, impact-proof, and vandal-resistant. One significant problem I found with these studios is their lack of soundproofing against the surrounding ambient prison noise that can infiltrate the studio. If the video link studios are situated close to holding cells or other well-populated prison areas, a 'soundtrack of incarceration'[77] can penetrate the studio and may then be transmitted to the remote courtroom, distracting the prisoner and providing an undignified and negative 'auditory spatial' environment[78] for the prisoner's court appearance.

In comparing courtroom space with prison video link space, it soon became apparent that there is a significant spatial disjuncture: the hard and taxing custodial endpoint of video link technology may be a legislated conceptual extension of the courtroom but it does not, at all, resemble or replicate a courtroom.[79] Prison video link studios are devoid of the atmospherics, aesthetics, and architecture of court. The disjuncture between courtrooms and their conceptual extensions in the form of prison video link studios is not only based on their divergent physical attributes, but also on their contrasting sonic worlds. While courtrooms privilege silence, solemnity, and even the 'sacred',[80] prisons are filled with hard,

76 Polycom, *Polycom Telejustice Solutions: Collaborative Solutions for Courts and Corrections* (2012) <www.polycom.com.au/content/dam/polycom/common/documents/data-sheets/polycom-telejustice-solutions-br-enus.pdf>.

77 McKay (n 63).

78 D Ihde, *Listening and Voice: Phenomenologies of Sound* (SUNY Press, 2007), 15, 194; see also JE Parker, *Acoustic Jurisprudence: Listening to the Trial of Simon Bikindi* (Oxford University Press, 2015).

79 ZM Hillman, 'Pleading Guilty and Video Teleconference: Is a Defendant Constitutionally Present when Pleading Guilty by Video Teleconference?' (2007) 7 *Journal of High Technology Law* 41; Bellone (n 22).

80 Leader, 'The Trial's the Thing' (n 12) 6.

reflective surfaces and clanging 'metal-on-metal',[81] making these enclosed spaces loud and chaotic.

The courtroom endpoint of video links

Graham[82] and Mulcahy[83] track the evolution of the courtroom from a co-present social space through to a space of strict segregation, particularly following the 'lawyerisation' of criminal procedure.[84] In this segmented and hierarchical space, courtroom custody docks delineate and contain the accused person while even the public gallery may be partitioned off.[85] Appearing from the courtroom dock, the defendant is spatially isolated from the other key actors and the advent of plexiglass-enclosed docks has meant that the defendant is further encased by secure, tangible barriers.[86] More recently, this *symbolic* isolation of the defendant in the courtroom has been reconfigured into an *actual* isolation through the progressive use of video links such that the defendant is completely marginalised by not being in the courtroom at all.[87]

Contemporary court design has been generally shifting towards the use of 'less authoritarian, more user-friendly' models, although Graham notes how, simultaneously, segregation and security have increased.[88] This has coincided with electronic and digital developments in criminal procedure and legal practice, with the consequence that the traditional designs and functions of the court estate are being challenged.[89] At the courtroom endpoint of the audiovisual link, there have been significant spatial transformations as screens, speakers, cameras, microphones, computers, and other electrical devices are integrated.[90] Less visible are the many legal support services that have similarly become digitised, such as online court registries, e-filing, e-discovery facilities, and legal databases. Defendants and a range of witnesses can now be electronically 'produced' at the courtroom endpoint,[91] appearing as flattened, two-dimensional images on a

81 Fairweather and McConville (n 2) 42.
82 Graham (n 16).
83 Mulcahy, *Legal Architecture* (n 1).
84 JH Langbein, *The Origins of Adversary Criminal Trial* (Oxford University Press, 2003); Hodgson (n 16).
85 Mulcahy, *Legal Architecture* (n 1).
86 See, for instance, *R v Benbrika & Ors (Ruling No. 12)* [2007] VSC 524; *R v Baladjam & Ors* [No 41] [2008] NSWSC 1462; *R v Dirani* (No. 7) [2018] NSWSC 945.
87 McKay, *The Pixelated Prisoner* (n 3).
88 Graham (n 16) 46; Hanson (n 23).
89 M Rossner et al., 'The Dock on Trial: Courtroom Design and the Presumption of Innocence' (2017) 44(3) *Journal of Law and Society* 317–344.
90 McDonald et al. (n 6); Donoghue, 'The Rise of Digital Justice' (n 6); G Hryncewicz-Lamber, 'The Computer-Aided Judiciary: How the Contemporary Technologies Change the Courtroom Design?' in *International Conference on Universal Access in Human-Computer Interaction* (Springer, 2013) 288–296.
91 See discussion in *Mendel & Mendel* [2018] FCCA 3256, Harman J at [7]–[14].

screen.[92] Both the witness stand and the courtroom custody dock are therefore structures that face obsolescence as courtrooms are increasingly being populated with screens and depopulated of humans. Furthermore, Hryncewicz-Lamber argues that the uptake of video links for both vulnerable witnesses and defendants will mean that other courthouse rooms will become redundant.[93] The 'rise of digital justice in the courtroom' has well and truly commenced and has already altered the mode and space in which justice is administered.[94] How the symbolism of the administration of justice is translated into new technologised spaces requires considerable reimagining.[95]

In 2012 I visited a 'virtual court' in Camberwell Green Magistrates' Court, London, to observe 'swift and sure justice'[96] in action. Gaining access to the court proved difficult and, when I was finally allowed in, I was surprised by the courtroom's small dimensions, informality, the proximity of all actors to one another, and the amount of computer hardware and tangle of computer leads, cords, and cabling. The emphasis was firmly placed on the procedural rather than the ceremonial. These video hearings allowed defendants, who had been charged at a police station, to have their first appearance before a magistrate by video link straight from the police station.[97] This can occur in a matter of hours of being charged, with the benefit that, if the defendant pleads guilty, he or she can be promptly sentenced. However, this court observation demonstrated to me how the remote defendants were not able to actively participate and were seemingly reduced to distanced and docile objects on whom justice was enacted.[98] Through this encounter with this emerging model of e-justice, the issue of adapting or retro-fitting existing court space to be able to handle technological needs became evident. As Hryncewicz-Lamber writes, the development of electronic courtrooms requires architectural attention to ergonomics, sightlines for screens, corrected lighting and acoustic conditions, and a means to aesthetically blend the technologies in keeping with the justice-based interior design.[99] My empirical study found that consideration must also be given to the other endpoints of the video links to ensure that spaces remote from the courtroom

92 McKay, *The Pixelated Prisoner* (n 3).

93 Hryncewicz-Lamber (n 90).

94 Donoghue, 'The Rise of Digital Justice' (n 6) 996.

95 Rowden, 'Distributed Courts and Legitimacy' (n 1).

96 Ministry of Justice, *Swift and Sure Justice: The Government's Plans for Reform of the Criminal Justice System*, July 2012, <https://assets.publishing.service.gov.uk/government/uploads/system/uploads/attachment_data/file/217328/swift-and-sure-justice.pdf>.

97 Donoghue, 'The Rise of Digital Justice' (n 6).

98 N Naffine, *Law and the Sexes: Explorations in Feminist Jurisprudence* (Allen & Unwin, 1990); Carlen (n 20).

99 Hryncewicz-Lamber (n 90); see also Lulham et al. (n 14); K Kashyap et al. (2018), *Court-Custody Audio Visual Links: Designing for Equitable Justice Experience in the Use of Court Custody Video Conferencing* (University of Technology Sydney, 2018), <https://www.designforsocialjustice.xyz/>.

provide suitable camera angles, soundproofing, and acoustic quality and a dignified environment.[100] From an architectural and phenomenological perspective, Rowden examines the rise of digitised justice and the diminishing significance of courtroom space. She reports on empirical findings that highlight some of the sensorial losses that occur when court participants are distributed across different spaces and linked only by technology.[101] Current video link configurations fail to convey court space environmental cues so that remote participants lose their sense of connection with other key actors, their sense of place in the 'social hierarchy of the court' and the communal process, thereby undermining the legitimacy of critical legal procedures.[102]

There are other spatial changes occurring, driven by risk aversion and cost-cutting. An interesting development in my own jurisdiction involves the increasing use of video link facilities within courthouses. In these instances, while defendants may be physically transported from prison to the courthouse, they still do not appear in the courtroom. Instead, they appear by video link transmitted from the court cells below to the courtroom above.[103] It seems strange indeed that these defendants, who have been physically brought inside the courthouse building, are not being afforded the opportunity of presenting themselves as citizens in the physical courtroom before the judicial officer. Rather, they are relegated to a form of 'constructive presence' (to borrow a term from complicity[104]) transmitted by video link from the court cells below.

Advances in courtroom technologies and e-justice are very much driven by pragmatic concerns around efficiencies and cost-savings.[105] Yet what is required is a critical analysis of how the transformed practices, procedures, and spatial relationships can be reconciled with procedural justice principles. Donoghue concludes that, while the technologised courtroom and the array of digital tools 'offer great promise for enhancing efficiency, participation and accessibility, they simultaneously have the potential to amplify the scope for injustice, and to attenuate central principles of the legal system, including somewhat paradoxically, access to justice'.[106] Nevertheless, the concept of the fixed site of justice that is 'spatially discrete and architecturally symbolic' is a notion that now seems almost quaint and conspicuously old-fashioned.[107]

100 McKay, *The Pixelated Prisoner* (n 3).

101 Rowden, 'Distributed Courts and Legitimacy' (n 1).

102 Ibid 276.

103 See, for example, *Evidence (Audio and Audio Visual Links) Regulation 2015* (NSW) – regulation 4 provides that people may appear for their bail proceedings from Wagga Wagga Court cells and Newcastle Justice Precinct cells, as well as from certain police station cells.

104 *George Pell v the Queen* [2019] VSCA 186, 1163 citing P Gillies, *The Law of Criminal Complicity* (Lawbook, 1980) and *R v Manners* (1837) 173 ER 349.

105 Leveson (n 7).

106 Donoghue, 'The Rise of Digital Justice' (n 6) 998.

107 Mulcahy, *Legal Architecture* (n 1) 12; Rowden, 'Distributed Courts and Legitimacy' (n 1).

Conflating court spaces with prisons

Building on Mulcahy's work and as I have argued elsewhere,[108] video links effect an intriguing spatial construction by conceptually extending courtrooms into prisons and other custodial spaces such as police cells. For instance, in my home jurisdiction, the legislation designates the enclosed, non-judicial, and carceral space of the prison video studio to be part of the remote courtroom.[109] However, this produces an uneasy conflation,[110] and Mulcahy questions whether this heralds a return to the now discredited nineteenth-century practice of courts of summary justice being physically proximate to police stations.[111] In this regard, the medium of video links has once again enabled justice to be, in effect, administered within police stations and prisons. But these are non-neutral and enclosed spaces of state prosecution and punishment (functions of the executive) that are being technologically conflated with the impartial space of legal adjudication (a function of the judiciary). This situation can be understood as a provocation to the 'separation of powers' that divides government functions into three distinct and independent branches – the legislature, executive, and judiciary – and which has even been influential on the placement of civic buildings.[112] This has not been consistently the case, of course, and I only have to look at my nearby Darlinghurst courthouse, a nineteenth-century building constructed immediately adjacent to what was the Darlinghurst gaol. But the progressive integration of courts and prisons brought about by technological networking renders the separation of powers less distinct,[113] which is perhaps particularly significant given the robust reticence of the courts to interfere with or be involved in the management of prisons.[114] When justice is administered in prison video link studios, being remote spaces of state punishment, the court cannot set the tone of the proceedings[115] and the judicial officer has a diminished presence, authority, and ability to exert control over the conduct of proceedings.[116]

108 Mulcahy, *Legal Architecture* (n 1); McKay, *The Pixelated Prisoner* (n 3).

109 *Evidence (Audio and Audio Visual Links) Act 1998* (NSW) s 5C.

110 Mulcahy, *Legal Architecture* (n 1); A Wallace and EL Rowden, 'Gateways to Justice: The Use of Videoconferencing Technology to Take Evidence in Australian Courts' (paper presented to the 9th European Conference on eGovernment, 2009), Academic Publishing Limited.

111 Mulcahy, *Legal Architecture* (n 1).

112 McDougall (n 24); John Hockings, 'Brisbane Supreme and District Court' (ArchitectureAU, September 2009) <http://architectureau.com/articles/brisbane-supreme-and-district-court/>.

113 S Elias, 'Managing Criminal Justice' (2017) NZCLR 316; LAWNEWS, 'Don't Allow Managerial Justice to Encroach upon Criminal Justice' (2017) <www.adls.org.nz/for-the-profession/news-and-opinion/2017/10/6/don't-allow-managerial-justice-to-encroach-upon-criminal-justice/>; J Galuszka, 'Manawatū Prison Set to Get Audio-Visual Links to Courts' (2017) <www.stuff.co.nz/national/98900389/manawat-prison-set-to-get-audiovisual-links-to-courts>.

114 C McKay, 'Digital Access to Justice from Prison: Is There a Right to Technology?' (2018) 42(5) *Criminal Law Journal* 303.

115 Mulcahy, *Legal Architecture* (n 1).

116 E Rowden and A Wallace, 'Remote Judging: The Impact of Video Links on the Image and the Role of the Judge' (2018) 14(4) *International Journal of Law in Context* 504–524.

Ultimately, because the state has a monopoly on the control of prisons[117] the conceptual conflation of courts with prisons represents a concentration of judicial and executive power, exacerbating the power imbalance between the prisoner and the state, and challenging the independence of the courts. The situation represents an awkward fusing of criminal procedure with penal policy and offender management,[118] demonstrated by recent industrial action by prison officers in NSW that resulted in significant court scheduling interruptions because prisoners were not being brought to the audiovisual link studios.[119]

Procedural justice in prison video link studios

In what way might the metaphysical court space in prison or police video studios alter the perceptions and the realities of open and impartial justice? If 'the space in which justice is done shapes what we think it means',[120] then does a custodial video studio reflect a 'just' space? If we assume that there continues to be a relationship between architectural design and procedural justice values,[121] the new digitised model must play a significant role in either 'dignifying or degrading' criminal procedure.[122] Are procedural justice values operationalised in the functional and sterile carceral design of prison video studios in the same way that they are in a public courtroom?

In my earlier empirical research project, I concluded that the conflation of prison and courtroom was problematic in undermining the fundamental common law principles of our criminal justice system, in particular open justice, equality of arms, the right to confrontation, and the presumption of innocence. Open justice requires that legal proceedings be subject to public oversight – a mode of surveillance of state authority[123] and a guard against 'bias, unfairness and incompetence'[124] as well as 'improbity'.[125] Open justice values require that

117 Fairweather and McConville (n 2).

118 KF Aas, 'From Narrative to Database: Technological Change and Penal Culture' (2004) 6(4) *Punishment & Society* 379–393.

119 S Rigney, 'Mass Prison Strike as Custodial Officers Walk off the Job from Jails in NSW' *The Herald* (online, 8 March 2019) <https://www.theherald.com.au/story/5944874/corrective-services-staff-strike-grinding-courts-to-a-halt/>.

120 Spaulding (n 22) 343.

121 E Rowden and D Jones, 'Design, Dignity and Due Process: The Construction of the Coffs Harbour Courthouse' (2018) 14(2) *Law, Culture and the Humanities* 317–336; B McKimmie, J Hays and D Tait, 'Just Spaces: Does Courtroom Design Affect how the Defendant Is Perceived?' (2016) 23(6) *Psychiatry, Psychology and Law* 885–892; Resnik and Curtis (n 23); Mulcahy, *Legal Architecture* (n 1).

122 Rowden and Jones (n 121) 319 citing Carlen (n 20).

123 P Butt and D Hamer, *LexisNexis Concise Australian Legal Dictionary* (Lexis Nexis Butterworths, 2011); Dennis, 'The Right to Confront Witnesses' (n 38); Resnik (n 23).

124 Zuckerman et al. (n 11).

125 J Bentham, 'Publicity in the Courts of Justice' (1843) quoted in *Scott v Scott* [1913] AC 417 (HL) at 477 per Lord Shaw.

procedures are held in open court, which is fundamental in ensuring transparency, accountability, and therefore the legitimacy of the criminal justice system.[126] Thus, the shift to court proceedings being administered, in effect, in prison video studios radically limits direct and unmediated public and professional oversight, and undermines impartiality, or perceptions thereof. One major element that is being lost is the ability to see certain key actors, particularly the defendant, in the open site of the courtroom. Instead, they remain behind the very locked doors of prisons. But, of course, the principles of open justice are not inflexible and there are occasions when the court may choose to deviate from them. For instance, proceedings may be 'in camera', matters or identities may be suppressed, and the use of video links may be specifically recognised as a departure from open justice.[127]

The principle of equality of arms advocates for a 'level playing field'[128] in criminal justice although the reality is such that there is an inherent inequality in any state prosecution of an individual.[129] Regardless, the principle of equality of arms is potentially challenged by video links as the physically present prosecutor in the courtroom has a privileged position over the physically absent and incarcerated defendant.[130] Moreover, the concentration of judicial and executive power within the space of the prison video link studio, discussed above, adds to this power imbalance.

There is a great attachment to the right to confrontation, which posits that an accused should be able to eyeball their accuser.[131] While the direct and unmediated ability to confront accusers is diminished by video links, courts have recognised that a level of unfairness and forensic disadvantage may be experienced by a defendant when a witness appears by video link. Yet there is no absolute 'right' to confrontation.[132]

Finally, the stigmatising effect of prisoners being electronically produced in court by video link wearing prison uniforms may evince perceptions of their criminality and dangerousness, thus undermining the presumption of innocence. The prisoner's carceral context is made clear to all those in the courtroom,

126 K Biber, *In Crime's Archive: The Cultural Afterlife of Evidence* (Routledge, 2018); Johnston (n 26); Mulcahy, *Legal Architecture* (n 1).

127 Kumar et al. (n 11).

128 Cassim (n 32) 290.

129 P Roberts and A Zuckerman, *Criminal Evidence* (Oxford University Press, 2010); Dennis, *The Law of Evidence* (n 33).

130 F Ridout, 'Virtual Courts: Virtual Justice?' (2010) *Criminal Law & Justice Weekly* 603.

131 Roberts and Zuckerman (n 129).

132 M Daniele, 'Testimony through a Live Link in the Perspective of the Right to Confront Witnesses' (2014) (3) *Criminal Law Review* 189–206; McKay, *The Pixelated Prisoner* (n 3); *R v Goldman* (2004) 148 A Crim R 40; *R v Wilkie, R v Burroughs, R v Mainprize* (2005) 193 FLR 291; *R v Terdputham & Anor (Rulings Nos 1 & 2)* [2015] VSC 411; *R v Governor of Brixton Prison* [2001] All ER (D) 239 (Dec).

manifesting 'presumptive guilt',[133] casting prisoners as abject subjects[134] and constructing a potent visual demarcation.[135]

In this increasingly technologised paradigm, the spaces and processes of criminal justice are radically changing and the administration of justice is becoming a 'spatially distributed event' in which the boundaries of courtrooms extend into other spaces.[136] Nevertheless, procedural justice principles must continue to structure and underpin court process 'so we hold onto the sense we are working within the bounds of a legitimate criminal court system'.[137] There is already more than a quibbling sense amongst scholars that fundamental and ancient legal principles are being tested. Certainly, the technologisation and digitisation of courts and the criminal justice system are not 'value-neutral'.[138] The power that any piece of technology wields is determined by its context and its operator[139] and this is particularly so in the context of, and operation by, institutions of state prosecution and punishment.

However, studies are being conducted in relation to the design of 'just' spaces in custodial situations and the challenge is to design networked physical and virtual spaces that reflect procedural justice values.[140] Given the great spatial disparities and differing functions, there are significant obstacles to mirroring a courtroom in a prison environment, although some European experiences suggest that 'equivalence', if not improvement, may be attainable.[141] This is an area that is deserving of further research.

133 A Grunseit, S Forell and E McCarron, *Taking Justice into Custody: The Legal Needs of Prisoners* (Law and Justice Foundation of New South Wales, 2008) <http://www.lawfoundation.net.au/ljf/site/articleIDs/4DC35D5A0C06F1C4CA25748D00131D8C/$file/TakingJusticeIntoCustody.pdf> 107; McKay, *The Pixelated Prisoner* (n 3).

134 M Brown, 'Visual Criminology and Carceral Studies: Counter-Images in the Carceral Age' (2014) 18(2) *Theoretical Criminology* 176–197.

135 McKay, *The Pixelated Prisoner* (n 3).

136 Rowden and Wallace (n 116) 504.

137 Ward (n 7) 354.

138 A Borgmann, 'Justice and Technology' in MR McGuire and TJ Holt (eds), *The Routledge Handbook of Technology, Crime and Justice* (Routledge, 2017) 677; Poulin (n 13); Hillman (n 79); Mulcahy, *Legal Architecture* (n 1); Rowden, *Distributed Courts* (n 1); Licoppe and Dumoulin (n 1); Dumoulin and Licoppe (n 13); Bellone (n 22); Donoghue, 'The Rise of Digital Justice' (n 6); McKay, *The Pixelated Prisoner* (n 3).

139 J Tagg, *The Burden of Representation: Essays on Photographies and Histories* (University of Minnesota Press, 1988) vol 80.

140 Kashyap et al. (n 99); GG Ashdown and MA Menzel, 'The Convenience of the Guillotine: Video Proceedings in Federal Prosecutions' (2002) 80 *Denver University Law Review* 63; Rossner and McCurdy (n 9); JUSTICE, *What is a Court? A Report by JUSTICE* (2016) <https://justice.org.uk/what-is-a-court/>.

141 Kashyap et al. (n 99); J Young, 'A Virtual Day in Court: Design Thinking & Virtual Courts' (paper presented at the RSA Projects and Cisco Systems Seminar, London, 2011) <www.thersa.org/globalassets/pdfs/reports/a-virtual-day-in-court.pdf>; R van den Hoogen and P van Rotterdam, 'True-to-Life Requirements for Using Videoconferencing in Legal Proceedings'

Conclusion

Given the embeddedness of technologies in our digital society[142] and the pervasiveness of the screen,[143] adhering to a binary paradigm of 'real' and 'virtual'[144] legal space is perhaps unhelpful. Instead, the boundaries and overlaps between the two are progressively blurred as online and offline social interactions are increasingly fused and our sense of actually *being* immersed in an environment is transformed by digital communication technologies.[145] In this human–technologised hybrid world with new 'technosocial practices',[146] distinctions cannot be readily drawn between 'real' and 'virtual' experiences, and the concept of the 'cyborg' (to borrow a term from Haraway[147]) court is a real possibility.[148] Indeed, in a not-too-distant speculative future, criminal procedure may be completely facilitated by ICT with no humans, at all, in any courtroom – that is, through 'an entirely distributed court network, with no centrally identifiable and locatable courthouse "hub"'.[149]

However, the growing technologisation of criminal procedure cannot be viewed as a simple addition to the old or a replacement with the new: these new technologies do not leave the space or spatial relationships unchanged. Instead, new forms of interaction are generated in the shift from terrestrial to digital environments. Video links mediate human interactions by 'stretching' legal procedures across space and mediate symbolic exchanges through a 'narrowing of the range of symbolic cues'.[150] This is not to say that the traditions or values of criminal justice are necessarily denigrated, but they are, at least, being transformed such that the 'ancient practice' of face-to-face adjudication is reconstituted[151] as virtual and digital. As to whether this is necessarily good, bad, or just different for procedural justice remains unclear: further research into actual legal outcomes is critical. Legal procedure has been shown to have great 'plasticity'[152] in its ability to evolve and, similarly, court space has, over centuries, adapted

in S Braun and JL Taylor (eds), *Videoconference and Remote Interpreting in Criminal Proceedings* (University of Surrey, 2011).

142 Lupton (n 4).

143 E Cashmore, J Cleland and K Dixon, *Screen Society* (Palgrave Macmillan, 2018); Ashdown and Menzel (n 140).

144 Stratton et al. (n 4); Rowden, *Distributed Courts* (n 1).

145 KJ Hayward, 'Five Spaces of Cultural Criminology' (2012) 52(3) *British Journal of Criminology* 441–462, 456. doi: 10.1093/bjc/azs008; Stratton et al. (n 4).

146 Stratton et al. (n 4), 27; S Brown, 'The Criminology of Hybrids: Rethinking Crime and Law in Technosocial Networks' (2006) 10(2) *Theoretical Criminology* 223–244. doi: 10.1177/1362480606063140.

147 D Haraway, 'A Manifesto for Cyborgs: Science, Technology, and Socialist Feminism in the 1980s' in *Feminism/Postmodernism* (Routledge, 1990).

148 C Leonetti and J Bailenson, 'High-Tech View: The Use of Immersive Virtual Environments in Jury Trials' (2010) 93(3) *Marquette Law Review* 1073–1120.

149 Rowden, *Distributed Courts* (n 1), 280; HMCTS, *Reform Update* (n 8); Courts and Tribunals Judiciary (n 9).

150 Thompson (n 21) 33–34.

151 Resnik and Curtis (n 23) 14–15.

152 Ibid 337.

and responded to contemporary needs.[153] Court space is 'far from being a stable concept'[154] and, without doubt, the spatiality of justice is radically changing and its icons are no longer terrestrially constrained.

Epilogue

Since first writing this chapter, the coronavirus or COVID-19 pandemic has caused seismic shifts in the administration of criminal justice. As the highly contagious virus took hold in early 2020, emergency public health measures as well as restrictions on human gatherings were enacted. Courts around the world were partially or completely locked down; trials and other procedures were adjourned. However, it soon became clear that gross injustice would eventuate if the wheels of justice were unable to turn for an indefinite period; the court system is considered an essential service.[155] The civil jurisdiction was particularly quick to embrace existing technologies and videoconferencing platforms including Skype, Zoom, and Microsoft Teams to facilitate remote hearings. Given that the focus of civil procedure is on the just, quick, and cheap resolution of disputes,[156] and recognising the uncertainty of the pandemic's duration and existing court backlogs,[157] civil courts swiftly adapted to a model of digital justice. Criminal courts, on the other hand, were slightly reticent to dive into the virtual courtrooms, more likely to adjourn matters due to repeated technical failures, and more focused on fair process and procedure.[158] Nevertheless, Herculean efforts by lawyers, judges, and court administrators minimised disruptions despite the fact that 'for the first time in living memory, personal appearances were essentially banned' in courtrooms to minimise contagion.[159]

At the time of writing, there is now some resumption of face-to-face criminal procedure with jury trials in my jurisdiction spread across two courtrooms to ensure social distancing.[160] Yet, the technological genie is out of the bottle and the functionality of digital or virtual justice has been tested in an unexpected and massive pilot programme. The space of criminal justice is being reconceptualised. The symbolic weight of criminal procedure is being dispersed across the networks, codes, protocols, and algorithms of a formless digital sphere where architecture and aesthetics are obsolete.

153 Rossner et al. (n 89).
154 Mulcahy, *Legal Architecture* (n 1) 7.
155 *Rakielbakhour v DPP* [2020] NSWSC 323.
156 *Civil Procedure Act 2005* (NSW) s 56.
157 F Dernikovic and M Wright, 'Adjournments and e-Trials in the COVID-19 Context' (2020) *Law Society Journal* June 01, 2020; *Capic v Ford Motor Company of Australia Limited (Adjounrment)* [2020] FCA 486.
158 *R v Macdonald; R v Edward Obeid; R v Moses Obeid (No 11)* [2020] NSWSC 382.
159 NSW Chief Justice Tom Bathurst, 'Media Release: NSW Supreme Court Moves Towards Resuming Face-to-Face Hearings' (2020) <http://www.supremecourt.justice.nsw.gov.au/Pages/coronavirus_covid19_announcement.aspx>.
160 Ibid.

INDEX